F ather Raphael Simon received his M.D. at the University of Michigan (Ann Arbor). He did psychiatric internships at Bellevue Hospital and Brooklyn State Hospital in New York City, and was psychiatrist at an institution for delinquent boys, Lincoln Hall, Lincolndale, NY.

He became a priest in the Cistercian Order of the Strict Observance and is a monk of Saint Joseph's Abbey, Spencer, Massachusetts. He has given retreats to the monks of his Order in the United States and Ireland and has been a retreat master and director for monks, priests and lay people. The story of his conversion from Judaism is told in his book *The Glory of Thy People*.

"*Hammer & Fire* is an accessible and inspiring guide to the riches of the Catholic faith. Those who have had the good fortune of having known Father Raphael as a spiritual director will appreciate that now many others can experience the clear, simple, and beautiful wisdom of his guidance. A son of Abraham and a psychiatrist, by God's grace Father Raphael became a most faithful monk and son of the Church. I highly recommend this excellent and very orthodox book."

— Father Matthew Lamb
Chairman and Professor
Department of Theology
Ave Maria University

Is not My word like fire,

says the LORD,

like a hammer

shattering rocks?

—Jeremiah 23:29

Hammer
& *Fire*

Way to Contemplative Happiness
and Mental Health in Accordance
with the Judeo-Christian Tradition

Father Raphael Simon

ZACCHEUS PRESS
Bethesda

ZACCHEUS PRESS and the colophon are trademarks of Zaccheus Press.

The Zaccheus Press colophon was designed by Michelle Dick.

The text is set in Usherwood; the display type is DIN Light.

Library of Congress Cataloging-in-Publication Data

Simon, Raphael, 1909-
    Hammer and fire : way to contemplative happiness and mental health in accordance with the Judeo-Christian tradition : liturgical prayer, charismatic prayer, contemplative prayer, transforming union / Raphael Simon.
        p. cm.
    Originally published: Petersham, MA : Saint Bede's Publications, c1987.
    Includes bibliographical references and index.
    ISBN 0-9725981-2-X (alk. paper)
    1. Spiritual life—Catholic Church. 2. Meditation—Catholic Church.
    3. Contemplation. I. Title.
    BX2350.3.S57 2004
    248.4'82—dc22
                                                                    2004020119

10 9 8 7 6 5 4 3 2 1

To learn more, please visit our webpage:

www.zaccheuspress.com

To The Father
in Whom all are one regardless
of color, race or creed

—that He may be known and loved
for the healing of all
for all are His children.

Acknowledgments

For permission to quote from publications to which they hold the copyright, I cordially thank Alcoholics Anonymous, Inc., Benziger Bros., P.J. Kenedy & Sons, the Newman Press, the Paulist Press, *The Pope Speaks* (American Quarterly of Papal Documents), the Society of the Divine Word ("Prayer for Priests" by Father Bruno Hagspiel, S.V.D.), and Sheed & Ward, Inc.

Scripture texts are taken from *The Jerusalem Bible*, copyright © 1966 by Darton, Longman and Todd Ltd and Doubleday & Company, Inc., and are used by permission of the copyright owner. All rights reserved.

Scripture selections marked "NAB" are taken from the *New American Bible*, copyright © 1970, by the Confraternity of Christian Doctrine, Washington, D.C., and are used by permission of the copyright owner. All rights reserved.

Quotations taken from the Documents of Vatican II are from the Abbott-Gallagher edition, reprinted with permission of America Press, Inc., 106 West 56th Street, New York, NY 10019 copyright © 1966. All rights reserved.

The author wishes to acknowledge gratefully assistance in typing this manuscript afforded by Sister Claire Cayer and Mrs. Marguerite Donovan.

References

References are almost always given in the text; footnotes are ordinarily reserved for more detailed explanations of the matters treated in the text.

"S.T." indicates the *Summa Theologica* of Saint Thomas Aquinas.

TABLE OF CONTENTS

A Prefatory Letter from
Leo-Joseph Cardinal Suenens

April 1987

Dear Father,

In this new and revised edition of your book on prayer you touch, in a deep and happy way, many aspects that situate prayer in the fullness of life and human happiness.

You should not be surprised that I appreciated particularly what you say to our dear charismatic prayer groups. You rightly insist on the fact that the gifts of the Spirit are meant to lead to an esteem and longing above all for the highest gift, charity, and for the sanctifying gifts of the Spirit. As you say: "Where charity and the sanctifying gifts of the Spirit are not primarily sought, the Charismatic Renewal becomes unbalanced and misdirected and loses the guidance of the Spirit." This is the message of Saint Paul for all the ages. Thank you for repeating it to all of us.

Your book touches a variety of aspects which bring prayer into the full context of human, liturgical and even ecumenical life.

May this book be a help for many, and equip them for apostolic fruitfulness in the various conditions in which they live. May this Marian Year—starting at Pentecost—teach our Christians to be united deeply with Mary, Mother of the Church, and thus to be open to the fullness of the working of the Holy Spirit.

Your book should be read in that light by many.

With my very cordial good wishes,

† L.J. Card. Suenens

Come, O Holy Spirit,
fill the hearts of Thy faithful
and enkindle in them the fire of Thy Love.

V. Send forth Thy Spirit and they shall be created.

R. And Thou shalt renew the face of the earth.

LET US PRAY

O God, who did instruct the hearts of the faithful by the light of the Holy Spirit, grant that in the same Spirit we may relish what is wise and always rejoice in His consolation. Through Christ Our Lord.

R. Amen.

Introduction

What This Book Is About & Who It Is For

One of the most encouraging phenomena of our times is a widespread spiritual hunger, a desire for prayer, a remarkable interest in meditation and contemplation. If this hunger is to be truly appeased, it must be put in the context of an authentic tradition.

Such a tradition has existed in Judeo-Christianity from its beginning. It is expressed in the Jewish Bible (notably in the psalms, the prophets, and the sapiential writings) and in the New Testament. In the age of the Apostles and immediately thereafter, there were "ascetics" living in their own homes, and these were followed by the monks, who have carried on this tradition to the present day. Its value, however, is not limited to monks. It is the tradition of the Church and it is founded on the Scriptures. It is meant for all.

The fullness of this Christian tradition is relatively unknown. I propose to put meditation and contemplation in this framework, and to make clear the goal to which this practice leads: a transformation of the human personality. When enough people have realized this transformation, society itself will be transformed.

The human personality can only be transformed by truth, goodness and beauty. Everyone seeks a real or apparent goodness. Everyone has an ultimate end which actuates his or her life, be it pleasure, self-enhancement, a career, service or goodness itself: God. This ultimate end is the person's religion. But there are false religions and true ones, authentic religions and inauthentic, a complete religion and incomplete religions.

The human personality is not fulfilled by the inauthentic, the false, the incomplete. On the contrary, these are the sources of dissatisfaction, frustration, warping of the mind and heart, anxiety, depression, neuroses, impulse and personality disorders.

This book is about the authentic, the true, the beautiful and goodness itself—the true ultimate ground of human existence and development. That is known by true philosophy which has the full use of reason and is harmonious with science, but it is known even more by the Revelation of God, Who Himself is the sure ground of truth and goodness. Moreover He has the power to make known to humankind His own inner life, which He has done in sending us His Own Son, Jesus Christ and His Spirit.

Authentic spiritual life, with which this book is concerned, is based on the reception of this Revelation and the response to it. Spiritual life is not a compartment of human life, it is the totality of human life when that life, fully lived, includes God as its ground and foundation.

"Contemplation" as used here refers to a form of prayer which is characterized by experience, love and the appreciated action of the divine. A gift of the Father, it is offered to everyone. This gift and the preparation for receiving it will be explained.

To become fully human and alive, to be integrated and mature, to be effective in our service and undertakings, we need to be transformed into Jesus Christ through a transforming union, through which we become truly ourselves. This book is about that transforming union.

I present what Revelation has told us about God's plan for our happiness, for our transformation, and of the practice that leads us to its fulfillment, as this practice has been known to the saints and as it has been preserved in Scripture and in the Church, and as it has been taught by Vatican Council II. Spiritual practice and doctrine are interdependent and cannot be separated from each other, without loss to both. Perhaps this is pertinent to some of the problems in the Church today.

I have striven for the most lucid, concise presentation. At the same time, I wish to show the mental health value of spiritual practice and its value for the integration and development of the human personality.

2

THE HUNGER FOR PRAYER which has surfaced recently finds many contemporary expressions. For this development to be fully satisfying to those who experience it and that it might be brought to fulfillment, it is necessary that people learn to ground their prayer in a deepening knowledge of Jesus Christ and of His Father and in the knowledge and fulfillment of the Father's will.

Thomas Aquinas has synthesized most penetratingly the teaching of Scripture and of the monastic and Church Fathers. He has articulated a profound understanding of human nature. He has clarified the relation of faith and reason, opening the way to integrating with the faith all genuine advances in knowledge. In this objective I have long been interested as is indicated in the story of my conversion, *The Glory of Thy People*, the story of a liberal agnostic Jew who came to know and love Jesus Christ (see Bibliography, page 311). My ensuing life and this book proceed from that conversion.

Thomas has been accorded a special preeminence as a teacher of Catholic doctrine by the teaching authority of the Church, by Vatican II, and the Popes of Vatican II, including John Paul II. Thomas's teaching is of outstanding and enduring importance. While basing myself on Scripture, I have made ample use of this teaching.

3

THE LITURGICAL MOVEMENT of the 20th century has been embraced by the Church in the renewal of its liturgy. Liturgical prayer is the prayer of the people of God. Its stuff, the psalms, have been the prayer of

Christians from the first century, as before that they were (and still continue to be) the prayer of the chosen people, the Jews. Liturgical prayer places our prayer and piety in an ecclesial, communal framework so important for a balanced spiritual development.

The lack of fruitfulness for many of liturgical prayer (when it is a true lack of fruitfulness and not just a seeming one) may stem from the failure to participate in it with the proper interior dispositions. Liturgical prayer reveals its riches when entered into by people whose spiritual life is authentic.

The Church's liturgy cannot renew the Church and society unless Christians bring to it the dispositions that come from leading a genuine Christian life, which it in turn will foster. This emphasizes the importance of the practice of the traditional means of spiritual growth for the fruitfulness of the Church's Liturgy and for that transformation of the people of God, upon which the transformation of society depends.

4

AN EXPRESSION of the hunger for prayer is the Charismatic Renewal movement. This has encompassed, it is estimated, nine million Americans. In this movement, the Father gave a new awareness of the Holy Spirit and poured out many gifts, in a manner which some believe is unique since early Christian times. The heart of the Charismatic Movement is the conscious acceptance through the power of the Holy Spirit of the relationship of the Christian to Jesus as Lord and Friend. Thus the promises made by Christians in their baptism and confirmation and in the reception of the Eucharist are consciously accepted and become central to the life of each. Such Christians wish to come together in prayer to nurture this pearl of great price which has been given to them.

Leaders of the Charismatic Movement recognize (with more or less acuteness) that this movement needs to be nourished and properly directed if its high promise is to be realized. The gifts of the Spirit, which were poured out so abundantly—and still are in some parts of the world—are meant to lead to an esteem and longing above all for the highest gift, charity, and for the sanctifying gifts of the Spirit.

These bring the Christian into a stable experiential union with Christ and are the indispensable source of apostolic and pastoral fruitfulness. The charismata are also important gifts for the building up of the Church. But their fruitful use depends on the presence of charity and the sanctifying gifts of the Spirit which perfect charity. It is one of the contributions of this movement that it has made the charismata better appreciated. And this alone makes it an important subject of consideration for those seeking to understand the spiritual life. But where charity and the sanctifying gifts of the Spirit are not primarily sought, the Charismatic Renewal becomes unbalanced and misdirected and loses the guidance of the Spirit.

To fulfill its high promise, members of the Charismatic Movement need to accept the fullness of love which the Holy Spirit is, and wishes to bestow. For that, group prayer, while good, is not enough. Like all spiritual movements, this one too needs to be placed in the context of the Christian tradition and to profit by all its means for attaining personal holiness. In particular it needs to seek with utmost earnestness and constancy the sanctifying gifts of the Spirit. I earnestly hope that this book will help to fulfill this need and so be of service to the Charismatic Movement.

5

AT THE MOMENT, a dialogue is taking place between monks of the eastern and western religions. Authorities of these religions recognize that the monks have a special affinity for each other and are in a special position to carry on the dialogue between their respective traditions. Those engaged in this dialogue need, and are seeking, to understand their counterparts. A book which represents the teaching on spiritual practice as found in authentic Christian tradition should be helpful to all parties to the dialogue.

6

IN SPEAKING OF GOD, I use ordinarily the personal form Father, referring to the first person of the Trinity.

The primary reason Jesus became man, the reason why He died and rose for us and sent us His Spirit (ushering us into a new age, the age of the Spirit) was to reveal to us the Father, and to make His Father our Father.

With regard to naming God as the Father, where the Son or Holy Spirit are not clearly indicated as the appropriate name, I am following the usage of the writers of the New Testament. Yves Congar reminds us[1] and Karl Rahner has clearly shown[2] that all but six uses of the term *Theos* (God) in the New Testament are references to the Father.

Because all perfections of creatures consistent with the deity are eminently present in God, those excellencies of women, such as their intuitiveness, sensitivity, tenderness, compassion, tact, endurance, are present in the Father, in the Son, and in the Godhead. Womanhood and maternity are given the highest place among humans in the person of Mary, the Mother of God.

In using the name of the first person of the Trinity, I recall that it is the Father from Whom all comes and to Whom all are called to return. I recall that He is indeed our Father.

There is increasing evidence, including psychiatric and sociological evidence, that the healing of individuals and of society awaits an increase in knowledge and love of the Father, a realization that He loves us, individually and as a planet of peoples, and wants to hold us and every aspect of our lives close in His embrace.

7

THIS IS A revised version of a book which appeared just before Vatican II, emerging from the same stream as did that Council. In it the need for union with the Father as our happiness and the means to fulfill that need are treated.

In Part One, Happiness, which is the goal of all human striving, is reflected upon first of all. In our society, in which product identification and specifications require careful examination, people need to consider with a similar care, and with deep reflection, in what their

[1] See Yves Congar, *I Believe in the Holy Spirit*, Vol. II, N.Y.: Seabury, 1983, p. 90.

[2] See Karl Rahner, "*Theos* in the New Testament," in *Theological Investigations*, Vol. I, N.Y.: Crossroad, 1961, pp. 79-148. See also the excellent work *The God Of Jesus Christ* by Walter Kasper, N.Y.: Crossroad, 1984, pp. 143-144.

true happiness consists. The first two chapters on "Happiness" are offered to assist this reflection.

Those who become convinced that they have an enduring happiness in God (and in God alone) find a new and stronger motivation which gives order, balance and meaning to their lives.

Some hints on doing spiritual reading are given here and in the Appendix. These hints may help the rest of the book to be absorbed and become an instrument of grace and transformation. Then prayer is discussed so that this reading may give rise to prayer, through which it becomes more fruitful. And since the obstacles to grace need to be removed in order for grace to flourish, this topic is treated next. Books such as this transmit the word of God, which is formative of the human personality.

In Part Two the knowledge of the Father and of His plan for our happiness ("the mystery of Christ ... now revealed in the Spirit" Ephesians 3:5) is set forth to win minds and hearts to Him and to an understanding of and cooperation with His plan.

In Part Three the role of the Church and its liturgy and sacraments in our human and spiritual development are explained. Liturgical prayer too is treated, that prayer which is most basic to an authentic Christian life.

Here too the states of life in which Christians may pursue spiritual practice are discussed: the married and lay single states, the priesthood and the state of consecrated life.

In Part Four is discussed a significant form of prayer of our time, in which anyone concerned with spiritual practice will have some interest: the Charismatic Renewal.

In Part Five are discussed our divine adoption and the infused virtues and the gifts of the Spirit by which divine life is communicated and grows in us. This in my opinion has very special pertinence to the charismatic movement, as I have indicated above. This section also treats of progress in the virtues and the gifts, true devotion, temptation, and the final outcome of human and spiritual life, classically known as "the last things."

Here too an account of the human psyche is given. Thomas Aquinas' doctrine is helpful in revealing the dynamic role of the virtues and gifts of the Holy Spirit which integrate the human personality psychologically, morally and spiritually.

If the spiritual life is pursued prudently, in accord with sound advice, it increases the psychological resources of people, and their mental health as well as human development. How it does so is indicated in the course of this book.

But in Part Six, particularly, psychological advice is offered, and the role of grace in maintaining and furthering mental equilibrium and personality growth is discussed.

Then all the degrees of the spiritual life are covered concisely in two chapters, from the stage of the beginner to transforming union. It is well to know the kind of union with Christ to which the spiritual life is tending with its trials and purifications. The advice appropriate to each degree is given. The new ways into which grace leads us are described. The dynamic center of the soul's action is lifted by the actuation of the sanctifying gifts of the Holy Spirit to a higher level, a more divine plane. This realizes human potentialities and happiness in an unexpected way, and confers a new capacity for action. A clear and brief explanation of the unfolding and fulfillment of the human personality through the spiritual life is thus presented in these two chapters.

Then a chapter on spiritual direction follows, for those interested in understanding it, or in giving or receiving it (including seminarians). This chapter indicates how this book may be made into a handbook of spiritual direction for directors and those who are directed, or who seek in this book the direction they may not find elsewhere.

Finally an integral program of the spiritual life is proposed in the last chapter. This is followed in the Appendix with a classified list of books for spiritual reading, starting with the Scriptures.

FEW CURRENT BOOKS have this perspective and cover this scope. May this book help many, including those ministering to others, the laity, lay ministers, permanent deacons, seminarians, the clergy and religious, to satisfy their hunger for prayer and to equip them for apostolic fruitfulness. May it help them to find depth and fulfillment in the various movements to which they belong, some of which are treated in a special way, and may it help these movements to prosper in accordance with the divine will.

This book is inclusive in the readership to which it is directed: to those who wish to enter into the fullness of grace to which Christ calls them, with its manifold benefits; to those who wish to profit by their Sunday observance and their participation in the liturgy or in religious services; to those in the Charismatic Renewal; to those involved in the East-West dialogue; to clergy, religious, permanent deacons, and laity who serve others; to those interested in human development, in fulfillment, in mental health.

The Father wants to help all His children, the entire human race, in all their varied needs, with a view of leading humankind into a new era, an age of universal holiness in one Spirit, one flock and under one Shepherd, and this book treats both of this initiative of His and of the response by which the benefits He wishes to pour out on the human family may be secured.

Part One:

Happiness
& The Way
to Happiness

You have made us for Yourself, O Lord, and
our hearts are restless until they rest in Thee.
— Saint Augustine, *Confessions*, Book I

1 The Way to Happiness

Our age is a time of crisis and change. Comfortable material well-being as an assured way and goal of life retains its attractiveness for many, but others are not satisfied with this as a goal. Today nothing is assured.

Indeed there is widespread anxiety about the future and an awareness of severe and difficult global problems. Still a hunger is breaking through human consciousness, a hunger for values, for decency, for prayer. The appeal of many of the movements of our day is their call for devotedness to the general welfare. True goodness is also an absolute and can have an appeal, even for the uncommitted. True goodness can be pursued in any state or condition of life.

When persons realize Who the Father is, and what His plan for them is, they are drawn to dedicate themselves to Him and to His design for their future. His design for the person, if accepted and

3

pursued, always has an influence on the renewal of society. His plan is one in which science and reason will cooperate with the divine wisdom for achieving a new world in which unselfish love is the mainspring.

This new world must take shape first in the hearts of individuals. Spirituality must rule human hearts. Then it will introduce into lives and conduct the divine order and the peace for which the world is looking. Then lives will be fruitful for bringing into existence a new age and widespread happiness.

Divisiveness and a shut-in view of sanctity are obstacles to this achievement. Too many believe that spirituality is for ministers, the clergy, the religious, but not for lay persons. Apart from those involved in such movements as the Charismatic Renewal, Cursillos, Focolare, the Legion of Mary, lay people who do feel God's attractiveness are apt to think at once that this is a call to the religious or clerical state. If one is opposed to embracing such a state, perhaps for very sound reasons, one is inclined to stifle this call, which is a call to union with God, our loving Father.

The Father invites all to come closer to Him in the lay state as well as in the priesthood and the religious life. Union with God is at once the road to personal happiness and to a new world, one which will be formed by lay persons, religious and clergy.

On Sunday January 20, 1985, John Paul II said:

> I am indeed convinced that the evangelical message bears an answer to crucial questions before the modern world and I feel the weight of the responsibility not to spare any effort to serve the cause of justice and solidarity for the children of the same motherland and for nations in search of a better tomorrow.

Church unity and the renewal of Church and society depend not only on the renewal of the clergy and religious, but also on the laity. The example and ministry of lay persons are needed if the world is to be made one in the love of Christ. Pius XII said on October 14, 1951, in words that are even more pertinent today:

> The Church has a threefold mission to fulfill for all: to raise up the fervent believers to the level of present day needs; to introduce those who hesitate on the threshold to the warm and salutary intimacy of the hearth, and to lead back those who have separated

themselves from religion and whom she cannot abandon to their miserable fate.

An inspiring task for the Church! But it is one rendered more difficult by the fact that, while the Church as a whole has grown greatly, the number of clergy has not increased in proportion. Besides, the clergy must above all keep themselves free for the exercise of the sacred ministry proper to the sacerdotal state, which no one else can do for them.

For that reason, assistance rendered by the laity to the apostolate is an indispensable necessity.

Of the universality of the call to sanctity, the Holy Spirit speaks clearly. "This is the will of God, your sanctification," He says through Saint Paul (1 Thessalonians 4:3).

All are invited to union with God. This invitation is applied to the individual whenever he or she reads or hears it, or feels within the attraction of the Holy Spirit. Day laborer, machinist, unlettered and learned, children, the aged, single and married persons are all called to holiness. The Father created the universe and keeps it in existence for this purpose, that all may have the opportunity to be united to Himself.

Through such a personal union with the Father and His Son, They are glorified and humans achieve their happiness.

The human personality is fulfilled when it is steeped in the divinity. It is healed, purified, elevated, and endowed with new energies and powers. Love becomes ascendant, wisdom shines from within, peace spreads abroad. The endeavors and conduct of such a one pour oil on the troubled waters of other hearts, mending the torn, refreshing the jaded, reconciling those who are estranged or hostile.

Self-love itself prompts to this goal. It is true that blind and inordinate self-love (ambition, envy, jealousy, anger, alcoholism, addiction, overeating, sexual license) are injurious. Self-love is destructive when it makes itself the goal or when it takes the wrong means to promote personal welfare.

But enlightened self-love, which is really charity towards oneself, seeks one's true welfare. It sets its possessor's goods in order and watches over them: the external goods of reputation and property, the good of the body, and the welfare of the soul with its goods of knowledge, virtue and friendship, and skill in various kinds of achievements.

Union with the Father is to the interest of everyone. It is to the advantage of each to love the Father more than oneself, to obtain from the Father for the mind the light of wisdom, and for the heart the harmony of well-ordered love. One cannot truly love oneself without loving others; nor find peace without being peaceable.

If we love the Father, we will desire to grow in His love and to benefit others. The danger of seeking to save one's soul by meeting the minimum requirements of salvation is explained by Christ in the parable of the money left by a master with his three servants. The one to whom five talents were left traded, and upon the master's return had gained another five. The one to whom two had been left gained another two. The third hid his talent in the ground and returned it to the master, who was displeased and took it from him because it had remained fruitless.

The Christian who is content with attendance at Sunday church services and the avoidance of deadly sin is burying his or her one talent of sanctifying grace and rendering it fruitless.

You are seeking happiness. Recognize then that happiness is to be found only in the Father and in the Father's will for you. Know that the Father's will for you is your sanctification. In seeking union with the Father you will find true happiness.

All the living, so long as they have their sanity and the use of their will, can embrace and fulfill this goal of life.

The past is no obstacle, whatever mistakes and sins it contains. Present limitations and problems are no obstacle. The very defects of the past and present will serve as means to accomplish this purpose. We can regard everything with the exception of future sins as part of the Father's plan.

Once our life has been dedicated to the Father, it takes on a very sublime purpose, which enriches and ennobles it, transforming even what is routine and monotonous. No occupation or form of life is incompatible with sanctity unless it be intrinsically evil. Most persons can seek their sanctification in the circumstances in which they find themselves. Yet many more than those who respond are called to the priesthood and to the consecrated state of life.

A vast multitude suffer from a lack of purpose in their lives, a lack of a purpose noble enough to remain a source of inspiration throughout life. Routine becomes enervating. Their courage to make the sacrifices for which life calls, falters. Then they are apt to be the prey of anxiety, discontent, temptation, and depression—of emotional, mental or moral disorders—as they take unhealthy ways of avoiding the painfulness of their lives. For the young and inexperienced, and the withdrawn, this has the added danger of preventing them from establishing good habits of thinking, willing and achieving, and a proper socialization with both sexes.

Only one purpose of life can inspire and animate the entirety of life. That is the purpose for which we have been made and which corresponds to the deepest aspiration of the human heart. For the deepest aspiration of the heart is not for satisfaction, but for values. Created desires do not fully satisfy the human heart. For the inner face of man and woman is turned of its very nature toward an infinite God Who alone is great enough and good enough to fulfill the infinite human longings. He alone can enter into the heart's innermost being to be possessed there in the intimacy of a mutual love.

2 Happiness Now & In Eternity

Most of us find it difficult to free our minds from preoccupation with ourselves. We feel unable to think of the Father and of Heaven. And yet we are not sufficiently serious about ourselves. Some feel unconsciously that an interest in oneself is contrary to Christianity, to nobility, and decency—that it is selfish. But a proper self-love is not selfish, nor contrary to the highest perfection. We fantasize about ourselves, we have feelings about ourselves, but do we seriously think about ourselves?

For many the way to a worthy life is to strengthen the basic instinct of self-preservation by consciously joining to it the force of the will, directed to one's true and fullest personal welfare. Thus the motivation and determination to act and strive and to do so aright is upheld. It is our duty to take care of our reputation, temporal interests, persons dependent upon us, our health, and personal welfare.

Action must be guided by reason and faith, if it is to be effective in procuring our personal welfare. Blind instinct alone is not sufficient; it must be enlightened. Now it is exactly through this enlightenment that selfishness becomes proper self-love; and that self-interest is guided to attain its proper ends. Eating, drinking, sleeping, working, playing will not benefit us unless done with judgment. The proper care of the body is an essential part of living and of loving.

So too there must be an order among the goals sought by the self. The body is of more value than the raiment, Our Lord teaches us (Luke 12:23). While promoting one's welfare, one must not neglect what is most vital, the soul. Without the soul there is but a corpse. Of what value is reputation or money to a corpse? It is the soul that experiences happiness, peace and joy. Those who report near-death experiences have no doubt about this. True self-love will consider first of all the attainment of the soul's end, God.

Can anything other than God be our end? Money, food, clothing and shelter of their nature serve us. They are not the master, the end. Power, too, is but a means to an end. Health and pleasure are important goods of the body, which is a part of human nature, and the instrument of the soul, to which it is joined. Knowledge and virtue are the goods of the soul which likewise are not the end but can serve to direct us to the end.

No matter how happy is our union with others, with spouses or friends, whatever our achievements: intellectual, economic, technological, social, or political, a part of us remains alone, unfulfilled. Freedom, peace and joy are the soul's when the soul knows, pursues and possesses God, Who alone is its end.

Our problem is that from adolescence on, we tend to pursue intermediate ends, without considering in what our happiness really consists, what is our ultimate goal. Only in mid-life, when, having attained (or failed to attain) these intermediate ends, do many people wonder what it is all about. Then they are apt to have a mid-life crisis, or a depression. Then only do many discover their ultimate end. But wisdom would counsel us to discover this as soon as possible, and to direct towards it our pursuit of intermediate ends.

When we know our ultimate end is God, we do not thereby disqualify ourselves from effectively seeking intermediate ends, such as having and raising a family, pursuing a career, or furthering social justice. Rather these intermediate ends become more meaningful because they are serving to bring us closer to the Father and to eternal happiness.

Wisdom comes from the Father. He gives it freely to those who ask for it. One then discovers that the purpose of one's existence is a union with Him which is only final and permanent after death in Heaven. Self-love, rightly ordered, leads the soul to find its joy in submission to the Father's will in the hope of the eternal possession of Himself, a possession which begins imperfectly, but really, in this life.

"You shall love your neighbor as yourself," says Jesus (Mark 12:31). Then we must love ourselves. In doing so we shall know what the measure of our love of our neighbor should be, what we should will for him and her. Loving ourselves truly, we shall also love our neighbor truly and desire for both of us the unending happiness of Heaven.

But what is this unending happiness? What has the Father revealed to us about it?

In the era before Creation, God alone existed—a bright intelligence and a flaming love; a single actuality, peaceful, joyous, wise and good.

This supreme Being is one and three: a society of three Persons in the one divine nature.

The first of these Persons is the Father. He is the ultimate origin of all that is. But He is not alone in the Godhead. "In the beginning was the Word, and the Word was with God"—that is with the Father (Prologue of Saint John's Gospel). The Word is the Father's Son.

The Father knows the divine nature with a complete knowledge. This knowledge *is* His Son, His Image. Thus the Son is begotten eternally of Him. The Father is forever gazing upon the Son, and the Son upon the Father.

The Father and Son look upon each other with infinite understanding and love. They have for each other and for all they love, the wonderful solicitude and tenderness of a woman, of a bride, of a mother. Their love breathes forth the third Person, the Holy Spirit, in Whom They are united anew. This Love is identical in nature with the

Lovers from Whom He proceeds. Like Them He possesses the divine nature. He is the Holy Spirit.

From all eternity there are three divine Persons, equal in dignity, united in supreme majesty and holy fellowship. This is the intimate, interior life of God.

God's existence, sovereignty, intelligence, will and providence are known from the things He has made, as an artist is known by his work. We reason from the effect to the cause. But the interior life of God is known to Him alone, and to those to whom He reveals it. So also, there is in the artist something of himself, of his interior life, which transcends his works and cannot be known from them. Only the Father can reveal the Son and only the Son can reveal the Father.

This revelation of Himself He gives in Christ and in the Church, and it is for all peoples. All are called to receive this gift. Yet many do not through no fault of their own, for example because of the tradition and culture into which they were born. They are not excluded from the Heaven which the Father has prepared for the human race. This is the universal perspective of the Catholic Faith, which recognizes the necessity of the Catholic Faith and of the Church for the salvation of those fortunate enough to be open to its teaching, or, because of a question in their minds, able to pursue this question and to receive the Faith, yet recognizing those not so fortunate as not thereby barred from Heaven.

God is what God is because He is God. His joy and contentment are an everlasting AMEN, a so-be-it, to this life of His. He possesses it all at once and entirely. Eternity is God's total and simultaneous possession of Himself, in contrast to our successive possession of our life, in a span of time past, present and future.

God was free to create or not to create. Since nothing was wanting to Him, why did He choose to create? The answer is found in His goodness. God communicates His divine nature divinely so that it is possessed by three divine Persons. He cannot communicate it in this way to another. But He could create angels and humans possessed of intelligence and will, capable of partaking of the divine nature and happiness. God is infinite goodness and goodness communicates itself to others. Goodness is diffusive of itself, like the fragrance of a rose.

Our happiness, then, is to be found on this supernatural plane where by faith and love we partake of God's nature and happiness.

God's happiness is so sublime that we have found another word to express it. We call it beatitude, or blessedness. It is to communicate this blessedness that He chose to create the angels, pure spirits, and humans, composite of spirit and matter. Happiness and union with Himself is our very end, the purpose of our existence. And He finds means of realizing His purpose despite the ignorance and disorder in us. Yet He will not force Himself upon persons whom He has gifted with free will.

We wonder about the disorder, the frustrations and afflictions which bruise and grieve our hearts. It is difficult for us to understand the purpose of life hidden as it is in the Being Whose will, seemingly, brings all this to pass.

With the aid of Revelation, we can go directly to the divine source of our life and being. With the assistance of the Father's grace, we see what His life is, and understand how good, pure and noble are His intentions in creating us. We can come to realize that the evils that entangle us are not from Him. Our hearts can enlarge with love of His infinite goodness as our suspicious and distrustful minds are set at rest. As the bitterness and uprisings of our hearts are quelled and their fears and forebodings quieted, we can submit ourselves lovingly to a divine will which is not the cause of sin and suffering, which wishes only our happiness, and which knows better than we how to bring this about.

How are these good intentions of the Father fulfilled? Having glanced with our mind's eye at the era before time, let us consider the era when time will be no more. At the General Resurrection, Christ will separate the just from the unjust. To all the deeds of all will be made known. Divine justice will be vindicated. Purgatory will cease to be. The blessed, bodies and souls reunited, will go with Christ to Heaven.

What we now hold by faith will then be evident to us, for we shall see God face to face. Of course, for many, this will occur from the moment of their death, when they will be introduced into Heaven and into this divine vision, before the General Resurrection and the General Judgment.

We shall see the generation of the Son from the Father, as His knowledge, and the procession of the Holy Spirit from the Father and the Son as the fullness of their love. We shall see that God could not be otherwise than three Persons in one divine nature.

It is in His own light that we shall see this intimate life of God, as He sees Himself. Then it will be impossible for us to consider God under any other aspect than that of His truth and goodness. He will exert an irresistible attraction upon us, eliciting from us an irrevocable love, like that which unites the divine Persons themselves. From this love will issue a peace and joy without limit. The freshness and intensity of this experience will never lessen. This light and love are the very light and love of the Father Himself, which we, His adopted children, inherit and possess whole and entire from the moment we enter eternity.

But we are human beings. It is as human beings that the Father will make us happy. In the beatific vision we shall see the union of the humanity with the divinity in the unity of the Second Person of the Trinity; the Mother whose Son is God; the divine power passing into the creatures whom the Father is conserving in being, and the divine sanctification sustaining souls in holiness.

As human beings we are a composite of body and soul. Our hearts will be captivated by the sweetness of the society of Jesus and Mary, our eyes by the loveliness of their countenances, our ears by their voices. In their company we will be at home at last.

There will be the joy of the companionship of the saints, including relatives, friends, and intercessors.

No one will be lost in this multitude, no one unknown, no one neglected. Each will be, as it were, the center of attraction of all, of all-embracing love and amiable companionship, without trace of discord.

Christ, in His risen body, showed us the characteristics which our resurrected bodies will have. They will be spiritual as Saint Paul remarks, the lower powers completely subordinated to the higher. In this docility of the sensible faculties lies their perfection. We shall never experience in the lower part of our nature a movement contrary to right reason or the Father's will, to which our wills will be completely conformed. Our bodies will not be subject to death, sickness, or pain.

Our Lord's body rose into the air in His Ascension. Our resurrected bodies, too, will no longer be subject to the law of gravitation. They will move where, and as quickly as, we wish—if we will it, at the speed of thought. Our bodies will also be able to pass through other bodies, as Our Lord did when He passed through the closed door of the Cenacle on Easter Sunday.[1] Finally, the glory of the soul will shine through the body as the splendor of Christ's soul shone through His in the Transfiguration.

Saint Peter tells us that there will be a "new heaven and a new earth." This new heaven and earth will excel our present habitations. In it there will be many mansions, our dwellings (John 14:2). Many will be the pleasures of Heaven, in which we will delight. Anything that we wish, the Father will give us, and in our desires there will be no disorder. We cannot portray the faintest image of the happiness which God has planned and which He will bring to perfection. Saint Paul tells us: "Eye has not seen nor ear heard, nor has it entered into the heart of man, what things God has prepared for those who love Him" (1 Corinthians 2:9). But if the Father has created such beauties for our temporary residence as we enjoy now on earth, we can be sure that our eternal home will be much grander.

We can return frequently throughout life to these truths. We admire God's wonderful attributes, the goodness, love, wisdom, power, and mercy which have conceived, willed, and are bringing to fulfillment this astonishing plan. Of course we desire that it be fulfilled in us, in our dear ones, in our enemies, in all. It inspires us with the courage and generosity to order our lives in such a way that this shall be accomplished. For it rests with us whether or not we shall share these joys.

In this light we can put into proper perspective the sufferings, frustrations, and privations of this life, which are not from the Father, but from original sin and human sinfulness. This life compared to eternity lasts no longer than the snap of a finger. For eternity is forever, time is not. All our pains will come to an end; borne for

[1] R.-M. Garrigou-Lagrange, O.P., *Life Everlasting*, St. Louis: Herder, 1952, Chap. xxix, p. 254. Also Saint Thomas Aquinas, *Summa Contra Gentiles*, Bk. IV, Chap. 1, xxxvii. See *Of God and His Creatures*, trans. by Joseph Rickaby, S.J., Westminster, Md.: Newman Press, 1950, p. 410 Footnote *.

His love, they will bring us and others an increase of everlasting joy.

This is the meaning of our days. Each hour is given us to merit a place closer to Jesus and Mary and to our dear ones for all eternity. Each suffering we endure speeds us on our way.

As often as we represent to ourselves this reality and enter into it with all the force of our soul, we shall understand the meaning of life and we shall renew our courage to do all that the Father wills us to do, and to suffer all that comes our way, with the graces the Father offers us to turn adversity into prosperity.

And since these truths are so helpful to us in combatting stress, anxiety, depression, and despair, and in moderating excessive highs and activism, and in preventing burn-out, we can see the importance of giving time to prayer and spiritual reading which lead us to absorb these truths and the energy-sustaining attitudes they engender, even if this means the elimination from our schedule of wasteful moments, such as the overuse of the media.

3 Hammer: Reading the Scriptures

Throughout the ages two means of spiritual practice have been paramount: reading the Scriptures and prayer. From the third to the 16th century, four little words expressed this primacy: *lectio* (the reading of the Scriptures), *meditatio* (mulling over one's reading), *oratio* (prayer issuing from this reflection), and *contemplatio* (contemplation coming into the prepared heart).

These are primary means of the Christian tradition for finding happiness, means which prayer movements need to make use of in order that they may flourish, means which need to be employed if church services, liturgy, are to be fully effective.

This chapter will speak of the nature of spiritual reading, of suitable reading matter, of the way to read, and of the fruits to be obtained.

Half the battle of life—of the spiritual life—consists in persevering in spiritual reading. We are constantly subjected to impressions from the world through what we see, hear and read. We are continuously influenced too by our temperament and imagination, which tend to make our thoughts subjective and misleading. We need daily contact with a source of divine truth, and this we have through spiritual reading. Through it we enter into an atmosphere of truth and reality in which the proper perspective on values is maintained, and this affects our judgments, desires, decisions, and conduct.

Without spiritual reading, prayer becomes empty and unfruitful, for spiritual reading supplies matter for our prayer. It reawakens memories and recollections, deepens true impressions, corrects errors, and extends our vision. While we continue to do daily spiritual reading, the relish for it increases; but when we let it drop out of our daily life it becomes distasteful, and only by repeated efforts do we recover its enjoyment.

The most excellent spiritual reading is the reading of the words of Christ; He is the Wisdom of the Father. This Wisdom dwelt among us and conversed with us. In order that the precious privilege of that one generation be not lost to its successors, divine Providence preserved for us the teachings of Christ in the New Testament and in tradition, and placed them in the hands of a divinely instituted society, the Church. And that this teaching might the better sanctify the lives of men, divine Providence has given us in all ages works of spiritual doctrine which contain and apply the teachings of Christ.

Spiritual reading is the reception of the divine truths from these written works. Sometimes spiritual reading not only enlightens the mind but also inflames the heart and strengthens the will. It is both food and medicine; without it the soul is feeble, sick, and often paralyzed.

What should we read? The Scriptures, the New Testament in particular, and especially Saint John's Gospel. Of special importance are Christ's Sermon on the Mount (Matthew 5, 6, 7), and His discourse at the Last Supper (John 13-17), The Acts of the Apostles and the Epistles. In the Old Testament, especially the Psalms, the Sapiential books (Wisdom, Proverbs, Sirach, Ecclesiastes) and certain beautiful sections of the Prophetical books (e.g. Isaiah, Chapter 49 to the end; especially noteworthy are Chapter 52:13-15 and Chapter 53).

In beginning in earnest the spiritual or interior life, and throughout the course of the spiritual life, books such as this one are helpful.

With the Scripture and books of spiritual doctrine rank lives of Our Lord. These help us to appreciate the Scriptures and to know Jesus better. Archbishop Goodier's works, *The Public Life of Our Lord Jesus Christ*, *The Passion and Death of Our Lord Jesus Christ*, and *The Risen Jesus*, are especially valuable for their portrayal of the warmth of the Sacred Heart of Jesus, into Whose interior sentiments they permit us to enter.

It is good to alternate books of spiritual doctrine with the lives of the saints, or to read them at the same time. The lives of the saints show the doctrine put into practice. They present us with very attractive examples which move us powerfully to make progress in the spiritual life. *The Story of a Soul*, the autobiography of Saint Thérèse of Lisieux, produced from her original manuscripts by Rev. Stephen Clark, O.C.D., ICS Publications, is such a work, suitable for many. Moving is Thomas Merton's autobiography, *The Seven-Storey Mountain*. More precise information and other suggestions for spiritual reading will be found in the Appendix to this book.

We should choose such reading as is adapted to our mentality and needs. It is possible to obtain spiritual food in a form suitable for almost everyone. Therefore, if we find that a particular book does not reach us, although it treats of the matter which we need, we can be fairly certain of finding the same matter in another book more suited to our mentality. But we should avoid fastidiousness and undue insistence upon personal taste, and the exclusive interest in the most recent or the popular.

The manner in which we read is also very important. It is advisable to begin our reading with a prayer, such as those to the Holy Spirit at the beginning and end of this book, to obtain actual grace. If possible this prayer should be said kneeling, and it should be intense. We pray because we wish the Father to speak to us through our spiritual reading: we wish Him to take our life into His hands and to change and conform it to the model of His divine Son, Jesus Christ. We should read slowly and deliberately, perhaps a chapter a day. We should avoid the haste which is born of curiosity, of the desire to know what the author is going to say in succeeding chapters. Spiritual reading is not done merely for knowledge or for the pleasure which are furnished by style and construction, or so that we will have matter for conversations. Love of the Father makes the soul eager to profit by whatever leads it to Him: humility makes truth and goodness attractive whatever their dress.

We should not hesitate to pass over to prayer if we feel drawn to do so. Our Lord is very much present to the person who reads with a right purpose. Thus we may converse with Him, adore Him, thank Him, make reparation for our past sins and defects, beg Him for the graces we need, and resolve to put the lights we are receiving into practice. Or our communication with Him may simply be the reception of His lights and graces.

The Spirit of Jesus makes suitable books read in this manner a channel of His personal guidance. He sheds light upon the divine truths, clarifying our intelligence. He warns us of dangers and obstacles, indicates the virtues we should practice and the sins and evil tendencies we should avoid. He may arouse in us new hope, holy desires and fresh determination, rectifying our will and reorienting our emotions. In the course of spiritual reading, as in prayer, He strengthens us to fulfill our duties and helps us to conform our will to the Father's, bringing about maturity of spirit and life.

The fruits of our spiritual reading are made more secure by reflection and prayer. In leisure moments, perhaps two or three times a day, we can reflect on those few points in our reading which promise to be most helpful to us. We can think over the lights received, the hopes, desires and resolutions formed, or which we would wish to form. Then we realize that more time is needed to assimilate these lights, to manifest to the Father our esteem for His wonderful goodness, to impress these good desires and resolutions upon ourselves so that our lives will be lastingly changed.

Thus, our spiritual reading may portray the admirable humility and meekness of Christ in a manner that affects us as never before: we appreciate how these divine qualities, so little appreciated, deserve to be praised, and how they would transform our lives. We realize that something more than our reading and reflection is needed to effect this. Then we may resolve to make the humility and meekness of Christ the subject of mental prayer. We know what we shall consider, admire and praise; for what we shall ask; what affections and resolutions we desire to deepen: we have a plan for mental prayer.

4 And Fire: Prayer

Mental prayer is divine fire that enkindles the soul with ardent and holy desires: without mental prayer it is difficult or impossible to be intimately penetrated by the Spirit of Christ.

This divine fire is often experienced by those in the Charismatic Renewal who are beseeching the Lord for the "Baptism of the Spirit"—a renewal of their baptismal consecration with awareness of the presence and love of Jesus and of the power of His Spirit. Then this fire introduces the person into sensible affections and consolations during which prayer is easy.

Everyone needs to be awakened to this need for mental prayer—a need which an Archbishop of Bordeaux in a pastoral letter to his people declared to be indispensable; for mental prayer, he asserted, is the only means which will enable the modern man to meet the difficulties and complexities of life in our day. Pope Pius XII, speaking to priests, has declared that there is no substitute for mental prayer.

This chapter may help the layman who has never practiced mental prayer, but it may be also useful to those experienced in prayer, who profit by reading on this subject from time to time, gleaning here and there useful hints, and forming a renewed zeal and courage in the practice of prayer and a deeper insight into it.

We shall speak of the nature and parts of mental prayer, giving an example and practical advice; then we shall discuss its trials, fruits and mental hygiene value.

NATURE AND PARTS OF PRAYER

What is prayer? Prayer is the lifting of the mind and heart to the Father. "Lifting" means the turning from creatures, which occupy our attention most of the time, to the Creator. "Mind" and "heart" signify especially the two faculties of intellect and will, which are engaged in the act of mental prayer.

The prayer of the just is holy converse in the intimacy of friendship with the God of our hearts, Who is closer to us than we are to ourselves. In prayer, the soul is endowed with power from above; it experiences a strength that is not its own, but Christ's. In prayer the soul acquires and exercises all the virtues, particularly (besides religion) faith, hope and charity. These virtues have God as their immediate object and so unite us directly to Christ and to the Father. By these virtues, the soul traverses the distance separating it from the Father; prayer is an actual participation of the divine Life; it is the child's sharing in the Father's and the Son's knowledge and love of each other.

Prayer takes its origin from our love of the Father, or of His Son, or at least from our desire to love God; and it is the great means of enkindling this love. It originates in love: it is the love of the Father or the desire for this love that leads us to pray—to apply our mind to Him. It results in an increase of love; that is its final purpose and ultimate effect.

What are the parts of prayer? From our definition, we can gather that they are acts of the reason and will. The intellect, or reason, considers the subject of prayer in the light of faith in order to arouse acts of the heart, that is, of the will and affections. Considerations—the acts of the reason—without acts of the will would be reflection, but not prayer. Acts of the will, except in the case of somewhat advanced souls, cannot be habitually elicited without these preliminary considerations. But it is the acts of the will which unite our soul to the Father by conforming our will to His in love, and it is in the loving conformity of will that union with the Father consists. This conformity extends to fidelity to the duties of one's state of life.

In this matter of prayer, as in many others, the Holy Spirit Himself will teach us what to do. Often He anticipates us by producing in us those very acts which are most suitable. This serves as a model of, and predisposition for, similar acts which we can make whenever we repeat our exercise of mental prayer.

Since prayer is conversation with the Father, or with the Son, we should introduce it with a realization of His presence. We may call to mind Who He is, and who we are. He is all and we are nothing. We humble ourselves before Him and adore Him; then we have begun to pray.

In our prayer, we fulfill our basic duties toward the Father by four acts which we may remember as a-c-t-s of prayer: Adoration, Contrition, Thanksgiving and Supplication or petition.

It is well to end our prayer with a particular resolution that will specify our determination to be faithful to the grace of the Father, especially if we are not advanced in the ways of prayer.

AN EXAMPLE OF PRAYER—FOR BEGINNERS

Let us give an example of mental prayer. First we place ourselves in the presence of the Father, realizing that He is close to us. We humble ourselves before Him and adore Him. Then we consider our subject. This may be chosen in advance from our spiritual reading and reflected upon in the evening before retiring and in the morning upon awakening. Let us say that it is the humility of Jesus, the Son of God, as this humility was manifested in His dependence upon His Mother during His sacred infancy. We may picture with our imagination the Infant and His most pure Mother as she adores Him lying in the manger wrapped in swaddling clothes shortly after His birth. If we wish, we are kneeling close beside her. The imagination can help us when used in accordance with faith; having truth as its measure, it in turn makes us appreciate humanly the reality of the things of faith. However, we contact God not by the activity of the imagination but by faith.

We consider that this Infant is truly the all-powerful God, in Whose hands are all things. Yet in all simplicity He remains where He is placed. He accepts His helplessness and waits for His Mother to attend to all His needs. God has placed Himself in utter dependence upon His own creatures for love of us. His wonderful goodness elicits from us loving admiration and acts of praise and adoration which we may prolong as long as we feel moved to do so. We rejoice to devote the entire energy of our soul to thinking of and praising Him, while forgetting ourselves.

We feel drawn to imitate such an example. Now we may compare it with our own manner of acting. God became one of us and depended on us. Do we put ourselves above others, are we unwilling to serve them, are we willing to acknowledge our dependence on God, our need for His grace?

The considerations from which we have already drawn acts of adoration now serve to help us elicit, for our pride and selfishness, acts of sorrow, which we again prolong.

We realize our need for Our Lord's humility, and for His grace, for which we beg, urging our petitions again and again. We understand that we must cooperate with His grace, and we make strong acts of determination to follow His example. Perhaps foreseeing certain opportunities to exercise humility, we determine to do so. Then we end by thanking God for the graces which He has given us during this prayer. Incidentally, psychiatrists affirm that a capacity for due dependence on others is part of maturity.

PRACTICAL ADVICE

Prayer should be spontaneous whenever possible; too detailed a de-scription of the manner of prayer is apt to impede the spontaneity of the soul in its relations with the Father, as if there were a certain etiquette or method it needed to follow. The characteristic of the prayer of Thérèse of Lisieux was that it had no method. Simplicity in the description of the method of prayer is helpful; it makes method more palatable and practicable. After all, the true Master of the spiritual life and of prayer is not a book, but the Holy Spirit. He is an interior Master, dwelling within us; we, prepared by spiritual reading, enter into contact with Him by recollecting ourselves at the time of prayer.

Attractions in prayer, which are in accordance with faith and right reason (including common sense), should be followed in preference to any prearranged plan of our own. However, it is well to have such a plan drawn from our spiritual reading (for some, during the first stages; for others, throughout the spiritual life); this will help us to focus our attention and overcome distractions and indecision, while we remain free to follow the attractions of the Holy Spirit. Should we—while occupied in making acts of prayer—find ourselves inclined to prolong any particular act, such as adoration or thanksgiving, we should not hesitate to do so, even for the entire time of prayer. When this ceases to be profitable or engaging, we can pass on to another act, eliciting it by fresh considerations.

While both the mind and heart act in prayer, we should not conceive of prayer as fifteen minutes of considerations and fifteen minutes of acts of the will. We can pass from one to the other as serves our purpose and in keeping with our attraction.

Prayer is conversation, and conversation requires two. We should not be too voluble, and we should stop from time to time to listen to the Father. He will speak gently and peacefully in His own manner; if we do not seem to hear Him, we can be sure that, nevertheless, He appreciates our pauses made in faith and loving expectation. The manner in which the Father speaks to the soul may simply be by communicating peace or joy to it, by strengthening the will in its love for Him and in its purpose of well-doing or He may draw it close to Himself in an affectionate hug.

We do not neglect to eat daily, because we realize the need for daily nourishment; our spirit's need for daily spiritual reading and prayer is just as urgent. Regularity in this matter is important. Common experience shows that the taste for spiritual reading is more easily cultivated and retained if reading is done daily; while serious mental prayer is in danger of being abandoned by those who do not strive earnestly to be faithful to a daily period of prayer. It would be well to give half an hour to each of these exercises. This is a time during the day in which the soul is withdrawn from its contact with the world and with creatures; a time in which, in holy repose and retreat, it keeps solitude and silence with God. A second period of prayer of at least 15 minutes during the day or evening is of very great value.

Incidentally, while this sacrifice is urged for the welfare of the soul and true happiness, it will also in most cases be very much to the advantage of the mind and body. Especially for men and women who cannot spare a moment, such an interruption will tend to procure much peace of mind that will reflect on the health of the body. This truth was expressed by a heart specialist and a psychiatrist who recommended at a medical meeting that a little time be snatched out of the midst of the day, even if only fifteen minutes, to be given preferably (according to one of these specialists) to spiritual reading, to prayer according to the other. Men and women will realize where they can get the time if they consider how much time they spend on television, radio, movies, magazines, newspapers and conversation.

For the reader who finds it difficult to engage in prayer for half an hour, a beginning of fifteen or twenty minutes is recommended. For most persons a more extended period is well worthwhile. It requires a certain amount of time for persons living in the world to recollect themselves and to concentrate their attention effectively on the subject. When less time is devoted to prayer, less profit is reaped from it.

Some cannot make mental prayer without the use of a book. They read, then bring home to themselves the truth of what they read as they pause to make acts of prayer. When unable to continue these, they resume their reading. Those who find it necessary to make use of this method should strive to make prayer predominate over reading.

Another alternative is to make the Stations of the Cross and dwell on Our Lord's love for us at each Station, speaking to Him in our own words, offering love for love.

It should be noted by those who say they cannot pray that they can always talk with someone. That is all mental prayer is. If we are convinced that Jesus, the good and loving friend of our heart, is present with us, why should we be unable to talk with Him?

There is a distinct advantage in choosing as the time for our half-hour of prayer the very first free half-hour in the morning. Then the mind is fresh and the preoccupations of daily duties and concerns have not laid hold upon the energies of the soul; consequently the soul can turn more easily to the Father and maintain itself in converse with Him. When at the very beginning of the day the soul directs its energies in a consistent manner to the Father, it gives to Him with firm determination the entire day with all that is to be done and suffered.

But to remain in this disposition it is necessary to return to the Father frequently during the day, for our good intention will diminish in strength as the soul begins to react to the stresses of daily life. We need to renew our supernatural intention and spirit from time to time or we will depart from the happy determination that we formed in the half-hour of prayer with God.

The period of spiritual reading serves to renew the soul's spiritual energies. If it is more convenient, this exercise may occupy two distinct intervals of fifteen minutes (or more). For some people, or during some days, only ten or fifteen minutes may be available. Then perhaps it would be well to use the Scriptures or a book which is very condensed, such as *The Imitation of Christ*.

Other moments of leisure, such as during transportation or walking, may be utilized for converse with the Father or for ordering in His presence the day's work and doings; and for determining to eliminate the faults which we foresee are apt to enter into them. Some may find it of advantage to single out two fifteen minute periods during their work in which they will strive to remain close to the Father, and eventually the length of these periods may be increased, strain upon the mind always being avoided, and freedom to devote one's energies to one's task being secured.

It is also worthwhile, in the midst of strenuous or engaging activities, to steal three or four minutes for the Father during which the stubbornness of one's will is broken, one's intention is purified, while the attention and energies are momentarily directed to Him Who desires to be with us more and more in all that we think and will and do. The prayer of Cardinal Mercier to the Holy Spirit, found at the end of this book, is recommended precisely for this purpose.

Another useful practice is the making from time to time throughout the day of aspirations, little acts of love or petition. Jesus and Mary, as also does the Father, wish to be our companions; we can make their desire a reality by turning to them our thoughts and desires and speaking to them now and again, and they in turn will help us to live in the Father's presence and to grow in His love. Thus, too, the good dispositions formed in prayer, and the spirit of prayer, can be maintained throughout the day, to influence our thoughts and conduct.

THE BEGINNER'S TRIALS: DISTRACTIONS AND DISCOURAGEMENT

Trials are to be expected by anyone who undertakes seriously to make a half-hour of mental prayer, or two periods of prayer, daily, particularly the trials of distraction and discouragement. The human mind has a capacity to wander without realizing that it is off the point. Thus, during mental prayer it may happen that we have spent several minutes thinking about some happening of the previous day or even counting the panes of glass in the church where we are making our meditation, before we realize that we are off on a distraction. As in the case of temptations to impurity and for the same reason, responsibility only begins when we realize with what our mind is occupied, and that, in this case, it is a distraction. Consequently our prayer has not been interrupted at all, since our intention to pray has remained. Without irritation, gently and peacefully, we should bring the mind back to the subject of our meditation, and as often as necessary. A prayer word, expressive of our faith and love, such as "Jesus" or "Father" may be helpful for this purpose. Sometimes we may spend the entire time of prayer in returning to the subject. But we need have no misgivings or feel discouragement; our time has been well spent in the sight of the Father, we have been exercising our will to pray all the time and hence have, indeed, obtained the merit of prayer, if not its refreshment.

If we are consenting to distractions when we become aware of them, we may seek a remedy. We may renew our determination to avoid deliberate distractions, for consent to distractions is a diminution or abandonment of our purpose to pray and an irreverence to God. We may slowly say the Our Father, Hail Mary or the Creed, dwelling meditatively on each phrase so long as we draw food for prayer from it; or we may read a little and then meditate on what we have read; or we may make the Stations of the Cross meditatively, reflecting on Our Lord's Passion and making acts of love and sorrow for sin, etc. However, indeliberate distractions are of no consequence, and should not be a source of concern or disquiet. They occur characteristically in the "nights," and to all at most times of prayer. This is how our imagination works! They do not impair the value of our prayer.

Discouragement attacks many persons who begin to practice daily mental prayer. It is well to keep in mind that all Our Lord asks of us is the continued effort, the persevering attempt to pray and to lead a spiritual life. If we persevere, Our Lord will know how to bring forth much fruit and to eventually transform us into His own likeness. That is His work; ours is only to make the intelligent and sustained effort.

We do not have to have beautiful thoughts and sentiments in order to pray well, nor do we need to keep up the pace set by an infrequent excellent and "fruitful" half-hour.

FRUITS

In prayer, by the acts of the will we direct our soul to the Father as to its true end. We embrace Him as the purpose of our life and as its goal. We make strong practical decisions and determinations to avoid sin and the near occasions of sin, which alone can separate us from God, and we choose, in preference to sin, the company and friendship of Jesus for time and eternity.

Through persevering mental prayer, the obstacles to our happiness in God are overcome. These are, on the part of the intellect, forgetfulness of our end and purpose, of eternity and the eternal truths; and forgetfulness or ignorance of ourselves, of our motives, desires and preoccupations, which, more than we may realize, are weaning our heart from God and turning hearts unduly to the things of the world.

Besides these obstacles on the part of the intellect, others on the part of the will and affections are also overcome by unremitting mental prayer. Besides the light to know our Supreme Good and ourselves, we need the strength to redirect our energies to this Good and away from what is useless, harmful or dangerous to us. We need to overcome worldliness, the undue love of honor, dignity, power, riches, comfort, and all forms of selfishness and sin. This mental prayer accomplishes, through arousing in us our natural and supernatural powers, by directing them to their true ends and objects, and by drawing divine help and strength into our minds and hearts. This is of immense mental health value. The Father, too, by His providence, favors the soul that perseveres in seeking Him.

There is a tendency on the part of our temperament to reassert itself, a tendency of our nature, with all its faults, to resume its ascendancy over our interior and exterior life. This tendency is overcome by the spirit of recollection and the practice of virtue consequent upon spiritual reading and prayer, which supernaturalize the soul.

MENTAL HYGIENE VALUE

From this account of prayer, we can readily understand its subsidiary value as mental hygiene, and for the resolution of certain mental and emotional problems.

Prayer establishes in us what we so much need in order to be mentally as well as morally healthy: a purpose for living.

Moreover, it leads to practical and effective choice of the means to accomplish that purpose. It makes us understand how sublime and noble this end is, and how efficacious are the means. From this comes a spirit of security and confidence, based not upon our own strength but upon the omnipotence and mercy of the Father and upon the help of His grace.

Everything in our life and contacts falls within the compass of this purpose without any distortion or unreality (or is eliminable), because the purpose of our existence and the existence of the universe is the union of our soul with the Father. The wholehearted pursuit of an end that is able to integrate our entire life makes for an integrated personality and mental health.

In prayer the soul which has made some progress is pierced by a two-edged sword which reaches into its joints and marrow. As Scripture says:

> The word of God is living and effectual and more piercing than any two-edged sword; and reaching into the division of the soul and the spirit, of the joints also, and the marrow, and is a discerner of the thoughts and intents of the heart (Hebrews 4:12).

Indeed, the Spirit of God searches the depths of the soul in prayer, making it aware of the obstacles to grace, of the hidden things in the deep heart of man which stand between him and the full flood of rationality, between him and his God.

In prayer, these twisted, hidden dispositions and movers of the soul's powers are uncovered and disclosed to the soul's gaze.

It realizes then its slothfulness and indigence, its prideful exaltation of self to which it deceptively bends certain activities; the envies, jealousies and antipathies which with some persons are the real or contributory grounds for certain conduct; its sensuality, which is the real or partial motive for certain friendships. The pretexts which, outside of prayer, it had accepted and offered in explanation of its activities are now disclosed to be pretexts. The soul is disentangled and delivered from its restraints as it becomes willing to sacrifice these persons, places, things, activities, and modes of conduct; freed from servility, its interior and conduct shine resplendent with a new rectitude. Thus occur changes in life which, in their turn, facilitate the soul's progress to the Father.

Prayer, then, is the Father's own psychotherapy for His sinful children. It is His method of uncovering unconscious motivations and of recalling to consciousness those things that have been excluded as painful and humiliating.

His two-edged sword reaches into the depths of the soul and divides the joints and marrow of the "old man," its secret "thoughts and intents." His Spirit of love enables the soul to see conflicts thus uncovered in the bright and mature light of the divine wisdom which is reflected in right reason and faith, and to solve them by a prudent act of judgment issuing into a strong and effective act of the will. These repeated acts of judgment and will eventually form in the soul the attitude of the child of God who is cheerfully submissive to the Father's will and who lovingly accepts all that it contains of circumstances, duties and sufferings. Such an attitude of soul is harmonious, integrated, effective and invulnerable throughout life's happenings.

In spiritual reading, the word of God, like blows of a hammer, breaks into pieces the indifference, pride and rebelliousness of our hearts, so that true contrition and devotion to the Father and His interests may spring forth in our soul.

In prayer, as these good dispositions are actualized, the fire of divine love descends from above. It inflames and molds into the image of Christ the soul which has placed itself upon the anvil of God's will.

5 The Obstacles to Our Happiness

The removal of the obstacles to our happiness by the repentance of sin is the first degree of conformity to the Father's will. Prayer and spiritual reading will help us to repent and become detached, and detachment will make these exercises more productive of good. But prayer and spiritual reading will not beget love in the soul without detachment from sin and its occasions.

Let us acknowledge that our efforts in prayer and spiritual reading will not bear fruit if we cling obstinately to sin or to the near occasions of sin. "No man can have two masters," Our Lord said. He cannot have two final goals, two final purposes in life. Sin contradicts the Father; it contradicts His plan for our happiness; it sets us at variance with our fellows, and even with ourselves.

The one who sins, and this book is written for sinners, is seeking happiness. But by sin one really departs from it; for one's happiness is in the Father alone. Hence in sinning one is making a mistake; sin is always a mistake. It is a mishap on the road to happiness.

First of all, then, we must make our prayer and spiritual reading bear the fruit of contrition and of a firm purpose of amendment. Unless we do this we cannot expect to make progress. Nonetheless if one cannot bring oneself to relinquish one's serious sins, one should pray and do spiritual reading. Especially should such a one be encouraged to pray perseveringly to the Mother of God that she may prepare the way for a return to her Son. Five decades of the rosary or even three Hail Mary's daily may mean the difference between eternal life and death. The making of a retreat or a mission is advisable in such a case.

Besides repudiating sin we must give up the near occasions of sin which are free, that is, possible to avoid. Otherwise we are wanting in true contrition and firm purpose of amendment. But even more than this, in the matter in which we are weak we must exercise a very special prudence and circumspection, for our weakness disposes us to two consequences. One is a lack of judgment, which leads us to yield to our attraction toward things connected with our sin; the other is a tendency to fall again because of the inadequate provisions made to avoid sin, the inadequacy of which the sinner is not apt to admit as readily as he or she should. Hence he or she will have no security unless he goes further than to relinquish the free (avoidable) occasions of sin; he must also be genuinely ready to give up legitimate pleasures bordering upon the near occasion.

This will require a spirit of mortification and sacrifice; sometimes one will not find the necessary strength outside of a retreat or without the help of a prudent spiritual adviser to whom one has disclosed one's case. Prayer and spiritual reading which dwell on the Father's goodness and love (and on the "last things") are also helpful in begetting the necessary love of God. Finally, such sacrifices of legitimate things as prudence suggests are a very pleasing reparation to the Father for past sins, and the Father will not be outdone in generosity.

The renunciation of sin is the first degree of conformity of the human will to the Father's will. In general, conformity to the Father's will supposes a certain knowledge and desire. It supposes the acknowledgment that the Father is truly God and that He has a plan which uniquely contains our happiness. It supposes our desire to pursue this plan and thus to place ourselves under His providence in a special manner.

And what is this plan? "For whom He foreknew, He also predestined to be made conformable to the image of His Son" (Romans 8:29). God's plan is that we be conformed to the likeness of Christ Jesus.

Such conformity requires humility, by which we acknowledge our faults and defects and consequent dissimilarity; it requires a willingness on our part to undergo change, correction, improvement, by which we become more Christlike and make our will agree with the Father's will. Conformity to the Father's will was the ruling principle of the life of Jesus Who gave us His example to follow; our will is conformed to the Father's will when we have in our hearts and deeds the charity of Christ. It is Jesus Who leads us to the Father.

The humble acknowledgment of our shortcomings and sins leads to peace of soul, not to the false peace of a deformed conscience or of foolish compromise but of a true adjustment to reality. The Father is the supreme Reality; all other reality is the effect of His will; He alone gives existence to all that is. Only the saint is fully adjusted to reality, because only the saint is fully conformed to the Father's will. The materialist, on the other hand, excludes from his or her life happiness and true adjustment to reality, for he or she fails to recognize or acknowledge the primary Reality and its chief effects, the soul, intellect and will, which are of the spiritual order and hold primacy over the material order. Such a one cannot even achieve the happiness of the brute animals, to whom he likens himself, because he has a soul, an intellect, a will and a conscience which he or she is trying to ignore, and which, although evaded or repressed, do not lose thereby their energy nor leave him in solid peace. In certain persons such repression may lead to mental and emotional illness. This discovery is the contribution of a school of psychoanalysis, existential analysis. Dr. Viktor Frankl of Vienna, one of its leading exponents, has found repressed religious tendencies in the irreligious, causing their psychological distress. These persons have consistently relegated to the unconscious the "voice of conscience," which, the research of these analysts shows, is such that it can only be explained by supposing the existence and activity of God as its cause.

It is true that some persons appear, and consider themselves, to be happy whose satisfaction is not in God but in material things—even, in certain cases, when they are conscious that they are abiding in mortal sin and are estranged from God. These people *are* miserable, but may not *feel* miserable. The hatred and malice of the devil are not directed so much at making people miserable in their feelings as in fact. Then they are more prone to remain in their pitiable condition without taking the necessary steps to become truly happy.

And yet experience with such persons proves that when they do set their consciences in order and return to the Father and find their peace in Him, they acknowledge that they were not really happy previously; they admit that something was lacking; there existed an emptiness, a void, a spiritual misery, the awareness of which they repressed or put out of their mind, but which made itself known at times, in some cases most of the time.

When we strive to see ourselves as the Father sees us we begin to have true peace; when we renounce sin we can truly accept ourselves. In the patient striving to correct our faults with the help of the Father's grace, we have assurance that we are doing what is in our power to become worthy of Him. Then the hidden motives of the heart will be revealed, and further progress will ensue as a result of increasing rectitude of will and life.

In all the circumstances of life we have but to do and suffer all that the Father wishes us to do and suffer. The spiritual life will not interfere with our other duties; rather it will enrich them and help us to fulfill them well.

We may be discouraged from undertaking the struggle against our faults and defects by the realization of our weakness. But the Father's help will strengthen us. He has given us means, some of which we shall discuss later, to overcome this weakness and to strengthen our wills. These means include the sacraments, the infused virtues, the gifts of the Holy Spirit—*and self-denial*. In self-denial in particular, we have the means to overcome the obstacles to happiness; by self-denial our wills are given power over our temperaments and faults; we are made capable of change, we are made free.

Part Two:

Plan of Happiness

God, Who through the Word creates all things (cf. John 1:3) and keeps them in existence, gives men an enduring witness to Himself in created realities (cf. Romans 1:19-20). Planning to make known the way of heavenly salvation, He went further and from the start manifested Himself to our first parents. Then after their fall His promise of Redemption aroused in them the hope of being saved (cf. Genesis 3:15).

Vatican II: *Dei Verbum*, Constitution on Divine Revelation, No. 3.

Through divine revelation, God chose to show forth and communicate Himself and the eternal decisions of His will regarding the salvation of men. That is to say, He chose "to share those divine treasures which totally transcend the understanding of the human mind."

Vatican II: *Dei Verbum*, Constitution on Divine Revelation, No. 6.

Although he was made by God in a state of holiness, from the very dawn of history man abused his liberty, at the urging of personified Evil. Man set himself against God and sought to find fulfillment apart from God. Although he knew God, he did not glorify Him as God, but his senseless mind was darkened and he served the creature rather than the Creator (cf. Romans 1:21-25). What divine revelation makes known to us agrees with experience. Examining his heart, man finds that he has inclinations toward evil too, and is engulfed by manifold ills which cannot come from his good Creator.

Vatican II: *Gaudium et Spes*, Constitution on the Church, No. 13.

6

The Angels,
Our First Parents,
& The Predominate Fault

Infinite love wished to communicate Its own beatitude to intelligent beings whom It would create. Love desired to be loved and to give Its lovers the opportunity to prove their love. Love desired to be won by victors whom It would reward divinely.

The angels are intelligent spirits whose mode of knowledge is by infused ideas received directly from the Father. They were constituted in a state of grace and were invited to share the divine life in glory, on condition of proving faithful under trial.

Some theologians teach that Lucifer, the highest of the angels by nature, envied the supremacy of God. He said in his heart: "I will set up my throne above the stars of God ... I will be like the Most High" (Isaiah 14:13, 14). He desired to be the supreme leader of all God's creatures and to receive their reverence for himself. He raised the standard of revolt with the defiant cry: "I will not serve."

Michael countered Lucifer's rebellion with the retort: "Who is like unto God?" In other words, why should we serve Lucifer when he is not even worth naming in comparison with our true leader, Who is God?

"I watched Satan fall like lightning from heaven," Our Lord testified (Luke 10:18), indicating the consequence of Lucifer's rebellion. Many of the angels, probably one-third, fell with him. Our Lord tells us of "the everlasting fire which was prepared for the devil and his angels" (Matthew 25:41).

By this grave sin of pride and disobedience, Lucifer and his followers lost eternal happiness; while Michael and the faithful angels, by their loyalty, humility and obedience won eternal bliss.

Men are confronted with the same choice. The Father created Adam out of the slime of the earth, gave him Eve as a companion, and placed them in the Paradise of Pleasure to dress and keep it. The Father commanded Adam: "You are free to eat from any of the trees of the garden except the tree of knowledge of good and bad. From that tree you shall not eat; the moment you eat from it you are surely doomed to die" (Genesis 2:16-17 NAB).

Eve tempted by Satan, and Adam by Eve, ate the fruit of this tree. By their sin Adam and Eve lost the most wonderful gifts and prerogatives with which a loving Father had endowed them. These gifts had lifted them by sanctifying grace to a share in the divine nature, had conferred on them freedom from sickness and death, and integrity: the perfect docility of the lower powers of sense to the higher powers of reason and will.

These gifts were a trust given to Adam, and would have been transmitted by him to his descendants had he proven faithful to God. Instead he transmitted to his descendants his sin and its consequences: they come into the world deprived of sanctifying grace (this is original sin as it exists in them), and with a fourfold wound of their nature: in the will is the inclination to evil and self (malice: wounded human nature without the gift of grace is unable to attain even to the natural love of God proper to human nature, the love of Him above self).[1] In the intellect is the wound of ignorance, by which man is deprived even of due knowledge, such as of his end and true happiness. In the

[1] S.T. (*Summa Theologica* of Saint Thomas), I-II, Q. 109, A. 3.

lower faculties is weakness, source of inordinate fear, sadness, anger; and concupiscence, the disordered love of sensible good.

The evils that we find in the world are many: wars, discord, injustice, hatred, sickness, death. They are paralleled by the evils we find within ourselves: a disorder in our powers, evil tendencies which overcome our good inclinations, selfishness, weakness, insecurity, inadequacy, ignorance.

These evils do not argue against the existence of an infinitely good and all-powerful Creator. His existence is too evident from creation, the work of His hands: the heavens with its wonderful order; the earth with its seasons and climates; plants and animals; and the marvelously constructed human body, apt for the works of the intelligence and will with which man is endowed. But these evils do point to the existence of original sin and to a corresponding punishment, which Revelation confirms. They are evidence that something went wrong, something that the good and omnipotent God permitted.

> The Lord God sent Adam out of Paradise of Pleasure to till the earth from which he was taken, lest perhaps he put forth his hand and take also of the Tree of Life and eat and live forever (Genesis 3:22, 23).

God placed in Paradise two trees of special significance. Disobedient man and woman ate the fruit of the Tree of Knowledge, tempted by Satan with the lure of obtaining a knowledge which would make them like unto God. Then, indeed, they obtained the knowledge of good and evil; they learned the bitterness of evil; and by contrast how good was the original justice which they had lost. God had also placed in Paradise the Tree of Life, but of this they were not permitted to eat. Because of their sin the earthly Paradise was closed to them. But their minds and hopes were elevated to a heavenly Paradise by the Redemption announced to them; through the Redeemer the new Paradise would be opened. The fruit of the Tree of Life of the new Paradise must first ripen, and be eaten—then through it a new immortality would be given to humans.

The malicious instigator of the first sin was deprived of the satisfaction of his victory when God decreed his overthrow and foretold the Redemption: "I will put enmities between thee and the woman, and between thy seed and her seed. She shall crush thy head and thou shall lie in wait for her heel" (Genesis 3:15).

The angelic intelligence, superior to the human, sees in one glance the alternatives of choice and their consequences. The angelic will is then fixed in its election. When the rebellious angels preferred disobedience they knew that they had made their final choice. It is not so with us, and to us alone God gave a Redeemer.

The Father's love for us is shown luminously in the Redemption. The Father would found on earth a kingdom of His love to which all would be invited. Here they would find freedom from the hard slavery of sin, from the kingdom of Satan. Here the very punishments of sin would be transformed into blessings: an increase of merit, virtue and eternal happiness. Humans would exclaim with Holy Mother Church: "O happy fault which has brought us such and so great a Redeemer" (Blessing of the Paschal Candle, Holy Saturday). Such is the way of the Father's love. Humble sorrow and obedient fidelity open the way for the guilty to greater blessings than were lost.

THE PREDOMINANT FAULT is that underlying fault, imbedded in our temperament, from which the majority of our other faults proceed. It is the avenue through which the enemy of our souls attacks us to move us to sin; for he knows that this tendency is apt to assume the upper hand in our soul; and that when it does it easily commands the soul's powers and energies.

Therefore it is important for us to discover our predominant fault, and to know the opposite virtue and remedy, so that we can correct it. Unless we act against it, progress in virtue will be difficult.

The Holy Spirit, Who sees what are the needs of our souls, often inspires in us the virtue opposite to our predominant fault. He protects the virtuous inclination of our soul, to which He adapts His inspirations.

The predominant fault can be discovered by observing the object to which our thoughts and desires habitually turn, by recalling the basic lifelong fault into which we most frequently fall. The criticisms of others that we have received from childhood on may also help us to identify it.

Usually persons who have not embarked upon the spiritual life identify this basic tendency with their "personality." They are not aware that it can be overcome. Indeed they view it as a virtue; their nature is on guard against being enlightened on this point.

As we have implied, faults are so related to one another that some spring from others, and the predominant fault is one from which others arise. Hence it is usually one of the capital sins, which are so named because from them most sins take their origin. Saint Thomas and Saint Gregory the Great consider pride not as a capital sin, but rather as the source and mother of all the capital sins, for pride strengthens self-love and makes self the beginning and end of all human activity. For them the seven capital sins are: Vanity (otherwise listed under pride), anger, sloth, envy, avarice (greed), gluttony, sensuality (lust).

In some persons pride itself is the tendency proximately under-lying their other faults. In many, another is the "proximate" predominant fault, while pride underlies this. With intelligent self-denial and progress in virtue, this fault and other faults springing from it are removed; the alcoholic attains sobriety, the incontinent man becomes continent, etc., and the numerous faults springing from this inclination are eliminated. Then the more deeply motivating tendency is exposed—e.g., pride—and this in turn can be overcome.

The predominant fault crystallizes certain aspects of an ego accus-tomed to act for and of itself. When a person "puts on Christ" he acquires a new principle of action, the love of the Father. Thus we, from being egocentric, become Christocentric. The opposition between egotism and the love of the Father must be understood and the will aligned with Christ and against "the old man."

If this egocentricity is not exposed and overcome, it remains like an underground, ready to join hands with the invader in the time of trial, and to betray us into the hands of our enemies, the world, the flesh and the devil. Just as an underground deserves attention in peacetime, because upon its uprooting depends the future security of the country, so the basic evil tendency of the soul, the head of the organism of sin, requires our attention (discovery and opposition) even though it is in hiding.

Our Lord went to the root of our malady: "If anyone wants to be a follower of Mine, let him renounce himself..." (Mark 8:34). God not self must be our beginning and end, the principle and motive of our actions.

7 Mary: Reflection of the Father's Happiness

What is the role of Mary in the Father's plan for our Redemption, sanctification and happiness? We know that it is Jesus Who is the sole Redeemer, Jesus gives us the Holy Spirit, and sanctifies us, and is our happiness, according to the Father's plan. Whatever role Mary plays in this plan is subordinate to that of Jesus, and is given to her in virtue of the foreseen redemptive merits of Jesus. He redeemed her as well as the rest of the human race, and indeed in a preeminent way. It was the shedding of His Blood, anticipated, which was the source of all the graces Mary had from her Immaculate Conception till her glorification.

It was the "Yes" of Jesus when confronted with His Crucifixion which saved us, and which is our model. The latest work of Karl Rahner points this out. His work in connection with Mary is discussed in an article by Elizabeth A. Johnson, C.S.J., of Catholic University, in *Église et Théologie*, 1984, 15, pp. 155-182.

Jesus' suffering unto death which redeemed us was His free, human act. At the same time, it was the act of the Second Person of the Trinity. His Resurrection by which He was established manifestly as Lord and Christ showed His Father's acceptance of this human and divine act. This is the Paschal mystery which is the center of the Church's liturgy. But Jesus could not have said His "Yes" which is the prototype of our "Yes" to the Father's plan and will if another "Yes" had not preceded it. This was the "Yes" which Mary gave to the angel when she was offered the conception of the Messiah in her womb through the overshadowing of the Holy Spirit.

Karl Rahner died before completing his last work on the Redemption, and before he had found a place for Mary in it. John Paul II pointed out that Vatican Council II showed Mary's place in the Redemption, as must any treatment of the Redemption if it is to be complete. Meanwhile we can be sure that if a method used results in eliminating truths of the faith, then there must be something deficient in that method.

While research and scholarship are important to the Church, we must live by faith, the faith of the Church, which is founded on Scripture and tradition, as it has been believed from the beginning until now, and as it is being handed on to us by the teaching of Vatican Council II. John Paul II has energetically promoted this teaching since participating actively in that Council, as did Paul VI before him, who was also one of its eminent members during its first year, and then Pope during its final three years.

By a small majority, the Council members voted to treat of Mary, not in a separate document, but in the Constitution on the Church in a final chapter, the eighth, as had been originally proposed by the preparatory commission. I am sure this decision pleased our Lady, who is certainly concerned not with what can be said of her for her own sake, but with what can be said of her in relation to Christ, the Church and us.

What the Vatican Council had to say about Mary was what the Catholic tradition, and especially what the Fathers and Doctors of the

Church have taught, and it is this teaching which I am interested in presenting. It is less well known, understood, and appreciated today, and so it is all the more important to be attentive to it, to be strengthened by it, and to respond to it. The teaching of the Vatican Council on Mary, briefly stated, sees her in relation to Christ as His associate; in relation to the Church, of which she is the type and the most eminent member; and in relation to us as our spiritual mother. She is the new Eve, as Christ is the new Adam.

AMONG CREATURES Mary was the most perfect reflection of the Father. His stars and earth, His plants and animals are all conformed to His will by their very natures according to which He moves them to their acts. They are in His hands, fulfilling the purpose for which they were created. But they bear only the traces, the vestiges, of His infinite perfections. He wished to have in His creation a mirror of Himself, a pure reflection of the divine beauty: Mary. Her faith, in its firm adherence to His truth, reflected the brilliance of His intelligence. She is the image of His love, goodness and mercy. All the bent of her will was directed to the doing of His good pleasure. She was His friend and companion, and called herself His handmaid, His slave.

Mary never failed in the fulfillment of the divine will. Her obedience flowed from her humility which kept her soul empty of itself and of creatures, of attachment to her own opinions and will.

God made this maiden worthy to be His Mother. At the moment of her conception when her soul was infused into her body in the womb of her mother, Anne, He prevented original sin from being transmitted to her in view of the foreseen merits of her divine Son, Jesus. Thus He made her conception immaculate and preserved her from the wounds of original sin. Already, through the Precious Blood of Jesus, the devil was vanquished in God's creation, which he had desired to dominate completely. For from the first Mary belonged to God in mind and heart. She lived the life of a pious girl of her age and time while remaining true to her divine Love. Her unmarred intelligence searched deep into the hidden meanings of the prophets, and her loving heart offered itself to the service of the Messiah.

It is easy enough for us to accept honor. We naturally desire to be elevated in the eyes of men. Mary treasured humiliation, humble situation and poverty. She was troubled, then, when the Archangel Gabriel told her that she was called to be the Mother of the Messiah. Acceptance was a sacrifice; yet more than humiliation and poverty, she loved the will of the Father. The story of her life is condensed into her response: "I am the servant of the Lord. Let it be done to me as you say" (Luke 1:38 NAB).

"Let it be done to me as you say," that is, "You, O Lord, have Your plan for me and for my life. I am Your servant. I have no other will but to fulfill Your will. I do not ask the details of Your plan. I know what You want now; that is enough. I shall do that. I accept Your will for me in its entirety, with all its consequences."

God, Who calls us to be His children, would have us be the children of Mary, whom *He* did not disdain to have as His Mother. He would have us imitate her; accept the divine plan as she accepted it; be His sons and daughters; do now what He asks us now to do; conform our will to His, fulfilling His will as well as we can.

Mary knew that Christ, the Messiah, was the Redeemer of all. "You shall ... give Him the name Jesus" (Luke 1:31 NAB), that is to say, Savior. She understood that He was the Head of the human race. If she was to be the Mother of Christ, she would be the Mother of the whole Christ, head and members. She would be the Mother of all human beings, our Mother.

This is what she accepted in her fiat. This relationship of people to Mary was confirmed by Jesus on the Cross when He said to Mary, who stood there with Saint John, our representative, "Behold your son," and to Saint John, "Behold your mother" (John 19:26, 27). We are the brothers and sisters of Christ because He died on the Cross to redeem us from our sins and to make us His members, and so it was fitting that this mystery of our relationship to Mary should be announced from the Cross.

We, too, must say our fiat. Hers was an acceptance of us as her children; ours is an acceptance of her as our Mother. She was elected to be the Mother of God and we are chosen to be the sons and daughters of the Father and of Mary. She showed herself worthy of her election and gave us the example. It is our part to show ourselves worthy of our election and to follow that example not in word and thought alone but in deed.

WHEN HER TIME was come, Mary brought forth her Son and laid Him in a manger. This Infant Whom she had carried in her womb, she could now hold in her hands and press to her bosom. She could gaze upon His lovely face and lavish her affection upon Him.

He was a true infant, utterly dependent upon His Mother's care. Yet despite all His awkward helplessness, how modest, composed, loving and understanding! To that Mother and to His foster-father, Saint Joseph, He directed tender glances. In His eyes shone forth the purity and strength of His noble soul, which had possessed from the first moment of its conception the full use of reason. From that first moment He had the beatific vision which the blessed have in Heaven, and infused knowledge, by which, as Head of the human race, He knew all individuals, all who were, and who were to be.

"When He cometh into the world, He said: ... Behold I come. In the head of the book is written of Me, that I should do Thy will, O God.... Behold I come to do Thy will.... I have desired it, Thy law is within My heart" (Hebrews 10:5-9; Psalm 40:8, 9). Such is the heart of Christ. In His infancy, this sentiment was manifested in His full dependence upon Mary and Joseph.

Mary read the secret depths of her Child's soul. She knew that He Who showed her His affection was not a human person. There is no human person in Jesus. A human nature, body and soul, yes. At the moment that His body and soul were united, no human person was formed by that union. A divine person, the Word, the Second Person of the Blessed Trinity assumed this humanity. She was looking into the eyes of God. God smiled upon her; God caressed her. She who held Him to her breast was held by Him in existence; and her soul was lovingly pressed to His infinite Bosom.

What food for thought! We can rejoice in the loving intimacy that existed between Mary and Jesus! We can learn by seeing Him through her eyes as she saw Him. She knew Him by faith just as we know Him. Her cousin Elizabeth at the time of the Visitation had said: "Yes, blessed is she who believed that the promise made her by the Lord would be fulfilled" (Luke 1:45). She believed; she adored in her Infant her God; she understood the lesson of His dependence upon her and Saint Joseph. She entered so fully into His sentiments and purposes that she was more than His disciple, she was His companion. More than ever Mary determined to acknowledge and love her own helplessness, her own dependence upon God. More than ever she resolved to fulfill perfectly His holy will. Surely before Saint Paul she said: "In Him Who is the source of my strength I have strength for everything" (Philippians 4:13 NAB).

FOR THIRTY YEARS Jesus Christ, the Son of God, lived a hidden life on earth, in the bosom of His little family. Mary was the devoted wife of Joseph, the carpenter, and the loving Mother of Jesus, who followed the trade of His foster-father. She cooked, kept the house, made their clothes, carried the water from the well, did those numberless little duties that mothers and wives do. These she accomplished with the utmost simplicity and love; the love of God alone was the motive in all her actions, no matter how simple and lowly; it was this love that gave them their value. Saint Louis Grignion de Montfort tells us that Mary was able to pick up a pin with such pure love of God as to do more good for souls than did the greatest actions of the Apostles. What merits she must have gained for us through her prayer and through her loving adoration and service of her divine Son!

Mary as mother and wife lived in the lay state, and she and Joseph are models for the laity. She was satisfied to live in a small village, to be the wife of a lowly citizen of that village, to wear the simple clothes of the time, and to do ordinary work throughout her life. She was satisfied that the greatness of her life be hidden. She knew that true greatness resided in the fulfillment of her daily duties out of pure love of God and in conformity with His holy will. Is not this example worthy of our imitation? Our station in life, no matter how lowly, our duties, no matter how commonplace, can help us to attain the highest holiness if we accept them as Mary accepted hers; if we elevate and ennoble them by performing our actions through the pure love of God (or at least through an increasing love of God, an increasing conformity to His holy will). The union of our actions with the merits of Jesus'

Heart and Blood invest them with a quasi-infinite value and make them capable of repairing not only our own sins but also those of others. None of the necessary circumstances of life will be obstacles to holiness. They are given by the Father and in accepting them for love of Him we will advance in His love.

The day came when Jesus left home. He might have said to her now as He said when He was twelve, in the Temple: "Did you not know that I must be busy with My Father's affairs?" (Luke 2:49). For thirty years He had lived a hidden life, much like that of the people whom He loved and whose lives He wished to sanctify by His example. In the three remaining years of His life He would converse with people of the secret and hidden things which He saw in His Father's bosom from all eternity. He would teach divine truths, win friends, lead them to Heaven. He would form disciples to carry on His work, He would found a Church and prepare it to receive the wonderful gift of the Holy Spirit. He would institute the sacraments—by which He meant to transmit His graces to us—and place them in the hands of priests whom He would ordain.[1] Then while He returned to His heavenly Father to take up His place as our Mediator at the right hand of divine Omnipotence, He would have a way to remain with us and give Himself to us, under the appearance of bread and wine. His name would be written in our hearts, and our hearts would speak in the intimacy of solitary prayer to His.

Mary understood His mission and did not detain Him. So parents must permit their children to follow their vocation in the Lord's service. If He had not gone she would have sent Him, for she was the partner of His mission and longed for its fulfillment.

Mary knew how it would end. She watched, prayed and offered sacrifices as He went about winning friends and lovers amongst His countrymen—and making enemies. Many of those in high places, then as now, were more concerned about their own prestige, holdings and ideas, than they were about the will of the Father. They identified the will of the Father with their own good, and they were not friendly to this Wonderworker Who went about preaching, teaching, and influencing people without their authorization. Gradually the full

[1] *Theology of the Priesthood*, Jean Galot, S.J., 1985, Ignatius Press, pp. 87, 172, passim. Also Vatican II: *Gaudium et Spes*, Constitution on the Church, Nos. 18, 28.

opposition between them developed. Jesus knew the potentiality for good that was in them, and wished to win their souls. He knew the evil that was in them, and wished to avoid provoking its increase as long as He could. When the time came, He resolutely set His face toward Jerusalem, and went to embrace His death, while Mary followed Him.

This was His moment, the moment for which He had come into the world. And hers too, the moment when her longings for our Redemption, for our deliverance from the bondage of Satan, would be fulfilled.

"I have a baptism wherewith I am to be baptized, and how I am straightened until it be accomplished!" (Luke 12:50). Thus He declares His burning desire to offer Himself in sacrifice to God. His love for us has brought Him from Heaven to earth. Now it takes Him to Calvary; and Mary's love for Him and us grows. Is it not for her, too, that He is laying down His life? Was she not redeemed by Him, were not her privileges of the Immaculate Conception and of the divine Maternity purchased by the foreseen merits of His Passion?

He had come to teach us how God loved us. When the last drop of His Precious Blood had been separated from His torn and mangled body, would we understand? Would we love Him in return? Our love for Him will fulfill the purpose of our existence, will lead us to Heaven, will comfort that Heart which so ardently desires to be loved by us.

At the end of His public life, Our Lord sat within the Temple area as the people cast money into the treasury. The smallest offering was given by a widow and consisted only of two mites. Jesus, calling His disciples together, said: "I want you to observe that this poor widow contributed more than all the others.... They gave from their surplus wealth, but she gave from her want, all that she had to live on" (Mark 12:43-44 NAB). Father Vincent McNabb, O.P. thinks that the widow is Mary, preparing for the Passion.[2] In His Passion Our Lord will be stripped of all. Even His garments will be taken from Him, to become the prize of His executioners. His Mother, this ardent disciple and companion of His, would not accompany Him in His Passion with anything in her possession. She would give her all too.

[2] *Mary of Nazareth* (N.Y.: P.J. Kenedy & Sons, 1940) pp. 27-28.

And we—shall we not be ashamed of our undue love of riches, honors, comforts? Shall we travel the road to Heaven overloaded with these things? Shall we not have the wisdom and prudence of Mary, the love and generosity to follow Christ, and to cast from us all that impedes and hinders our ascent?

The counsels of Christ—poverty, chastity and obedience—cannot be embraced in their full extent by all. Those who follow Christ should realize that honors, possessions and comforts are not evil in themselves, but good in the measure that they are necessary or useful for a virtuous life lived in the world. However, the spirit of the counsels, the spirit of detachment, is for all. If our love for creatures is to be rightly ordered, we must have the spirit of sacrifice, the readiness to make sacrifices, and we must make real sacrifices from time to time. Nor should we measure ourselves by the value of the work we do, nor by our positions or honors; that measure is too small to measure the sons and daughters of God.

Near the cross of Jesus there stood His Mother.

— John 19:25 NAB

8 The New Adam & Eve

The night before He died, Jesus and His twelve Apostles together ate the Passover meal. Then "Jesus took bread, blessed it, broke it, and gave it to His disciples. 'Take this and eat it,' He said, 'this is My body.' Then He took a cup, gave thanks, and gave it to them. 'All of you must drink from it,' He said, 'for this is My blood, the blood of the [new] covenant, to be poured out in behalf of many for the forgiveness of sins'" (Matthew 26:26-28 NAB).

Thus was given what was promised when He said: "For My flesh is meat indeed: and My blood is drink indeed. He that eats My flesh and drinks My blood, abides in Me and I in him" (John 6:56-7).

At this time Jesus conferred upon His Apostles the power to do what He had just done—to offer the Sacrifice of the Mass. His words transmitted the capacity to do what they commanded: "Do this as a remembrance of Me" (Luke 22:20 NAB).

The Last Supper was followed by the shedding of His blood: What had been offered at the Last Supper, and there immolated mystically, was immolated on the Cross in fullest actuality. Here was the reality foretold by every lamb sacrificed on the altar of holocaust since the institution of the Old Testament. To many of His followers, like those who took the road to Emmaus three days later, the Crucifixion of Jesus Christ was inexplicable. They had been hoping that this was the prophet foretold by Moses, the promised Redeemer, but they did not know that the price of Redemption was His own Precious Blood. Deep gloom settled over their spirits when Christ was delivered into the hands of His enemies, cast out of the city, and executed upon a gibbet.

But to Mary this depth of degradation was a revelation of divine glory and strength. She understood that precisely at the moment when the serpent struck, the serpent's head was crushed, and his captives were freed. She understood, and it was wonderful in her eyes, that to redeem us Christ needed no miracles, no precious materials, no machinery; He simply permitted Himself to undergo a hideous and shameful criminal's death. The wood of the cross which bore Him, the iron of the nails which pierced Him, joined together by His cruel executioners, these were the materials He used to redeem us. His wisdom and power were thus made manifest. Never was Christ greater, more glorious, than in His Crucifixion; never was He more completely Master. He had come unto His own creation which had been dominated by another, the fallen Archangel Lucifer, "the prince of this world." In the very moment when the devil thought himself victorious, Jesus overthrew him in the singlehanded hard combat of His painful death, and took possession of the kingdom of our souls.

Now the fruit of the Tree of Life had ripened.

WAS MARY IGNORANT of the role she was playing in her *compassion*? Surely she knew that a new race would arise from this new Adam and this new Eve. Jesus was thinking of this, too, in the unutterable desolation of the Cross. Overwhelmed with the grief and pain consequent upon our sins which He had made His own, He cried out: "My God, My God, why have You forsaken Me?" (Matthew 27:46 NAB; Psalm 22:1 NAB). Jesus knew in its entirety this psalm which He had just intoned; His, too, were the sentiments with which it concludes: "I will proclaim Your name to my brethren, in the midst of the assembly I will praise You. So by Your gift will I utter praise in the vast assembly.... All the ends of the earth shall remember ("Do this in remembrance of Me"), and shall turn to the Lord.... For dominion is the Lord's, and He rules the nations.... And to Him my soul shall live; my descendants shall serve Him.... Let the coming generation be told of the Lord that they may proclaim to a people yet to be born the justice He has shown."

This moment of the Crucifixion was a fresh start for the human race. The Cross, so narrow and straight, was the way to the new Paradise. Adam and Eve's Paradise had witnessed their sin; they had succumbed to temptation; moved by pride they had disobeyed and eaten the forbidden fruit. Christ's Cross was the witness of His fidelity, obedience even unto death, motivated by humble reverence for the will of the Father. His helpmate, Mary, the Co-redemptrix, was united with Him in the accomplishment of the Father's will.

"I shall put enmities between thee and the woman.... Thou shalt lie in wait for her heel, and she shall crush thy head" (Genesis 3:15). The dragon who had led Eve into sin had heard this divine sentence pronounced in Paradise; on Calvary it was fulfilled.

OUR PRIDE, sloth, and disobedience now have their remedy. We see the dreadful effects that followed upon the original sin of pride and disobedience: death, suffering, privations, unbelief, evils of all kinds. Then we join Mary at the foot of the Cross and behold our remedy with her. There we see humility outraged, yet still humble; obedience crucified, yet still obedient; death issuing into eternal life.

From the divine heights the heavenly Physician diagnosed our ills. He saw the excessive love of self at the root of all sin. He saw the pride which strengthens this self-love; pride which tends to make us consider ourselves our own beginning and our own end. Pride in its deadly form, scorning to recognize a supreme Being above itself, or to subject itself to those who are His representatives; pride in its less deadly form, yet still turning the soul from God and His commandments, urging on to the satisfaction of self-love, hindering the restraining influence of conscience upon excessive desires for temporal goods and flight from temporal evils. Pride—not the beginning of every *individual* sin—but the beginning of every *kind* of sin and a host of individual sins of every kind.

From pride He saw springing especially sins of presumption: inordinate desire and hope that leads men and women to attempt things beyond the strength of their nature, knowledge, virtue or means, due to too high an opinion of themselves; and sins of ambition, the inordinate love of position and authority over others; and sins of vanity: the excessive desire for recognition of their excellence, from which easily arises envy of others whose excellence is taken as a threat against the recognition of one's own.

From His vantage point, He saw pride giving rise (besides to vanity and envy) to the other capital sins: spiritual sloth, that evil sadness at the effort required in striving after happiness in God; anger, the desire for revenge of injury; greed, the excessive love of possessions and riches; gluttony, the excessive pleasure in eating and drinking; lust, the inordinate desire for sexual pleasure.

Stemming from these He saw the host of other sins:

From *vanity*: hypocrisy, boasting, contention, disobedience, obstinacy;

From *envy*: hatred, tale-bearing, detraction, joy at our neighbor's misfortunes;

From *sloth*: faintheartedness (shrinking from the means to eternal happiness), despair (of the end itself), forgetfulness of the commandments, rancor or spite against those who lead souls to eternal happiness, detestation of eternal happiness, seeking after forbidden things;

From *anger*: indignation, preoccupation with vengeful thoughts, abusive and injurious words (insults against one's neighbor, blasphemy against God), quarreling and strife (as angry thoughts pass to words and deeds);

From *greed*: insensibility to mercy, excessive anxiety and cares over temporal goods, violence, falsehood, perjury, fraud, treachery;

From *gluttony*: dullness of mind, frivolous joy, talkativeness, unrestrained lightness of behavior, impurity;

From *lust*: blindness of spirit, thoughtlessness, inconstancy, rashness, self-love, hatred of God, love of this world, despair of the future world.[1]

He saw how these sins attacked the virtues which united souls to Himself; how faith was contradicted by unbelief, heresy, apostasy; hope by despair and presumption; love by hatred of God and humans.

He diagnosed our ills and resolved upon the remedy. At the root strengthening this self-love was pride. He, Himself, would teach us how to be humble, and through humility all the obstacles to His graces would be removed. He chose as His Mother the humblest of His creatures. He, humility Incarnate, taught us humility by His birth, life and death. He showed us on the Cross how the malice of our enemies and the sufferings which befall us could become the way to happiness. We have but to accept them as He did, in union with His intentions. The very evils strewn through life would be the means of making us humble and of striking at our enemy: the pride and self-love within us. Nothing then would be able to impede the conformity of our will with the Father's will—and of our peace and eternal blessedness. Humility would lead to and result from obedience; obedience would win the victory.

God emptied Himself, taking the form of a servant—our human nature—and was made obedient even unto the death of the Cross. He took upon Himself our sins as if they were His own. By His example we in our turn are helped to acknowledge and avow humbly our sins, faults, defects and limitations. Self-examination is made easy for us; we realize that we can please the Father by this manifestation of humility, that all His fatherly mercy requires of us is the humble acknowledgment of our faults, together with sorrow for them and a firm purpose of amendment. Then the painfulness of, and consequent resistance to, self-knowledge diminish; then those nagging, anxious, half-perceptions of our defective acts and tendencies, of our faults and limitations which we tend to banish and keep from consciousness are admitted into the focus of our attention. The sting is

[1] We have followed the concise articles on the capital sins in the *Summa Theologica*. Very helpful on this subject is Tanquerey's *The Spiritual Life*, Bk. II, Chap. iv, "The Struggle against the Capital Sins," p. 392. Also excellent is Father Garrigou-Lagrange's *The Three Ages of the Interior Life*, Vol. I, Chap. xxi, "Sins to Be Avoided"; Chap. xxviii, "Healing of Pride"; Chap. xxix, "Healing of Sloth."

taken out of them; far from shattering our security and sense of adequacy, they contribute to it.

Here are the truths about ourselves which help us to be humble and hence to be pleasing to the Father. Having duly evaluated our sins in the light of faith and right reason, we confess them to a representative of Christ who has the power to give us absolution; in making them known, we assure ourselves and the Father of our sincerity and good-will. Thus for the Catholic, humility, self-examination and confession—in the framework of the other practices of the spiritual life—work against the neurotic tendency of repression and the disposition to neuroses, as well as against other deformations of personality and emotional disturbances. So our psychological resources and mental health are increased. Yet without prayer and spiritual reading, without the strong conviction that the Father Himself is our happiness that comes therefrom, without the enlightened effort to conform our will to His in all things, humility is more difficult, self-examination is less satisfactory, and confession bears less fruit of amendment.

When Mary, the women with her and Saint John, with Joseph of Arimathea and Nicodemus, hastened to bury Jesus that Friday afternoon before the sabbath rest set in, Mary knew the horror of sin. It was sin that had made those marks upon the body and had wrought the death of her Son. For our sins He had died. It is by accompanying Mary at the death of her Son that we can realize how evil our sins are, that we can obtain a hatred of sin, a real detestation residing not in the feelings but in the will.

Sin is the one great detestable thing. It is the one thing that stands against the majesty, beauty, and goodness of the Father. It stands in opposition to Him as if it would kill Him, as it did His Son; as if it would destroy and annihilate His being, against which it rebels. We do not see sin with the eyes of our body; it is only through faith and grace that we are enabled to see it in all its malice with the eyes of our soul. It is an evil so horrible that if we could see it we would certainly hate it.

The sins that we should hate most are not those of our neighbor but our own. These are the only sins over which the Father has given us immediate power, for through His grace we can bring about their complete annihilation. Though sin is forgiven, the tendency to sin remains—the tendency which has been strengthened by our indulgence in sin. But in the Father's grace, and in particular in the sacramental grace of a good confession, we receive helps to fight against these tendencies to sin.

Sin is the one thing that can deprive us of our eternal happiness. It is the one evil that we should hate above everything else, that we should rather die than commit. Our hatred of sin should extend to all sin, mortal and venial. For fully deliberate sin, whether it kills the soul, whether it is a serious offense against the Father or not, is always ugly. It is an insult to the Father, and although when venial it does not deprive us of the Father's friendship, it strikes Him and displeases Him.

We should also resist our faults of frailty, our habitual failings, impatience, discourtesies, and so forth. However irksome they may be to us or others, so long as we are resisting them, determining our will contrariwise to them, all is well; there is correspondingly little sin in them, as there is little will in them. They are unpremeditated and sudden movements, work or actions that escape us without much realization, at the moment, of their nature. We repair these easily by an act of sorrow such as, "My Jesus, I am sorry," joined to the sincere will to avoid them. We should not be disturbed by these "slips," nor attribute to them a greater degree of voluntariness than they actually possess.

If we repair them generously by true sorrow for offending the Heart of Christ, united to His infinite reparation, we are closer to Him afterward than if we had never committed them. Hence they should never cause us discouragement. We shall continue to have faults of frailty throughout our life although we can and should decrease their frequency, and we should banish all *fully deliberate* sin from our lives.

9
Life from the Dead

Did Jesus ascend to His Father on the day of His Resurrection, as John seems to imply, or forty days later as Luke states? This question has been broached in the Church from its early days. Scholars have pointed out that John and Luke are not in contradiction. Jesus risen would be with His Father. In fact, is there a good reason why His soul did not go to His Father as soon as it left the body? Dying, Jesus said: "Father, into Your hands I commend My spirit" (Luke 23:46). And to the good thief Jesus said: "I assure you: this day you will be with Me in paradise" (Luke 23:43 NAB). Not tomorrow or the third day nor in fifty days, but *this day*.

On the day of His Resurrection Jesus gave the Holy Spirit to His Apostles to forgive sins. Ten days after His Ascension He sent the Holy Spirit in its fullness upon His disciples to inaugurate publicly the mission of the Church.

There is a question of distinguishing, on the one hand, the glorification of Jesus, which included His Resurrection and presence with His Father and which did not need any delay, and, on the other hand, His formal leave-taking (His Ascension) and public inauguration of the Church (Pentecost). The Church celebrates these events separately in its liturgy as Easter, the Ascension, and Pentecost.

When Jesus rose, did He rise in the same body which had suffered and died? The Gospel accounts and Saint Paul indicate that there was a bodily difference after His Resurrection. Henceforth His body was "spiritual"—but this transformation does not at all exclude a transformation of the body that had died. In fact, a similar transformation had occurred temporarily when He was transfigured before Peter, John and James on the Mount.

Jesus took pains to show the disciples, who feared that they were seeing a ghost, that He had a human body like we have, and the same body which had died. This is the full meaning of the term "Resurrection"—a rising from the dead of the same body, though now in a new state, no longer subject to death. To doubting Thomas He pointed to the wounds in His hands, feet, and side; in the presence of the Apostles, He ate fish.

What must have been the joy of Jesus and Mary when they met face to face after His Resurrection, after His holy soul had rejoined and vivified His body and passed with it through the rock sealing the sepulcher! What must have been the exultation of her heart, revivified after the cruel suffering and desolation of His Passion and Death!

She soon found that His companionship in the Resurrection was to be different from the companionship of His mortal life. In the forty days after His Resurrection, He appeared to His disciples a number of times, but He did not remain with them. Now He was glorified, immortal, no longer capable of suffering, His body radiant and subject in its movement to His will. When He disappeared the exultant joy remained in Mary's heart, for she knew that her Son would nevermore die, and that the day would come when they would be eternally reunited in Heaven.

Mary rejoiced also for herself and for us. She realized that Christ's Resurrection was the model of ours; that we would experience the reunion of soul and body, adorned with the glorious privileges that now were His. We should often contemplate Jesus, not only in His Passion and Death, but also in His Resurrection and Ascension. Then our faith, our hope, and love will be strengthened, our joy quickened; we shall better understand the happiness that awaits us and believe it with more certitude.

Forty days after the Resurrection Jesus blessed His Apostles and bade them goodbye (Luke 19:50-51; Acts 1:9). To their astonishment He gradually ascended until a cloud hid Him from sight. It would take Him then little longer than the speed of a thought and the act of His will to pass from this cloud to Heaven, to bring to His Father the trophy of His victory, those Sacred Wounds which plead for us until we shall all be reunited with Him. In Heaven He offers to the Father in loving adoration the Kingdom He won by shedding from those wounds His Precious Blood.

Ten days later in the Upper Room, the Apostles, the disciples and Mary received the Holy Spirit, Who descended upon them under the form of tongues of fire and with the sound of a mighty wind. Peter, the Vicar of Christ, now presided over the infant Church; but Mary remained in its midst for many years living a life of prayer, sacrifice and good example to obtain for the Church the graces it needed and to strengthen and encourage it.

If we are faithful in sanctifying our daily life after the example of Mary of Nazareth, and if we accept our humiliations, frustrations, and tragedies together with Mary at the foot of the Cross and in union with the Precious Blood which was shed there, we shall have some part of that fruitfulness which she had in the infant Church after Pentecost. We shall draw down graces upon priests and missionaries; we shall obtain the gift of faith for unbelievers and the gift of perseverance for believers who are sorely tried. First we must expiate our own sins and make progress, but we can have the intentions of Jesus and Mary from the start, in prayer, sufferings and duties done; and although our lives remain very ordinary in the sight of others they will become very pleasing to God and helpful to souls. Mary's apostolate— that of prayer and sacrifice, the mightiest apostolate of all—is not limited to cloistered souls; it belongs also to Christians who embrace with generosity a spiritual life in the world.

Mary had seen her Son die, and she would not have it otherwise with herself. Like Him, she who had not contracted original sin was not subject to the penalty of death. But she would imitate Jesus in all things; she embraced death with joy, desiring at last to taste for love of Him what He had accepted for love of her and us. Although her Son permitted her to undergo death,[1] He did not permit her body to see corruption, but brought about the reunion of body and soul and her Assumption into Heaven, where He crowned her Queen of Heaven and earth. Then He received in Heaven the one who had received Him on earth, to honor there her who had so honored Him here. Then He released the final outpouring of His gifts which His love had been hard pressed to withhold. On earth He had allowed her to suffer privation, affliction and desolation; in Heaven He bestows upon her the most sublime and unending joys.

Mary's power is measured by the power of her Son. She is still His Mother and has a mother's rights over Him, and He is no less obedient to her now than He was on earth. In Heaven, Mary hears our prayers; she knows that God made her His Mother for our sake, for God became man in her to redeem us from our sins. She who had received sublime privileges for our sake does not forget her duties to us, though we forget ours toward her. We wound and afflict her by our sins, for what offends the Son offends the Mother; but her heart is a heart of mercy and forgiveness, which looks to the day when she will brush the dirt off the clothing of our soul, straighten out its wrinkles, or better still, give us a complete change, dressing us in the garments of her Son. She does this by bringing about the conformity of our spirit with His. She prepares us for Holy Communion, for the reception of that sacred flesh which she brought forth for love of God and love of us. Then Jesus is given to us truly. She helps us to act through His virtues and graces instead of through our own defective tendencies, supplying all that is wanting in us that we may do all things in Him and may be made worthy of His promises.

CATHOLIC SENSE, which is a sense of all reality both natural and supernatural, understands the central role of Mary in our salvation and sanctification. We know it is through her that we are saved, in the sense that God made our Redemption dependent upon her consent to

---

[1] At the moment theologians dispute whether Mary underwent death.

His plan, announced to her by the Archangel Gabriel. It was Mary who gave to God the flesh with which to suffer and die, and so redeem us. It was Mary who was the Co-redemptrix, offering the Sacrifice of the spotless Lamb together with the High Priest, Jesus, receiving from His sacrifice the grace to fulfill her role. For in all things she was dependent on and subordinate to Him, the one sole Redeemer and Mediator. It was around Mary that the Apostles and disciples persevered in prayer and obtained the promised gift of the Paraclete. She, whose humility and ardent charity had brought down the Holy Spirit when He overshadowed her to form Jesus in her chaste womb, once again—surrounded this time by her children—with them drew down the Holy Spirit that the Church might enter upon its public life.

As IT WAS in our Redemption, so it is in our sanctification. The Holy Spirit has one unique spouse, Mary, in whom He will form Jesus in us. For Mary is truly our Mother in the spiritual order, just as truly as our earthly mother is our mother in the natural order. It is through Mary that we have a spiritual life, and that spiritual life progresses in us. How ardent is her wish that this life should come to full maturity! As spiritual infants we have the utmost need of her. It is our part to remain mindful of this need and dependence; Mary desires to be with us, but we must will it too. It is our part to make her the companion of our life by turning to her frequently in thought and desire and conversing with her. We must think of her, love her, speak to her, keep in her company. To us, as well as to Juan Diego at Guadalupe are addressed the words: "Am I not here, I, your Mother?"[2]

Mary does not think of herself; she is not interiorly filled with Mary but with Jesus. When we unite ourselves to her and are drawn by the Holy Spirit into her interior, we are drawn to Jesus and we shall find ourselves thinking not of Mary but of Jesus. That is what she wants. We can be sure that if we make her our companion she will make us His companion. Then when we lose track of Jesus, we can turn once

[2] Rev. George Lee, *Our Lady of Guadalupe* (N.Y.: Catholic Book Publishing Co., 1947). The entire Indian narrative is contained in Chap. 7. Also *The Image of Guadalupe* by Jody Brant Smith, Doubleday Image Book, 1984.

more to Mary, think of her and draw close to her. She in turn will draw close to us, bringing Jesus with her.

Mary's heart is within the heart of Jesus as the lining of a purse is within the purse. If we put ourselves in Mary's heart, we are certain to be in the heart of Jesus. All that is hers Mary takes good care to make belong entirely to Him. We should consecrate ourselves entirely to her most pure Heart. This was done for us by the Popes Pius XII, Paul VI and John Paul II. When we consecrate ourselves to her we ratify what they did in our name. The case is the same with the consecration to the Sacred Heart of Jesus; and this consecration too is renewed in a new manner by that to Mary's Immaculate Heart. The Brown Scapular (see Chapter 35) is the sign of our consecration to Mary.

We may give her our bodies, with their senses, to keep pure and recollected, our hearts with their affections, our intelligences with their judgments and opinions (to be brought into conformity with truth), and our wills. We may give her our merits to preserve and increase, our satisfactions and prayers to distribute as she pleases.[3] Thus we shall be like the little child who brings all its earnings to its mother, and receives from her in return all the loving care that it needs. But we must persevere in striving to belong to Mary, and we must imitate her practice of virtue. To one person who kept praying to Mary to show herself a mother, Mary one day appeared and said: "Show yourself my child." We must show Mary we are her children by imitating her virtues and those of her Son, Jesus. This we do through the Holy Spirit Who has been given to us.

[3] See Saint Louis Mary de Montfort, *True Devotion to Mary* (N.Y.: Montfort Fathers, 1954).

10 "I Am the Way, the Truth, and the Life"

The essential elements of the knowledge of Jesus Christ were established by ecumenical councils in the first centuries of the Church. Thus Chalcedon defined that two natures, the divine and human, exist in one divine person in Christ. Later councils defined that there are two intellects and wills in Christ, the divine and the human.

Saint Bernard and Saint Francis developed the knowledge of the humanity of Christ and devotion to it. Saint Thomas in his *Summa Theologica* treated of the mysteries of the life of Christ. In our day theologians are engaged in the important task of filling out these human aspects of the man Jesus, even of His consciousness. In pursuing this objective, theologians have the assistance of Scripture scholars and their interpretations (exegesis) of the Gospels. This is called Christology from below or ascending Christology. The knowledge of Christ as defined by the early Councils of the Church, and deduced from the theology of the Trinity and the fact of Christ's humanity is called Christology from above or descending Christology. Descending Christology, by including the fact of Christ's humanity, His human intellect, will and emotions, etc. includes what is pivotal to ascending Christology, and what forms a point of junction between the two Christologies.

Confusion in the faith is engendered when Christology from below contradicts or seems to contradict the doctrine of the Church as established by its Councils and teaching authority. Before suggesting a few guidelines to help the reader avoid such confusion, I wish to quote authentic Catholic teaching, adapted to our times, from different documents of Vatican Council II, to indicate how Jesus Christ is spoken of by that Council.

> Then, after speaking in many places and varied ways through the prophets, God (that is the Father) "last of all in these days has spoken to us by His Son" (Hebrews 1:1-2). For He sent His Son, the eternal Word, Who enlightens all men, so that He might dwell among men and tell them the innermost realities about God (cf. John 1:1-18). Jesus Christ, therefore, the Word made flesh, sent as "a man to men," "speaks the words of God" (John 3:34), and completes the work of salvation which His Father gave Him to do (cf. John 5:36, 17:4). To see Jesus is to see His Father (John 14:9). For this reason Jesus perfected revelation by fulfilling it through His whole work of making Himself present and manifesting Himself: through His words and deeds, His signs and wonders, but especially through His death and glorious Resurrection from the dead and final sending of the Spirit of truth. Moreover, He confirmed with divine testimony what revelation proclaimed: that God is with us to free us from the darkness of sin and death, and to raise us up to life eternal.
> —Constitution on Divine Revelation, No. 4.

> For Jesus Christ was sent into the world as a real Mediator between God and men. Since He is God, all divine fullness dwells bodily in Him (Colossians 2:9). According to His human nature, He is the new Adam, made head of a renewed humanity, and full of grace and of truth (John 1:14). Therefore the Son of God walked the ways of a true Incarnation that He might make men sharers in the divine nature. He became poor for our sakes, though He had been rich, in order that His poverty might enrich us (2 Corinthians 8:9). The Son

of Man came not that He might be served, but that He might be a servant, and give His life as a ransom for the many—that is, for all (cf. Mark 10:45).... Now, what He took up was our entire human nature such as it is found among us in our misery and poverty, though without our sin (cf. Hebrews 4:15; 9:28). For Christ said concerning Himself, Whom the Father made holy and sent into the world (cf. John 10:36): "The Spirit of the Lord is upon Me because He anointed Me; to bring good news to the poor He sent Me, to heal the broken-hearted, to proclaim to the captives release, and sight to the blind" (Luke 4:18). And again: "The Son of Man came to seek and to save what was lost" (Luke 19:10). But what was once preached by the Lord, or what was once wrought in Him for the saving of the human race, must be proclaimed and spread abroad to the ends of the earth (Acts 1:18).... Thus, what He once accomplished for the salvation of all may in the course of time come to achieve its effect in all.

—Decree on the Missionary Activity of the Church, No. 3.

The truth is that only in the mystery of the incarnate Word does the mystery of man take on light. For Adam, the first man, was a figure of Him Who was to come, namely Christ the Lord. Christ, the final Adam, by the revelation of the mystery of the Father and His love, fully reveals man to man himself and makes his supreme calling clear.... He Who is "the image of the invisible God" (Colossians 1:15), is Himself the perfect man. To the sons of Adam He restores the divine likeness which had been disfigured from the first sin onward. Since human nature as He assumed it was not annulled, by that very fact it has been raised up to a divine dignity in our respect too. For by His Incarnation the Son of God has united Himself in some fashion with every man. He worked with human hands, He thought with a human mind, acted by human choice, and loved with a human heart. Born of the Virgin Mary, He has truly been made one of us, like us in all things except sin.

—Constitution on The Church, No. 22.

There is a balance in the way the Council speaks of the divine and human in Jesus. This balance reflects the unity existing in Jesus. According to Vatican Council II, Jesus is conscious of being divine, comes to heal the poor and broken-hearted, to raise up man and woman, and to save humankind. At the same time He is a man with a human mind, heart and hands.

As the first principle demanded by our faith, an account of the man Jesus must not deny His divinity nor the unity in which the two natures human and divine exist. He is a divine person with divine consciousness, Who accordingly knows Who He is and what is His mission. He has divine knowledge which makes Him an infallible teacher and witness to the Father, and capable, with the Father, of sending to His Church the Holy Spirit, which He did after He rose from the dead and ascended to His Father. He lives forever, and is present in the Eucharist and in our tabernacles, and gives Himself to us as food. Nothing can be said of Jesus by a Christology from below, if it is to be true to the faith, which does not agree with His divinity and the unity in His person of the two natures.

Secondly and following from this, the human and divine in Jesus must be in harmony with each other and not in contradiction with each other. Whatever is disruptive of this harmony is unacceptable from the viewpoint of faith.

Thirdly, since Jesus took a human nature and is like us in everything but sin, everything human but sin and what is not fitting to the divine (certain effects of sin) must be allowed of Him.

We must recognize in applying this third principle, that the sin which is *not* present in Jesus is not only personal sin, but also original sin. Like Adam before the Fall, He has original justice. There is hence a harmony between the higher and lower levels of His human nature as well as between His humanity and divinity. Like us He knew through His senses, understood what He experienced, and weighed the evidence to form judgments. In this process we have certain principles and convictions in whose light we weigh out the evidence. In this same process of weighing out the evidence attained through the senses, He, however, had divine light, unimpeded by original sin, which permitted Him to attain the truth in His judgments. In this way, like us, He could grow in human wisdom and knowledge. This growth was compatible with the sight of His Father, which He had according to the teaching of Saint Thomas and Karl Rahner and indeed, according to the (undefined) doctrine of the Church (*Encyclopedia of Theology*, edited by Karl Rahner, 1975, p. 769). Thus He could be the secure teacher of humankind for all ages. While His will remained free, He had the privilege of being free from the possibility of sinning, a possibility which is a limitation, not a prerogative of freedom. This privilege supplemented the grace with which He freely cooperated to merit our Redemption. Thus He was the secure way to the Father and our perfect exemplar of virtue, while remaining fully and truly human. Certain defects that follow sin are not befitting a divine person: among these, Saint Thomas includes ignorance, error and sickness, but of course not immunity from injury (which brought about His death) or death itself.

Intermediate between Christ's knowledge through His senses, by which He could grow in knowledge, and the sight of His Father, Saint Thomas predicates infused knowledge. This is the kind of knowledge the angels have and which we will have when our souls are separated from our bodies. Then the present mode of knowing, which requires the brain for its functioning, will no longer be possible for us. We have empirical knowledge of this kind of knowing from the systematically collected "near-death experiences." These people, clinically dead but resuscitated, tell us of a kind of knowing hard to express. Their very rapid thinking seems to be independent of the brain and their perception is independent of their senses.

But these privileges, which were hidden and not apparent, should not blind us to the fact that Jesus was a man like us. As a boy He was obedient to His parents (Luke 2:51). He was taught by Joseph the carpenter's trade. His parents taught Him the Scriptures. He laughed and cried, played and conversed. He was subject to fatigue (John 4:6). So ordinary did He appear to His fellow villagers that when at the age of thirty He began preaching, they asked: Where did He get all this? (Mark 6:2). When He began gathering crowds around Him and working miracles, His relatives thought He was out of His mind and came to take Him away (Mark 3:21).

However, without attention to these guidelines, the effort to make Jesus thoroughly "human" easily transgresses the boundaries of faith, and cannot help but cause the weakening and loss of faith, which characterize the present time. With the weakening and loss of faith there follows the loss of priestly and religious vocations and the confusion of the faithful, which are all too common.

JESUS CHRIST is the Son of God. From all eternity He proceeds from the Father as the Father's Word, the complete, full, adequate expression of the Father's thought, a divine Person possessing the divine nature. This Word contains all the Father's knowledge: His knowledge of Himself and His knowledge of all creatures that can, do, or shall exist. All creatures are ways in which God imitates the divine nature in creation; all are resemblances of the Word. Just as there is in the workman an idea of the work which he will perform, so there is in the Word the types of all creatures, and God fashions creatures to these types. But men and women and the holy angels, are conformed by grace to the Word Itself;[1] at first in living faith and then in vision.

All humans who live or shall live are either actual or potential members of Christ; it is the Father's saving will that all should be conformed to Christ in grace and glory.

In Jesus Christ we see the truth, the mercy, the forgiveness of the Father made corporeal. "And eternal life is this—to know You, the only true God, and Jesus Christ Whom You have sent," said Jesus (John 17:3 NAB). To know the mysteries, sayings and deeds of Jesus is to know the Father. "To have seen Me is to have seen the Father ... Do you not believe that I am in the Father and the Father is in Me?" (John 14:9, 10). If we know Jesus, we shall also know the Holy Spirit, for they too are one; we shall know the Blessed Trinity, the three divine Persons existing in the unity of one divine nature. Jesus is the glory of the Father and also the way to the Father.

If we would know the way, we must look to the fundamental interior dispositions of the Sacred Heart, from which Jesus' actions proceed. Jesus has an ardent, tender, consuming love of His Father. Everything He did was done for His Father; He came to earth to do His Father's will, not His own. The object of His Father's will is the happiness of persons. Jesus had a burning desire for their happiness. He knew that they would find this happiness through loving Him; He desired the salvation and sanctification of all without exception. He

---

[1] "Adoptive sonship is a certain likeness of the eternal Sonship ... adoption, though common to the whole Trinity, is appropriated to the Father as its author; to the Son, as its exemplar; to the Holy Ghost, as imprinting on us the likeness of this exemplar" (S.T. III. Q. 23, A. 2, ad 3). Reprinted from the *Summa Theologica*, Benziger Bros., Inc., publishers and copyright owners. Compare also Romans 8:29.

loved His enemies and His executioners. "I am not come to call the just, but sinners" (Matthew 9:13).

The Sacred Heart's love is not daunted by the sins, even the oceans of sins, of men and women. He pursues sinners as justice pursues criminals; but whereas justice pursues criminals to punish them, He pursues sinners to forgive them. Sin repented does not sadden Christ, rather He rejoices in the repentance of sinners. Though a sinner offends Him a million times a million times, He will wash away the last sin as completely as the first—never does He tire of repentant sinners.[2]

The Heart of Christ has a most ardent, indulgent, affectionate love of souls. He loves you *as you are*, with a threefold love: with a sensible affection, a burning love of the will, and a divine infinite love. This threefold love is directed by a divine and a human (supernatural and natural) light.

The Heart of Jesus is saddened by sinners who will not return to Him and take refuge in His Heart, by sinners who persist in remaining apart from Him in their own misery. He is saddened more by the children of His Church than by those outside it, and more by the sins of those whom He has loved with a special and unchanging love of predilection—those He has chosen for a life of close union with Himself, either in the lay state or the consecrated state as His priests and religious. He never repents of the choice He has made, and having loved them with a special love, He is the more wounded by their sinful defection. Nor will He fail to bless them with His choicest blessings if they will return to Him in fervor—nothing will be too good for them, as He shows in the story of the prodigal son.

Though His Heart is saddened, torn, oppressed especially by the obstinacy in sin of priests and religious, yet it is not embittered or punitive. Rather does pity toward them prevail. "Poor souls, they little know where they are going." Knowing the terrible pains of hell, which are so much the worse for unfaithful priests and religious, He wishes at all costs to spare and save them. Souls must not be lost. Hence His own most bitter Passion and Death, hence His willingness to accept the sufferings of others offered in their behalf. He wishes all souls to

[3] Josepha Menendez, *Way of Divine Love* (Westminster, Md.: Newman Press, 1949).

seek union with Him, all souls to be purified, all souls to help others by making their actions and sufferings effective by purity of intention and union with His infinite reparation. His desire to render efficacious the actions of persons goes so far as to invest their acts of reparation for their own faults of frailty with the power to save souls.

Jesus has a special love for the truly just, justified by faith and grace, who are typified by Mary and Saint Joseph (the two closest to Him) and by Saint John the Evangelist; and their justification is the effect of this special love. His Heart went out especially to the afflicted: to the widow of Naim, who had lost her son; to lepers, the outcasts of their society; to the blind and paralyzed; to the poor. Jesus identifies Himself with the poor and embraced their condition Himself. He wishes them to accept their poverty; to become poor in spirit and in so doing to turn their poverty into spiritual riches, while bettering their condition as and when they can.

The Heart of Jesus was emptied by the adoration of His Father in humble selflessness and in complete submission to His will and is filled by the beautiful twofold love of God and humans, which He gives us as ideal and precept. Humility removes all the obstacles; obedience practices all the virtues, it promotes and fulfills that twofold love.

Our supernatural merits do others good, but they are incommunicable. The merits of Jesus, the Head of humanity, alone are communicable; He communicates His merits and virtues to us through His grace. We have but to acknowledge our utter poverty, our helplessness, our incapacity for any good. Then we are free to be enriched by His graces, to act through His virtues. Then we can be humble with His humility, obedient with His obedience, and loving with His love. Nothing is wanting to us if we are humble. All graces of the way shall be ours.

In Jesus, in His mysteries, words and sayings, we have a model on which to think, and to which to conform ourselves. In grace, we have His merits and virtues through which to follow His example, and while doing so we may offer our good works and our sufferings in union with His, so that they may be acceptable to His heavenly Father despite their deficiencies.

More, in Jesus we have a never-failing Companion. He says: "Behold, I stand at the door and knock. If any man listen to My voice and opens the door to Me, I will come in to him and will sup with him, and he with Me. He who overcomes, I will permit him to sit with Me upon My throne; as I have also overcome and have sat with My Father on His throne" (Revelation 3:20).

"Any man": this invitation extends to all. "I will sup with him": Jesus will eat at the table of our heart. The bitter and sparse food of our complaints, grievances, difficulties, will be a matter of joy to Him to listen to. And then He will give us to eat with Him at His table ("and he with Me"), feeding us on the divine lights and graces of His divinity, which will truly refresh and strengthen us. After this repast, having partaken with Him at His table, should we not overcome our weaknesses? And if we do overcome them, and persevere in the right path to God, despite our trials and difficulties, Christ will give us to sit with Him upon His throne. Such is the life which Jesus invites us to live.

As His friends or as His enemies, all ultimately serve Him. He patiently awaits the turning to Himself to become His friends of those who are evil-doers. Meanwhile what they do through ignorance, error, misguided zeal, or malice works for the benefit of those who love Him. The latter, who fulfill His designs of benevolence and merciful kindness as His companions, grow in His image and likeness by suffering the misunderstanding and assaults of the former. With Him they reign forever in His Father's Kingdom. This is what He desires for all; for this He endured atrocious sufferings and rose from the dead.

Constantine was given a sign of victory—the Cross shining in the sky—and the persecuted Church emerged triumphant from the catacombs. So today another sign of victory shines in the firmament, as Leo XIII, Pius XI and Pius XII have said: the Sacred Heart—and this time the victory shall be the reign of Christ over humankind. For He shall reign in love, His kingdom will come. To this end are and shall be offered the prayers, actions and sufferings of a legion of loving hearts to whom, despite their frailty and miseries, He is all in all.

> CHRIST, GOD, IS THE HOMELAND TO WHICH WE GO.
> CHRIST, MAN, IS THE ROAD BY WHICH WE GO THERE.
> St. Augustine, *Sermo* 123, c. 3.

11 Fire on Earth

The Holy Spirit, the mutual love of the Father and Son, is the "heart" of the Blessed Trinity. In It, He is personalized love, intelligent, radiant, serene. "I have come to light a fire on the earth," exclaims Jesus, "how I wish the blaze were ignited" (Luke 12:49 NAB). This fire which Jesus is come to cast upon the earth and which He wants to enkindle in our hearts, is nothing other than the charity of the Holy Spirit, Whom He sends from the heights of Heaven. Having ascended to the right hand of the Father, He cast this fire into the hearts of His Mother, the Apostles and the disciples in the Cenacle on Pentecost Day. It filled the Apostles with unutterable joy and strength, and sent them bounding out of the Cenacle to bring the tidings of eternal joy to all.

Thus the Kingdom of God was established in the reign of the Spirit, Who sweetly mastered the hearts of men and drove them onward to their sanctification and happiness in God. This was foretold by the prophet Ezekiel: "And I will pour upon you clean (baptismal) water, and you shall be cleansed from all your filthiness ... and I will give you a new heart ... and I will put My spirit in the midst of you: and I will cause you to walk in My commandments, and keep My judgments, and do them" (Ezekiel 36:25-27). It is this Spirit which makes us brothers of Jesus, and children of Mary and the Father; and which gives us a new, more abundant and supernatural life with new powers and new energies. It leads us freely to put off the old man of self-love, the threefold concupiscences and the seven capital sins, and to "live decently as people do in the daytime: no drunken orgies, no promiscuity or licentiousness, and no wrangling or jealousy" (Romans 13:13).

The Holy Spirit is the Spirit of Jesus because He proceeds from the Father and the Son, and because the Spirit animated the holy soul of Jesus in His actions. Thus we read, "Then Jesus was led by the Spirit into the desert" (Matthew 4:1). The Holy Spirit is come to us to be our Spirit. "The charity of God is poured forth in our hearts, by the Holy Spirit, Who is given to us" (Romans 5:5).

The Holy Spirit is the Master of the spiritual life; we should strive to be His disciples. He knows us intimately and loves us with a tender love. He enters into our hearts, shedding therein His light, love, peace and joy, strengthening our wills in their good determinations and acts, prompting, warning and consoling us. He is truly our friend, a friend Who is always within us so long as we remain in the state of grace. He is the soul of our soul and grieves when He is repulsed, for love is saddened by rejection. To prevent this we must be quick to follow His inspirations and the good resolutions that He prompts in us, and to turn from the tendencies to sin and self-love. We cannot play fast and loose with the Holy Spirit. We must give Him our love and refuse Him nothing once we are assured that it is He Who asks. To refuse Him what He repeatedly asks is to stop our progress; we shall not advance until we make the sacrifice He is persistently demanding. Moreover we must open our eyes and ears that we may see in His light and hear His voice. We must be sensitive to the impressions made on our soul by our lower nature, reading them aright when they have something of value to say to us, and rejecting them when they do not. Thus we will follow Christ and His Spirit in love.

The way to God for each of us is known by the Holy Spirit, and He desires to lead us all, both as a community, and as individuals. We are presenting the principles of the spiritual life contained in the doctrine of faith, but their applications must be individualized. This the Holy Spirit helps us to do. With His assistance we must each work out our conformity to the Father's will in the circumstances of our lives and according to our own particular character and temperament. By accepting our daily sufferings and performing our daily duties out of love for the Father and in union with the Heart of Jesus, we shall be molded in Him. There is much that we can imitate in the saints, in holy persons and in others with whom we come in contact. But we should not follow them in their idiosyncrasies, or in their exceptional actions, or in a mode of life adapted to *their* circumstances but not to *ours*. We must take for imitation that which is suitable for us; we must ask the Holy Spirit to help us in our choice; we must be supernaturally ourselves.

It is to the Holy Spirit that we should pray before spiritual reading; and it would be well for us to turn to Him in the midst of our activity for a minute or two to recollect ourselves and put our will in His service.

Just as the Father's power is shown in the Creation and the Son's wisdom in the Redemption, so the Holy Spirit's love is shown in our sanctification. He is the Spirit of sanctity and He calls us to sanctity; the way to save our souls is to sanctify them progressively. Here we may make a mistake, under the influence of the devil and of the worldliness that he fosters. We may say: "Sanctity, that is not for me—I don't want to be a saint." Do we know what we are saying? We wish to be happy, and happiness lies only in God; happiness lies only in sanctity therefore. None have eternal happiness except the saints. All Christians are called to be saints. In the days of primitive Christianity, Christians were called "the saints"; we find this manner of speaking in the Acts of the Apostles and the Epistles.

People who speak in this way mean to say, I think: we don't want the revelations, visions, power of working miracles and the extraordinary happenings that we find in the lives of the saints.[1] We don't want

---

[1] We should not depreciate extraordinary graces, charismata, which are given for the upbuilding of the Church. However sanctifying grace, and acts of faith, hope and charity are of a higher order. This should be borne in mind especially by those in the charismatic movement, where, sometimes, the extraordinary is desired at the

their extraordinary mortifications and sufferings. We don't want to be singular or conspicuous.

This is good Catholic sense and common sense, but none of these things are sanctity, all (with the exception of heroic suffering) are accidental to the sanctity of the saints. These saints were saints because they were heroically humble, modest, pure, obedient and charitable. They were saints because they carried out the tedious, common, monotonous duties of life for love of Jesus, and endured the sufferings of daily life for His love. This made them saints and it can make us saints, too, without extraordinary mortifications and extraordinary graces.

Divine Providence assures us of this teaching through Saint Francis de Sales, a Doctor of the Church. He, with Saint Jane de Chantal, founded the Visitation Order, whose rule of life was so mild that it could accept those who had not the health, youth or capacity to live the life of the stricter religious orders then existing. When young, strong nuns of his Order wished in their generosity to do more than the common rule, Saint Francis did not permit it, but said: "That is all you have to do to become saints." We are further assured of this by divine Providence when It gives us, in our times, Saint Thérèse of Lisieux as our teacher and example. Saint Thérèse did not follow the example of the nuns of her convent who at that time used prickly plants to mortify their bodies. Her little way was to have nothing extraordinary in it; it was to be a way that all souls of good-will could follow. In her prayer there was no method. In her life there were no extraordinary self-inflicted mortifications, no charism of miracle-working, no levitations or stigmata. But there was love, love which could efface itself, which could endure sweetly (but not without a struggle) the exasperating rosary-rattling of the sister next to her, or the inconsiderate water-splashing of a fellow-worker in the laundry, or the fussiness of a sick nun whom she was helping. Thérèse washed, ironed, mended and nursed for the love of God. Such an example all can follow.

---

expense of charity and virtue. For the importance of the charismata for the building up of the Church in faith and love and for the renewal of the Church, see Chapter 20, The Charismatic Renewal. A balance is needed.

It is the Holy Spirit Who gives us an attraction to the things of God and to the spiritual life. He it is Who leads us to spiritual reading, prayer, the frequent reception of the sacraments, and the practice of the virtues. The attraction to silence and solitude comes from Him, as does the desire to sacrifice useless, legitimate pleasures—especially those which are in their very nature distracting, such as shows, dances, radio, television, the excessive reading of newspapers and overmuch talking or chattering.

The devil's action, on the contrary, produces perplexities, scruples, doubts, paralyzing uncertainty and discouragement. He lifts us up in pride and self-exaltation—even during prayer and our other spiritual exercises if we permit it—making us self-reliant, self-sufficient, and leading us on to a fall. Or else, seeing our generous dispositions, he prompts us to indiscreet mortifications which will injure our health or place a strain upon our mind. He wishes us to undertake too much; if he cannot make our consciences lax, he tries to make them overstrict, so that we shall become discouraged.

The spirit of the world leads us to place our end in creatures, to love them unduly. It leads to self-indulgence in food, drink and recreations, to vanity, the mutual giving of glory, to flattery and hypocrisy, to pride, ambition and avarice. So, men wear themselves out in mind, body and soul, and neglect their families in the service of honor or material gain.

Devotees of the world and the devil have the illusion that they are free, but theirs is the hardest slavery. Their freedom is an illusion, for as Our Lord says: "Whosoever commits sin, is the servant of sin" (John 8:34)—and sin is a hard taskmaster. John Wu points out in an admirable book, *The Interior Carmel*[2] that the Church calls a fast and follows it with a feast; the world offers a feast and it is followed by a headache. In each case there is pain, but the pain of sacrifice for the love of God is followed by a true joy, whereas the false joys of the devil and the world are followed by pain and sorrow. Devotees of the world and the devil have their special duties and obligations, their special rules and regulations to which they must conform. They have many sacrifices to make for the sake of promises of happiness that are not

[2] N.Y.: Sheed & Ward, 1953.

fulfilled. But when their sacrifices are made and they have gained their ends, they find that these are not so satisfying as they had expected, and they start off on the chase again. They seek to get into a higher income bracket or more important job; the more important they become, the greater their duties and responsibilities and the more they are taken up with them. If they did all this for the love of God, they would have their reward and it would be lasting and worthwhile, but when it is done for the love of themselves and creatures they are left in the end unrewarded.

Psychoanalysis has brought to the attention of men who pride themselves on being self-sufficient and free, that they are more the slaves of hidden springs of motivation than they realize. Indeed, it is those who, in their pride and obstinacy, think they are doing their own will who are in the deepest slavery. The devil does not want to shatter their illusions until he has them safely as his eternal own. He wants them to be miserable in truth without realizing their sorry state, so that they will remain in it until it can never more be bettered.

"You shall know the truth, and the truth shall make you free," says Our Lord (John 8:32). He knows that we are not entirely free until we know the truths of His doctrine and live them, practicing self-renunciation.[3] Then will be uncovered those hidden springs of motivation, the seven capital sins, rooted in self-love and pride; and the enlightened person—fighting against these tendencies in his or her nature—will win through the grace of Christ and His Holy Spirit an ever-increasing capacity to be humble, obedient, truly loving and happy.

---

[3] But I do not mean to suggest that humans, even proud and sinful humans, do not have a truly free will. Indeed, men are freer than they often think. We are apt to shift the responsibility to our heredity, early life, and environment. It is true that temperament inclines us in certain directions, that unconscious ideals and patterns of response are established in early childhood, etc. We may come to understand ourselves better through becoming conscious of, and accurately judging such factors. But it is our free will that yields to our tendencies, or resists them. We are free to say to them, "yes" or "no," especially when they are habitual, and so repeatedly come to our attention. We must learn to recognize and evaluate our tendencies and to exercise our freedom for our eternal advantage, and then we shall have peace and happiness in our lives. To do this, we must know the truth.

12 Saint Joseph

Saint Joseph has a special role to play in God's plan for human happiness, just as he had a special role to play in the life of God Incarnate. Of all men, he was chosen as the foster-father of Jesus and the chaste spouse of the Blessed Virgin Mary. God wanted a man upon whom He could depend, to speak in a human manner; a man whose qualities of mind and heart would fit him to be a father to Jesus and the spouse of Mary, the safeguard of her consecrated virginity in wedlock.

As the chaste husband of Mary, Saint Joseph was joined to her in union of soul (S.T. III, Q. 29, A. 2) and community of life. Mary's chief good, her divine Son, Jesus, she shared with Joseph, who had a special relationship to Jesus unrivaled by any other, second only to that held by His Mother. God gave Saint Joseph the gifts and graces which would enable him to fulfill this office worthily and to live in terms of holy intimacy with Jesus and Mary. Saint Joseph was the head of the family and Mary referred to him as the father of Jesus, for he was His legal father, and truly father, even though he had no part in the begetting of Jesus. So we hear Mary saying to Jesus, on finding Him in the Temple, "Son, why have You done this to us? You see that Your father and I have been searching for You in sorrow" (Luke 2:48 NAB). Joseph had the humility to accept his position and to command; Jesus "was obedient to them" (Luke 2:51 NAB).

Saint Joseph possesses the same paternal authority in the Church as he exercised in the Holy Family of which the Church is the extension, for all Christians are the brothers of Jesus and the children of Mary.[1] He is the patron, the protector of the entire Church. His role was prefigured by the Old Testament Joseph. Pharaoh declared that Joseph was "full of the spirit of God" and enlightened by God in all he said (Genesis 41:38-39). He put him over all his household and over all his land, so that all things in Egypt were subject to Joseph and all went to Joseph for their needs in time of famine. "I am Pharaoh," said the king to Joseph, "without thy command no man shall move hand or foot in all the land of Egypt" (Genesis 41:44). The chastity of Saint Joseph is also prefigured in the chastity of the patriarch.

We may single out a few special virtues attributable to Saint Joseph. His prompt obedience was manifested when the angel solved his dilemma concerning Mary's pregnancy, telling him not to fear and to take Mary as his wife; and again when the angel roused him from sleep and told him to flee to Egypt, which he immediately did. Prompt obedience is an evidence of humility. We may well believe that he acknowledged himself unworthy of the choice God made of him, while accepting it in all simplicity, with complete conformity to the divine will and with unchanging gratitude for this choice and for all the gifts and graces which were his because of it. His justice was shown in his quandary in regard to Mary's pregnancy, when, knowing her virtue but also the law of Moses, he considered putting her away privately as

---

[1] *Quamquam pluries*, Encyclical letter of August 15, 1889 of Pope Leo XIII, on devotion to Saint Joseph. See *Papal Documents on Mary* by William Doheny, C.S.C., and Joseph Kelley, S.T.D. (Milwaukee: Bruce, 1954).

a solution which would fulfill the law without jeopardizing Mary's reputation. Saint Joseph was prudent, taking counsel with God in his actions, allowing himself to be led by the Spirit of God and by the divine will made known to him by faith and reason. Thus, upon his return from Egypt, he did not go back to Bethlehem but rather to Nazareth because, "he heard ... that Archelaus had succeeded his father Herod as king of Judea, and he was afraid to go there. Instead, because of a warning received in a dream, Joseph went to the region of Galilee" (Matthew 2:22 NAB). In his intimacy with Mary and Jesus he lived a life which exercised the purest faith, hope and charity, and it was in their company that he is believed to have died his holy death.

Saint Joseph is a powerful father and patron to whom we should be devoted in all our necessities, spiritual and temporal. Devotion to him will help us to lead an interior and supernatural life. This he and Mary desire us to do; they have the mission to care for Jesus in our souls, to help us to grow in Jesus, and to help Jesus to live in us. A prayer expresses this life of Jesus in us: "O Jesus, so live in me this day, that all I do may be done by Thee." It requires time and correspondence with grace to bring about the fruition of such a daily prayer. Saint Joseph will obtain great confidence in the Father for us, and if we imitate his virtues, if we do all in imitation of Saint Joseph, he will help us to live in Jesus, so that Jesus may live in us.

Part Three:

Means to
Happiness

13 From the Side of Christ: The Church

From the side of Christ, dead on the cross, pierced by a lance, flowed blood and water (John 19:34). The Fathers of the Church saw in the blood and water the sacraments of the Church: Baptism and the Eucharist. Saint Augustine says that just as in the sleep of Adam, God took from his side the rib from which He made for him a companion and spouse, so as Christ slept the sleep of death, the Father fashioned from His side His bride, the Church.

While through the sacraments the ministers of the Church transmit the life of Christ to humankind, the Church herself, companion and bride of Christ, is also the sacrament of Christ. She is a sign of His salvation to the nations. It is His purpose that in her all humankind be gathered together as a people made one by the unity of the Father, the Son and the Holy Spirit, dwelling in all and in each.

Thus He desires humankind to be His people, a people who form a living and lifegiving community, growing in the grace of Christ until it reaches its fullness in a life that goes on forever.

Christ died as a witness to the truth which He had brought to earth for humankind. But this He did not do for His own generation alone. There are three ways in which He could have transmitted these truths to succeeding generations, as Duane Hunt perceived as he struggled from Protestantism to the Catholic Church, in which he became the Bishop of Salt Lake City diocese, and as he tells us in *Where I Found Christ* (convert stories, edited by Father John O'Brien).[1]

Jesus could have made these truths the matter of private revelation, communicating them to men of all times as individuals. Certainly then He would have required only sincerity and good-will and the desire to know His truths as conditions for this private revelation. In this case we would expect all who possess these qualities to have received this revelation and to be in agreement. But there is no such agreement: there are many Protestants in the various denominations, and even in the same denomination, who are sincere and seek Christ's truths and good-will and yet who disagree with one another.

Christ could have placed these truths in a book, so that all sincere seekers of His truth would learn it there, and then too we should expect agreement. But although there is an inspired book—the Bible— sincere believers disagree as to the teachings of Christ it contains. This, then, was not the way He chose to give to all of good will the knowledge He had brought to earth.

Finally, He could have established a society of persons to whom He would confide these truths and who, in their turn, would teach others. But if this were to succeed, this society would have to last to the end of time—be indefectible. And, if the truths entrusted to it were to remain unaltered and uncorrupted, it would need the power of transmitting without error Christ's teachings.

Now, we know from the Scriptures, as well as from tradition and history, that Christ did form such a society with just such a mission, on the foundation of the twelve Apostles whom He personally trained and instructed, and who were witnesses of what He did and of what

[1] N.Y.: Doubleday, 1950.

befell Him. And we know that one of these Apostles, in particular, was singled out to be the mainstay of all the others and of the entire society. Simon Peter confessed at Caesarea: "You are the Messiah, the Son of the living God" (Matthew 16:16). Jesus replied: "You are 'Rock' and on this rock I will build My Church, and the jaws of death shall not prevail against it" (Matthew 16:18 NAB).

Again, the night before He died, Jesus said to Peter, "Simon, Simon! Remember that Satan has asked for you, to sift you all like wheat. But I have prayed for you that your faith may never fail. You in turn must strengthen your brothers" (Luke 22:31-32 NAB). It was for Peter's faith then that Christ prayed, and Peter would have the function of confirming his brethren in the faith. Finally, we may recall that after the Resurrection and before His Ascension, Our Lord said three times to Peter: "Simon, son of John, do you love Me more than these?" and three times Peter answered: "Yes, Lord, You know that I love You." Three times Jesus charged him, "Feed My lambs, feed My sheep" (John 21:15-17 NAB).

Peter was to be the chief Shepherd, to whom the sheep would all be entrusted; he would feed them the true doctrine and the true Bread that came down from Heaven. He would also be the shepherd of his co-pastors, the bishops, strengthening them in the faith. Our Lord in speaking thus to Peter fulfilled the promise He had made when He declared to Peter that upon him He would build His Church: "I shall give to you the keys of the kingdom of heaven. Whatever you declare bound on earth shall be bound in heaven. And whatever you declare loosed on earth shall be loosed in heaven" (Matthew 16:19).

Christ did found a Church. He founded it upon the rock of Peter. Peter and the Apostles united with him form a college through which Christ transmits His truth to all generations. Peter and the Apostles provided for the succession to this college by appointing men like themselves—bishops—to carry on the work and teaching of Christ.

The preservation of Christ's truth could only successfully be accomplished through a provision of divine providence by which these successors would be enabled to persevere in teaching the truth Christ had entrusted to Peter and His Apostles. This provision is the charism by which the Holy Spirit protects His Church from error. It belongs first of all to the Church itself, that is to all the people of God. And it belongs to the Church's spokespeople—the Pope and the bishops. This charism is not the charism of revelation or inspiration. It is simply the protection from error in teaching the truths of the faith—and of morals through which that faith is expressed in lives.

This charism is called infallibility. When the Pope or the bishops united to the Pope define a teaching of faith or morals for the whole Church, then it is protected from error. Likewise the agreed upon ordinary teaching of the Pope and the bishops united to the Pope proclaimed as the revelation of Christ is protected from error. "This is so, even when they are dispersed around the world, provided that while maintaining the bond of unity among themselves and with Peter's successor, and while teaching authentically on a matter of faith and morals, they concur in a single viewpoint as the one which must be held conclusively" (Vatican II's Constitution on the Church, No. 25).

In this manner the teachings of Christ are preserved. As Vatican II's Dogmatic Constitution on Revelation says:

> The task of authentically interpreting the word of God whether written or handed on (that is by tradition) has been entrusted exclusively to the living teaching office of the Church, whose authority is exercised in the name of Jesus Christ. This teaching office is not above the word of God but serves it, teaching only what has been handed on, listening to it devoutly, guarding it scrupulously, and explaining it faithfully by divine commission and with the help of the Holy Spirit; it draws from this one deposit of faith everything which it presents as divinely revealed.
>
> It is clear, therefore, that sacred tradition, sacred Scripture, and the teaching authority of the Church, in accord with God's most wise design, are so linked and joined together that one cannot stand without the others, and that all together and each in its own way under the action of the one Holy Spirit contribute effectively to the salvation of souls. (No. 10)

While the fullness of unity and of the means of salvation exist only in the Catholic Church, Vatican II's Decree on Ecumenism states:

> Nevertheless all those justified by faith through baptism are incorporated into Christ. They therefore have the right to be honored by the title of Christian, and are properly regarded as brothers in the Lord by the sons of the Catholic Church. (No. 1)

Moreover some, even very many, of the most significant elements or endowments which together go to build up and give life to the Church herself can exist outside the visible boundaries of the Catholic Church: the written word of God; the life of grace; faith, hope, and charity, along with other interior gifts of the Holy Spirit and visible elements. All of these, which come from Christ and lead back to Him, belong by right to the one Church of Christ.... It follows that these separated Churches and Communities, though we believe they suffer from defects already mentioned, have by no means been deprived of significance and importance in the mystery of salvation. For the Spirit of Christ has not refrained from using them as means of salvation which derive their efficacy from the very fullness of grace and truth entrusted to the Catholic Church. (No. 3)

Hence on the one hand, there are many outside the Catholic Church seeking the unity of Christians, and Catholics are, likewise urged "to participate skillfully in the work of ecumenism" (No. 4), that all may be one as Christ prayed they should be, and as we should so pray, that the world may believe the Gospel.

In fact we should recognize all men and women as the children of the Father, regardless of color, race or creed (divided not by God, but by man), and pray for all.

We acknowledge that the Catholic Church has the functions of teaching, governing and administering the sacraments. In her government she has but one objective, the salvation and sanctification of souls; her end is to lead all to Heaven. This is clearly reflected throughout her Code of Canon Law. Through His disciples, Jesus continues His saving mission.

This Catholic Church is the Mystical Body of Christ; it is, together with Him, its Head, the whole Christ; and whatsoever is done of good or evil to the least of its members is done to Him. His loving Heart lives in each of His members who are in the state of grace, and ardently seeks to reign in love, as sovereign King over each and all the living, in the unity of His Mystical Body.

Already there is union, if not full, of all Christians in Christ through faith and baptism; already Christians are related to those who first received divine revelation, the Jewish people; and already Christ is present in some way to all persons, as Vatican Council II has declared.

Saint Thomas teaches that in assuming a human nature, the Word wed all humanity.

By the expression, the Mystical Body, we mean to say that Jesus is united to the men, women and children who constitute His Church, the Roman Catholic Church; that He is living in them by His grace (insofar as they are in the state of grace), by which they cleave to Him and through which He, His Father and His Spirit dwell in them; that He is in the Hierarchy of His Church by His living and divine authority to serve the faithful; and that His Spirit of Love, which is the soul of His Church, is ardently seeking to bring through His Church and in His Church all to the highest union with the Father. This is the end the Sacred Heart has in view, this will be the universal coming of His Kingdom for which we pray in the Our Father. This also is the end of the ecumenical movement, in the words of Vatican Council II's Decree on Ecumenism: "that there may be one visible Church of God, a Church truly universal and sent forth to the whole world that the world may be converted to the gospel and so be saved, to the glory of God" (No. 1).

We should review these truths from time to time. We believe what the Church teaches, because Christ Who is Truth Itself entrusted His teachings to her. We should frequently renew our loving submission and fidelity to the Church through whom we receive so many and so great blessings. And we should preserve an attitude of respect and loyalty toward her priests, in whom Jesus lives for us and who are exposed to severe trials and temptations for our sake. We should not take it upon ourselves to be their judges whose judgment is reserved in a special way by Jesus to Himself. He Himself shall call them to a strict account. And for the universal reign of His love which they promote, we should, together with them, pray, work and suffer.

14 The Sacraments: Channels of Grace

Our sins are the finite acts of finite creatures, but their malice is measured by the infinity of Him Whom they offend. Adequate reparation requires the offering of something of equal value, something that will please the infinite Majesty as much as the sin offends Him. Since all our acts are finite, and all the service and love we could offer the Father are due Him anyway, we cannot make adequate reparation: this requires an infinite person, the value of whose acts is infinite, acting in our name, as our representative. Now the Father willed that there be adequate reparation for our sins. The Second Person of the Blessed Trinity, a divine Person Whose acts have infinite value, took a human nature in which He could suffer and atone as our representative.

Thus the merits of Jesus Christ repair the sins of us all from the beginning to the end of the world. He is the Savior of the human race; He became man to save us from our sins. He bore the stripes of the chastisement that should have fallen upon us, the guilty ones. These merits, which He distributes through Mary, the Mediatrix of all graces, He communicates to us through the channels of the sacraments.

Christ has put the sacraments into the hands of His Church, more particularly, into the hands of His priests; priests are "administrators of the mysteries of God" (1 Corinthians 4:1 NAB).

The sacraments are sensible signs to which Christ attaches invisible grace, which, through these signs, He confers upon humans. Only God can give grace, and only He can attach grace to sensible signs, to material things. In doing so He has regard for our human nature, which is a unity of body and soul. In this unity the senses communicate with the mind and the mind communicates through the senses, for example in speech.

In the sacraments an effect is produced which is above the capacity of the material thing used by the Father to convey grace. Christ Himself is the Sacrament of sacraments, since in Him there is a human nature through which grace is conveyed above the capacity of human nature to do. He Himself is present in the conferral of the sacraments to render them fruitful of His grace to their recipients.

The sacraments also stir up in those who participate in them the dispositions proper for receiving them. They produce their effect by the action of Christ so long as no obstacle is placed in the way by the recipient, and this effect is greater, the greater the receptivity of the recipient.

The sacraments are conferred according to rites established by the Church, and these rites are liturgical celebrations. Therefore the sacraments are properly conferred in an ecclesial community participation; they are an event of the church community. Thus in baptism, confirmation, the Eucharist, marriage, holy orders, anointing of the sick, the rite of these sacraments are appropriately celebrated in the Church with the participation of the faithful. And even the sacrament of Reconciliation, in which the penitents are bound to confess their sins individually to a priest and hence privately, has a communal and social aspect, and is a reconciliation of the penitent not only with the Father, but also with the Church.

The Constitution of the Sacred Liturgy of Vatican II speaks of Christ's sending the Apostles filled with the Holy Spirit to preach the gospel to every creature and to proclaim that "the Son of God by His death and Resurrection had freed us from the power of Satan (Acts 26:18) and from death, and brought us into the Kingdom of His Father," and says that Christ had as His purpose also "that they might exercise the work of salvation which they were proclaiming, by means of sacrifice and sacraments, around which the entire liturgical life revolves" (No. 6).

This Constitution goes on to say: "To accomplish so great a work, Christ is always present in His Church, especially in the liturgical celebrations" (No. 7).

In the sacrament of baptism (by infusion), the sensible sign is the pouring of water over the forehead together with the words: "I baptize thee in the name of the Father and of the Son and of the Holy Spirit." This sensible sign, together with these words, denotes the washing away of original sin (and actual sin in the case of adults) from the baptized soul, which the invisible grace of the sacrament accomplishes. Thereby humans are made members of Christ's Mystical Body, His Church. Thereby the merits of His Holy Passion and Death are applied to them for their sanctification. The priest drives away the evil spirit, so that the Holy Spirit, unimpeded, may enter to possess and dwell in the soul of His elect.

Baptism is an election, a choice, to which all are called: Christ died for all. The baptized, either himself or by proxy, solemnly promises to renounce the devil with all his pomps and works, and the world (its maxims and false practices), and engages himself, or herself, to take up his cross and follow Jesus Christ. By Baptism the elect of God undergoes a mystical death with Christ: with Christ he or she is nailed to the Cross, dies and is buried. One dies to self, to the world and to the devil in order that one may rise with Christ in the newness of Christian life and have one's glory with the glory of the Only Begotten Son.

This sacrament imparts a character upon the soul of the recipient, and configures the Christian to the Passion, Death and Resurrection of Jesus Christ (S.T. III, Q. 66, A. 2; Q. 69, A. 9 ad 1) so that the Eternal Father sees in the Christian His Only Begotten and most dear Son. Nevertheless the baptized should seek to maintain harmony between the character imparted by Baptism and his, or her, own mind, outlook and deeds. In other words, the baptized should keep close to the mind of Christ through spiritual reading and prayer, should die to self daily, and rise in Christ to fulfill the Father's will in duties and good works, with docility to the inspiration of the Holy Spirit. Thus we renew and fulfill daily the renunciation and pledge of this sacrament and walk in the grace of our Baptism. This grace is the grace of the spiritual life, for Baptism is a sacrament of regeneration, and what is born again in us is *the spiritual life* (S.T. III, Q. 69, A. 5), which we lost by original sin through Adam and which we regain by our incorporation in Christ by Baptism. We ought to rejoice and thank our Lord for having numbered us among His followers. "It was not you who chose Me, it was I Who chose you" (John 15:16 NAB), and we should resolve to be His followers not only in name but also in deed.

The sacrament of Confirmation is conferred ordinarily by the bishop. By this sacrament we are made mature Christians, capable of fighting in defense of our faith and of bearing witness to it with our lives if necessary. By it we are strengthened to fight against the maxims and bad example of the world, the vehement desires of the flesh and the strategies of the devil. The confirmed Christian should stir up the grace given by this sacrament, and fight as a soldier of Christ not only for his, or her, own salvation but for that of others, by the witness of his, or her, own life, by prayers, sacrifices and good works.

Like Baptism and Holy Orders, the sacrament of Confirmation places a permanent character upon the soul, an indelible mark which configures it to Christ. Through this sacrament the Holy Spirit is given in a special manner; His gifts are more deeply rooted in the soul. When we live and grow in this Spirit through cherishing our spiritual life for our own welfare and that of others and for God's glory, we act in accordance with our dignity as confirmed Christians.

The Eucharist together with Baptism and Confirmation completes the initiation of the Christian and his or her incorporation into Christ. The sacrament of the Anointing of the Sick is given to the baptized Christian in danger of death from illness or old age.

Saint James says in his epistle: "Is any among you sick? Let him call for the elders (priests) of the church, and let them pray over him, anointing him with oil in the name of the Lord; and the prayer of faith will save the sick man, and the Lord will raise him up; and if he has committed sins, he will be forgiven" (5:14-15).

The Council of Trent cites this text in declaring that "this sacred anointing of the sick was instituted by Christ our Lord as truly and properly a sacrament of the New Testament."

This sacrament is available to the sick at the beginning of their danger of death, or to the old and infirm. The sick do not have to be at the point of death to receive it. Formerly called the Sacrament of Extreme Unction, it was considered reserved for those at the point of death. Since Vatican Council II, this sacrament is recommended for those who are seriously sick and for the elderly who are weak. Its use is also approved for sick children who have sufficient use of reason to be comforted by it.

As Paul VI said quoting the Council of Trent, this sacrament "takes away sins, if any remain to be taken away, and the remnants of sin; it also relieves and strengthens the soul of the sick person, arousing in him a great confidence in the divine mercy; thus sustained, he may easily bear the trials and hardships of his sickness, more easily resist the temptations of the devil 'lying in wait' (Genesis 3:15), and sometimes regain bodily health, if this is expedient for the health of the soul" (Paul VI Apostolic Constitution, *Sacram Unctionem Infirmorum*).

The sacrament of the anointing of the sick is another manifestation of the divine thoughtfulness and of the tender mercy of our Lord, Who wishes to give His special graces to those who are seriously ill and to be with them in a special way at such times.

To profit more fully from this sacrament, we should live for God, accept sickness lovingly from His hands in reparation for our sins and the sins of others, understand the sacrament, and not delay in receiving it with faith and piety. But lacking such preparation, the sacrament itself may serve to help us enter into the dispositions of acceptance of illness and of bearing its burdens with Christ.

For further reading on the sacraments, *The Teaching of Christ, A Catholic Catechism For Adults*, published by Our Sunday Visitor, may be consulted.

15 The Liturgy & Liturgical Prayer

The liturgy, liturgical prayer and the liturgical renewal of Vatican II are experienced by the greatest number in the Sunday eucharistic liturgy, the Sunday Mass.

The purpose of this renewal was to increase the influence of the liturgy on the spiritual life of the Catholic Christian, and ultimately on all Christians and all humankind. Thus, at the beginning of its Constitution on the Sacred Liturgy, the Council says: "It is the goal of this most sacred Council to intensify the daily growth of Catholics in Christian living; to make more responsive to the requirements of our times those Church observances which are open to adaptation; to nurture whatever can contribute to the unity of all who believe in Christ; and to strengthen those aspects of the Church which can help summon all of mankind into her embrace" (No. 1).

How can the eucharistic liturgy of the Sunday Mass, that part of the Church's Liturgy that is best attended, be expected to accomplish this? The Council goes on to answer this question:

> For it is through the liturgy, especially the divine Eucharistic sacrifice, that the 'work of our Redemption is exercised.' The liturgy is thus the outstanding means by which the faithful can express in their lives, and manifest to others, the mystery of Christ and the real nature of the true Church. It is of the essence of the Church (and we might add of her head, Jesus Christ) that she be both human and divine, visible and yet invisibly endowed, eager to act and yet devoted to contemplation, present in this world and yet not at home in it. She is all these things in such a way that in her the human is subordinated to the divine, the visible likewise to the invisible, action to contemplation, and this present world to that city yet to come, which we seek (cf. Hebrews 13:14). Day by day the liturgy builds up those within the Church into the Lord's holy temple, into a spiritual dwelling for God (cf. Ephesians 2:21-22)—an enterprise which will continue until Christ's full stature is achieved (cf. Ephesians 4:13). At the same time the liturgy marvelously fortifies the faithful in their capacity to preach Christ. To outsiders the liturgy thus reveals the Church as a sign raised above the nations (cf. Isaiah 11-12). Under this sign the scattered sons of God are being gathered into one (John 11:52) until there is one fold and one shepherd (cf. John 10:16).[1]

The liturgy is the public act of the Church through which she worships God in the name of all, offering the adoration, reparation and thanksgiving due Him, and petitioning for the graces needed by all.

Charismatic Catholics should recognize that as helpful as are their prayer groups, it is in the gathering of all the people of God, all of whom receive charismata in their sacramental baptism, that the Church is most properly represented. Hence they place a high priority on their participation in the parish liturgy, together with their brothers and sisters of the parish. While they may indeed dignify their prayer group meetings with the eucharistic liturgy, still they do not constitute an elite parallel to the people of God, but are members of this people, and express their membership by their participation in the parish liturgy.

The Church's worship of God is the most efficacious means of sanctification Pope Pius XII asserted in his encyclical *Mediator*

---

[1] Constitution on the Sacred Liturgy, Documents of Vatican II, Walter Abbott, S.J., America Press.

Dei,[2] which is recommended for meditative reading, as is also the Constitution on the Sacred Liturgy of Vatican II. Vatican II says that "the liturgy is the summit toward which the activity of the Church is directed; at the same time it is the fountain from which all her power flows" (Constitution on the Sacred Liturgy, No. 10). The liturgy requires our personal cooperation and participation. The principal act of this worship is the Holy Sacrifice of the Mass at which the priest communicates in the fruits of the Sacrifice by receiving the divine Victim as his food—and at which all the faithful are invited to likewise communicate, so long as they have a right intention in doing so and are not in a state of mortal sin (whether or not they have been to confession recently). "No other action of the Church can match its claim to efficacy, nor equal the degree of it" (No. 7). Baptism fits the Christian to participate in this worship which individuals and society owe to their Sovereign Lord, Creator and Father.

The liturgy presents the teachings of Scripture and of the Church—and particularly the mysteries of Christ—in a manner not only apt to enlighten the mind but also to communicate love and devotion to the heart, while serving as a vehicle of worship.

The liturgy is truly the fount of the Christian spirit, as Saint Pius X called it. The Church urges the participation of all in the liturgy, so that all may be nourished by the Christian spirit which issues from it. Our spiritual life does not flourish best when we isolate ourselves from others; rather, we are a people, members of one another, and God desires our common sanctification insofar as this is practicable. This is fostered particularly when we participate in common in the liturgy, where humility and charity, through the recognition of our membership in one Mystical Body, is promoted. To repeat: "For it is through the liturgy, especially the divine Eucharistic Sacrifice, that the work of our Redemption is exercised. The liturgy is thus the outstanding means by which the faithful can express in their lives, and manifest to others, the mystery of Christ and the real nature of the true Church" (Constitution on the Sacred Liturgy, No. 2).

In other words, in the liturgy we do not come together as a group of individuals each pursuing his or her individual prayer apart, but as

---

[2] Obtainable from the U.S. Catholic Conference, 1312 Massachusetts Ave., N.W., Washington, DC 20009.

a people performing a common action, joining in a common prayer. The external ceremonies and action are invested with those interior dispositions which each brings. Our entire spiritual life outside the liturgy contributes to our participation in it. In turn, the liturgy strengthens us with graces for pursuing our spiritual path during the course of the day. Thus the liturgy presupposes a common faith, and a common membership in one body, and expresses it. This is the reason the Church cannot invite our separated brethren to communicate without reserve in the sacraments together with us, while nevertheless feeling the pain of this separation, and praying that it will be mended by our all being reunited in the unity of one faith and one Church.

The lay person's minimum participation in the liturgical life is attendance at daily or Sunday Mass. The principal elements of the liturgy are to be found in the Mass. Certain parts, called the Ordinary of the Mass (including the Canon), vary less than other parts, the Proper. The Proper varies with the season or the mystery or the saint commemorated. Christ Himself teaches us through the readings and the Gospel. By listening to these the Christian receives enlightenment and direction adapted to the liturgical season or time. This is appreciated by those who follow the beautiful daily Masses during Lent, a practice not uncommon among our faithful, and to which non-Catholics are invited, as they are also to all Church services throughout the year.

The liturgical year begins with the season of Advent. Then the Church, with Mary and the prophets, gives vent to ardent longing for the coming of the Savior. During the season of Christmastide the Church rejoices in the birth of Jesus. It follows Him in His hidden life, and then throughout Lent in His public life to His Crucifixion on Good Friday and His Resurrection on Easter Sunday. It follows Him in the forty days after the Resurrection to His Ascension, and then perseveres in prayer with Mary and the disciples till the descent of the Holy Spirit on Pentecost. Trinity Sunday follows Pentecost Sunday; the work of Jesus and His Spirit are consummated in the worship of the Blessed Trinity.

Thus the Christian follows Christ by following the liturgical year with the Church. Attached to each of His mysteries commemorated by the liturgy are graces coming from His Sacred Heart to do a special work in the soul. So during Christmas, there is the grace of spiritual childhood: humility, simplicity and great joy in salvation; during Lent, the grace of the spirit of penance, amendment of life, personal love of and loyal devotion to the Crucified Redeemer; during Easter, the grace to rise in invincible newness of life, in the new creation all are called to be; on Ascension Thursday, the grace "to mind the things that are above, where Jesus sits at the right hand of the Father," and with Jesus, to abide with the Father.

The liturgy of Holy Week follows the drama of our Redemption in a moving manner, as the Savior celebrates the Last Supper, is delivered up to death, and goes to be crucified, then is buried in the sepulcher from whence He rises on Easter Sunday. With Christ on Easter Sunday, the Christian comes forth from the tomb to newness of life. As He rose before daybreak, so too the Church, unable to postpone its great joy, celebrates His Rising with a nocturnal Mass, the Easter vigil.

Christ Himself presides over the liturgy in the Blessed Sacrament. He is present also in the assembled faithful who are the real Church, for the church is not a building but a people. Our Lord knew of our participation in His mysteries while they were being enacted, through His divine nature and through the beatific vision and infused knowledge of His holy soul. Thus He experienced our following of Him. Time and space are annihilated as Christ and the Christian are present together in the experiences of His Sacred Life, His Nativity, Passion, Resurrection and Ascension.

The liturgical year contains, besides the Christocentric cycle, a Marian cycle commemorating the mysteries of Our Lady's life: her Immaculate Conception, December 8th; her Nativity, September 8th; the Annunciation, March 25; her Assumption, August 15.

There is also the calendar of the saints. Christians, by their attendance at the Mass which honors the saint in question, make the equivalent of a pilgrimage. It is as though instead of going to visit the tomb of the saint they meet the saint at the Mass celebrated by the Church in his or her honor.

The gem of the liturgy is Holy Mass; the setting of this gem are the Hours of the Divine Office which sanctify the hours of the day. Matins (vigils) and Lauds are the night and morning office of the Church; the traditional time for reciting Matins is the last hours of the night; for Lauds, daybreak; Terce, 9 o'clock (the third hour, Roman time); Sext, twelve (the sixth hour); None, after the noonday meal (the ninth hour, or 3 o'clock); Vespers at eventide; Compline before retiring.

The Divine Office has as its principal constituent the one hundred and fifty psalms so distributed that all may be recited within two to four weeks. Attached to the psalms are antiphons which show the psalms' particular application in the Church's use, for example, in the commemoration of a particular mystery or feast; then there are responsories, and lessons containing teachings from Scripture or from the Fathers of the Church or from the lives of the Saints.

While some lay persons recite the Divine Office daily, many will find it impossible or inadvisable to do so. All however may do reading on the liturgy. (A few suggestions will be found on pages 99-100.)

ANOTHER MEANS of obtaining some of the benefits of the liturgy (but in no way substituting for it) is the use for spiritual reading and prayer of the stuff of the liturgy, the psalms. These are found in the Old Testament of every complete Bible; they are also published separately in a form that permits their easy use.[3] The authorship of many of the psalms is traditionally attributed to David whose life bore so many resemblances to the life of Christ that he is called a "type" of Christ. Scripture tells us that he was a man according to the heart of God. He knew by prophetic light the mysteries of Christ which are declared in the psalms. Thus Psalm 21 (or 22) begins with the words of Christ on the Cross, portrays the Crucifixion with the detail of an eyewitness, and enters into the sentiments of Our Lord's holy soul.

To understand the psalms, "the prayerbook of Christians," and make them our own as generation upon generation of Christians have done, we must recall the mystery of the Mystical Body of Christ: Christ is the Head, we are the members, sharing one life, with the same intentions and sentiments insofar as we conform ours to His. He took upon Himself our weaknesses and sins, and made them His own. These interior sentiments of Christ are expressed for us in the psalms, for their authors entered into His dispositions. Many of the psalms are best understood when we apply them to Christ; in saying

[3] For example, *My Daily Psalm Book* (Monastery of the Precious Blood, 5300 Fort Hamilton Parkway, Brooklyn, NY 11219).

them we identify ourselves with Him and with His sentiments. Further, the psalmist utters all the sentiments of the human heart in its needs, joys and exultation; hence the universal applicability of the psalms and their usefulness as prayers in all the circumstances of our lives. Dale Carnegie recalls the successful use, for anxiety and insomnia, of Psalm 22 (or 23): "The Lord is my shepherd I shall not want."

Other psalms can be understood as referring to Our Lord, although they are literally expressions of the Psalmist concerning the events of his own life. Many of these events typified the events of Christ's life. Thus Psalm 3 has as its subtitle: "The Psalm of David when he fled from the face of his son Absalom." At that time Absalom had rebelled against his father and wished to be king in his place. This psalm begins: "O, Lord, how many are my adversaries! Many rise up against me!" It ends: "Salvation is the Lord's! Upon Your people be Your blessing!"

The rebellion of his son Absalom against King David is a type of the rebellion of Judas and the high priests and scribes against Christ's spiritual Kingship; and this psalm can be understood in this spiritual sense to refer to the Passion and Resurrection (so particularly, "Now I can lie down and go to sleep and then awake, for Yahweh has hold of me"). It may be noted that to escape Absalom, David fled from Jerusalem across the brook Cedron; while after the Last Supper Jesus also crossed this brook to gain the refuge of Gethsemane. We can also understand this psalm as treating of the enemies of our soul—first of all, our own disordered passions led by our predominant fault: "O, Lord, how many are my adversaries! Many say to my soul: There is no salvation for him in God. But You, O Lord, art my shield, my glory." Leagued together with our evil tendencies are the devil and the false maxims of the world; sometimes too the persecutions of men, as in the Communist countries, where the Church cries out: "Why, O Lord, are they multiplied that afflict me? Many are they who rise up against me."

In order better to understand the circumstances of David's life, reflected in many of the psalms, we may read the first and second book of Kings which relate his story. There we learn how truly meek and humble he was. When the psalms by their language call upon God for revenge against the psalmist's enemies, we can understand this as a prophecy of the divine justice which will befall his enemies, rather than as a prayer that he be so vindicated. Furthermore, we can apply these "vindictive" texts to our spiritual life by considering the enemies inveighed against to be the spiritual enemies of the soul: the world, the flesh (including our passions and sinful tendencies) and the devil. Then we can bring to bear all the energy of our soul in praying the Father to overcome these enemies, while setting our will against them. Thus the psalms may be brought into conformity with the high sentiments of charity and mercy that the Christian seeks to nourish by his prayer and spiritual reading.

There are then various ways to complement one's prayer life. There is the charismatic renewal, a wonderful initiative of divine love and mercy, with its prayer groups and prayer communities. Through it the Father wishes to bring about an awakening to the Third Person of the Trinity, the Holy Spirit, Who is the fullness of love of the Father and of the Son.

But above all is the liturgy, and especially the Eucharistic liturgy, by which all the people of God are called together to participate in the Redemption and its fruits.

Finally there is the divine office, and its stuff, the psalms, which from the beginning have been the prayer of Christians.

Wisdom has built herself a house, she has hewn her out seven pillars. She has slain her victims, mingled her wine, and set forth her table. She has sent her maids to invite to the tower, and to the walls of the city: Whosoever is a little one, let him come to me. And to the unwise she said: Come, eat my bread, and drink the wine which I have mingled for you. Forsake childishness, and live, and walk by the ways of prudence.

— Proverbs 9:1-6

16 Jesus in the Eucharist

Wisdom is an appropriate name of the Son of God; the house which He has built is the Church; the seven pillars are the seven sacraments; the table is the altar where the Victim, Jesus, mingled with wine—His Precious Blood—is given to the little ones called thereto by Wisdom's maids, the priests.

This text is also applied to Mary, the Seat of Wisdom. Her house is Jesus, Whose Mystical Body is the Church, in which are the seven pillars, the sacraments. She calls out through her servants: "Whosoever is a little one let him come to me. Come, eat my bread and drink the wine which I have mingled for you. Forsake childishness and live (with everlasting life) and walk by the ways of prudence (which will lead you to eternal beatitude)."

He has not dealt thus with every nation; nor are the gods of other nations so close to them as our God is close to us, Saint Thomas reminds us. For we Catholics live around a holy table, the altar, on which our God is present. There we eat and drink receiving Him into our hearts. In so doing, we are united not only with Him but with each other. For the Sacrament in which we receive Him also signifies and promotes the union of charity among those who are gathered together at His table.

THE EUCHARIST is the greatest of the sacraments, for in the sensible sign of this Sacrament is contained not only grace but the Author of grace. The excellence of the Sacrifice of the Mass resides in this, that it is the self-same sacrifice as the Sacrifice of the Cross. In both there is the same High Priest, for Jesus is the principal Priest Who offers the Mass through the instrumentality of the visible priest; and there is in both the self-same Victim. On the Cross the Sacrifice was offered for all by Jesus, and in a bloody manner. On our altars the Sacrifice is daily offered for all in an unbloody manner. On Calvary, Jesus was capable of suffering and endured torments as His Precious Blood was separated from His spotless flesh. In the Mass He suffers now no longer, and His flesh and blood are separated not physically but sacramentally by the twofold consecration, "This is My Body," "This is My Blood." On Calvary, Christ in His beatific and infused knowledge saw each of us, loved each of us, died for each of us individually. He foresaw each Sacrifice of the Mass, each Holy Communion which was to follow, and through which the merits of the Cross would be communicated to us for our salvation and sanctification. He could not have given us a greater proof of His love than He did on the Cross. He could not give Himself to us more completely than He does under the form of food at Holy Communion.

A sacrifice is an external sign of the adoration of the heart. It is the worship of God through the immolation of a victim, attesting to the sovereignty of the divine Majesty, and to the homage and submission of the creature. No one could possibly have a greater adoration and spirit of oblation than that which was present meritoriously in the Heart of Christ from the moment of His conception to the moment of

His death but especially when He offered Himself upon the Cross. Then He was filled with a desire to be utterly annihilated before His heavenly Father in testimony of the infinite excellence and beauty of God. This oblation of His Heart was fulfilled exteriorly in the bloody, cruel death that He willingly and gladly suffered.

Sacrifice (like prayer) has four ends which fulfill the duties of religion to God: *a*doration, *c*ontrition (or reparation), *t*hanksgiving and *s*upplication (a-c-t-s). In the case of the sinless Christ on the Cross and in the Mass, this reparation made for our sins is fully adequate and more than adequate (it is not contrition properly speaking, for Christ had no sins of His own to repent).

So, too, are His thanksgiving and supplication fully adequate; and at Holy Mass, His supplication obtains for those for whom the Mass is offered and for those who assist at it, in communion with the Church, the graces they need, if they are fervent and place no obstacles thereto. The Mass has great value for all who attend, even those who are not of the Faith or who are not in a state of grace—it may obtain for them the graces of faith, of contrition and confession. (Pope Benedict XV teaches that it is more beneficial to Christians to have Masses celebrated for themselves while they are living than after they are dead.)

Thus we see why the Christian who can do so should begin each day with attendance at the Sacrifice of the Holy Mass. Then he unites himself with the oblation of Jesus Christ in this greatest act of religion. Then he stands with Mary and John at the foot of the Cross. Here he can offer his adoration and thanks, his contrition or reparation, his petition for all the graces that he needs for the day.

Throughout the day, the true worshipers strive to fulfill their morning oblation by doing and suffering all that the Father wants them to do and suffer, by conforming their will to His.

When we consider what Holy Mass is, as we should from time to time, we experience wonder and admiration at the goodness of the Father Who wanted to give us the opportunity to stand by the Cross of His Son, Jesus. He did not wish this great privilege to be reserved to Mary, John and the holy women; He wished us also to have the joy and the daily joy of sharing it with them. Surely Mary would have preferred to have been torn to pieces rather than to have missed one moment of her Son's Passion. We can well be ashamed of the lack of faith and coldness of heart which keeps us away from daily attendance at Holy Mass.

Nevertheless the will of the Father must be sovereign here too, and if the circumstances of our life prevent us from attending Holy Mass daily, we must willingly make this sacrifice. Thus a mother who neglected her husband and her children to attend daily Mass would be practicing a false piety.

When we are downcast and overburdened with the thought of the flood of sin that covers the face of the earth and outrages the gentleness and loveliness of the Father, spoiling the beauty of His creation, we can unite ourselves to the Mass being said at that moment, reflecting that in the Mass more honor and glory are given to the Father than all sins together take from Him. When He promised that the New Covenant would never be revoked but would endure forever, He must have had in mind the Precious Blood by which that New Covenant was sealed.

In the post-Vatican II Church, all are called to active, responsible participation in the Mass. We may follow the words of the priest while making the responses proper to the faithful. We may stand in spirit at the foot of the Cross. We may lovingly unite ourselves interiorly to the Hearts of Jesus and Mary. We should all unite ourselves with the priest in the principal parts of the Mass: in offering the oblation at the Offertory, in uniting the oblation of our daily lives with the oblation of Christ at the Consecration, and in receiving Christ sacramentally or at least spiritually at the Communion. And all should unite themselves with their brethren present and absent with whom they form one body, one flock, and toward whom they have the sacred duty of charity and mercy which they must exercise faithfully if they are to draw fruits from the Sacrifice for themselves. This is something we may profitably reflect on from time to time, arousing in ourselves a more active charity and directing it intelligently to the welfare of our brethren. The unity of the members of the Mystical Body is represented in the unity of the Host, composed as it is of many grains of wheat and consecrated by the priest in the name of Christ, but this unity can be realized only by Christians who love one another in truth and in deed. We cannot be united to Christ if we are indifferent to our neighbor; fraternal charity is the Lord's own commandment. This unity and charity is promoted too by our common participation in the other exercises of the liturgy. But it is especially when we gather together around the Lord's altar and banquet table to offer the spotless Lamb as our sacrifice to God and together to partake with Him of divine refreshment that we should experience our oneness in Christ and resolve to be truly devoted to our neighbor's welfare.

For it was not to be solely the victim on our altars that Jesus instituted the Eucharist. He desired that we should not only share His Sacrifice but also partake of its fruits in the reception of the Holy Eucharist. "Anyone who eats My flesh and drinks My blood has everlasting life and I will raise him up in the last day.... He who eats My flesh and drinks My blood lives in Me and I in him. As I live by the Father, so he who eats Me will draw life from Me" (John 6:55-58).

We must believe in the love of Jesus for us when we realize that He laid down His life for us and that He gives Himself to us under the form of food. We cannot doubt but that He desires to be with us and to assimilate us to Himself. He wishes to strengthen our languid faith, inflame cold hearts, increase the bond of union among us, strengthen us in every virtue and diminish the force of concupiscence and all our vices. His presence excites in us a lively faith, strong hope and ardent charity; the most precious moments of our life are the moments when we receive Holy Communion and remain with Him during our thanksgiving.

Likewise we can believe the love the Father has for us when we realize that He gave of His best for us: His well-beloved Son, and to the torture of the Cross.

Holy Communion communicates grace to us according to our disposition. The more desire and hunger we arouse in ourself for this holy Bread, the more fruit we receive from the Sacrament. The ten or fifteen minutes after receiving, while Jesus in the Sacrament remains with us, are priceless moments that should be spent with Him in love and thanksgiving (in the Church, unless some special circumstance requires us to leave immediately after Mass). Then we can converse with Him familiarly, or in silence remain united to Him, and receive the special graces He brings with Him.

JESUS' LOVE for us was such that He would find a means whereby He could still remain amongst us with a real, true and substantial presence after His ascension into Heaven. This means His divine ingenuity found in the Holy Eucharist. Not content to be offered on our altars and received into our hearts, He would also be present in our tabernacles so that during the hours of the day and night we might have the pleasure of His company.

How precious is this divine Presence amongst us! There in the tabernacle is the same loving Friend with Whom men consorted in holy, familiar companionship during His mortal life. The same Jesus—Who wept over the widow's dead son and raised His friend Lazarus to life, Who cured the ten lepers—is present there awaiting our visit.

17 Forgiveness: The Sacrament of Reconciliation

Jesus manifested something of the depth of His understanding of our human nature when He instituted the sacrament of Reconciliation, as our own age has come to realize.

Those who have perfect contrition are thereby freed from their sins. God could have been satisfied with this manner of granting forgiveness without creating an obligation of confessing to a priest and of receiving absolution from him. He did so, however, not for His sake but for ours, as we can appreciate after due consideration. We know ourselves well enough to realize how deep-seated is our tendency to deceive others. Moreover our subjective norms of right and wrong often do not correspond with the objective truths of morality: our conscience may be too strict, too lax, or otherwise erroneous. Each of us, when examining his conscience before God without the purpose of manifesting it to His representative, is apt to make a very inadequate examination. Furthermore, without the sacrament of Reconciliation, we could not so readily assure ourselves that we had been forgiven. It would not be easy for those in whose consciences memories of misdeeds rankle to retain the reassurance of forgiveness if the divine forgiveness had never been externally manifested to them.

Now the sacrament of Reconciliation answers all these needs and difficulties. We know that just as in the Mass the principal priest is Christ, so in the confessional it is Christ in the person of the priest to Whom we are confessing. This act of faith is very important. We know too that Jesus (and the Holy Spirit) are present in the priest to manifest the mercy, love and forgiveness of His Sacred Heart. The priest should know the truths of morality according to God's Revelations and the teaching of the Church, and he is assisted by the grace of his state. As we examine our conscience before God, the shadow of Jesus living in His priest to Whom we are going to make our confession, as well as the external reality of the act of confession which we are about to perform, stir us to examine our conscience faithfully and to awaken true contrition through supernatural motives.

We know that our sins are truly forgiven when the priest gives us absolution if we have done our part in contributing to the sacrament the acts which it is our duty to make. "Whose sins you shall forgive, they are forgiven them," Jesus affirms (John 20:23); "I believe in the Holy Catholic Church, the forgiveness of sins," the Creed says. This forgiveness is an annihilation of sin; it no longer exists, although some temporal penalty due because of the sin may remain as well as the tendencies to sin. Absolution is an external and audible act; we have sensible experience of this sacrament. And though scrupulous people have difficulty in believing their sins forgiven even after this, how much more would they, and we, have difficulty in believing our sins forgiven had we not the sacrament of Reconciliation? This absolution is a balm, a relief, a lightening of the soul.

As we prepare before the Father for confession by examination of conscience, we know what is expected of us, that we must submit to the power of the keys all mortal sins that we have not confessed, their number, kind and the circumstances changing their kind by adding an additional element of malice. We know that in the absence of mortal sin, venial sins committed since our last confession, or sins committed at any time since Baptism even though they have already been confessed, provide sufficient matter for the sacrament.

There is an objective morality which enlightens us to perceive truly and objectively what is upon our conscience. We may have recourse to the enumeration of the seven capital sins to discover the underlying principle or motive that prompted our sins, and this examination leads us to discover our predominant fault, the source of most of our sins—the underlying tendency of our nature that frequently betrays us. This examination of conscience, with the help of the Father's grace, for which we pray, becomes like a mirror which reflects the actual state of our soul, providing us with precious self-knowledge. For the person who leads an interior life and who seriously fights against his sinful tendencies, this knowledge becomes ever more complete throughout life. This increasing self-knowledge is most important in preserving the soul from tendencies to mental disease, acting as it does to oppose the tendencies to repression and regression which so often characterize loss of mental health. At the same time we should check every *undue* tendency to introspection and self-examination. We shall gain more light about ourselves by doing so. If Jesus and Mary are the object of our thoughts more frequently than ourselves, we shall come to greater self-knowledge. We shall see ourselves more clearly through comparison with Them.

We must keep in mind that supernatural sorrow for our personal sins is a more important part of the sacrament of Reconciliation than the examination of conscience and confession. In our preparation for confession we should give more time to acts of sorrow than to self-examination, without slighting the latter if we have serious guilt upon our soul. We elicit acts of sorrow in the manner explained when we treated of prayer, that is by considerations such as how much Jesus loved us, and how ungrateful we have been; how we have wounded Him. "I was wounded in the house of my friends" (Zachariah 13:6). We can also dwell on the hatefulness of sin, which opposes the Father and which is also opposed to our supernatural happiness and without which there would be no hell. To feel sorry is not always in our power; to be sorry is. True contrition is essentially in the will, not in the feelings.

Our part in confession includes the willingness to accept the penance imposed. Having humbly confessed our sins, received our penance, made a sincere act of contrition, we should not fail to perform our penance and to give thanks to God for this sacrament and the graces we have received.

Each time it is received the sacrament of Reconciliation restores, or confers an increase of, sanctifying grace. It also confers a special sacramental grace that strengthens us to fight against the tendencies to sin that remain after the guilt of sin has been removed.

If the sacrament of Reconciliation is to be a great help in our spiritual life and a source of peace, we must accent three things: the sincere desire to correct our faults, to avoid the occasions of sin and to make progress; an intense act of faith that we are making our confession to Christ; and faith in the forgiveness of sins, and appreciation of the sacramental graces which help us to fight the tendencies to sin that remain. In this sacrament we are reconciled, not only to the Father, but also to the Church: to our brothers and sisters, who, because of the solidarity of the people of God, have also been offended by our sins. In the plan of God the sacrament of Reconciliation is intended to be a source of peace; it is up to us to make it such in our lives.

It is interesting to note the experience of members of Alcoholics Anonymous. Only after having resolved to tell their faults to another human person and after having actually done so, do many experience the forgiveness of God and the sense of His presence. It is worth quoting at length from *Twelve Steps and Twelve Traditions*,[1] a book which has value for all true students of human nature and religion. We shall then perhaps better appreciate the divine wisdom of the sacrament of Reconciliation. We shall also value more that humility which leads us to seek advice and direction from the priest after manifesting our anxieties and troubles of conscience to him, a disposition which is necessary for anyone desirous of making spiritual progress. The quotation follows:

> Step Five: "Admitted to God, to ourselves, and to another human being, the exact nature of our wrongs." Most of us would declare that without a fearless admission of our defects to another human being, we could not stay sober. It seems plain that the grace of God will not enter to expel our destructive obsessions until we are willing to try this.... Our moral inventory has persuaded us that all-around

---

[1] N.Y.: Alcoholics Anonymous Publishing Inc., pp. 58-63. Grateful acknowledgment is here made of permission to quote these pages.

forgiveness was desirable, but it was only when we resolutely tackled Step Five that we inwardly knew we'd be able to receive forgiveness and give it, too.... It was most evident that a solitary self-appraisal, and the admission of our defects based upon that alone, wouldn't be nearly enough. We'd have to have outside help if we were surely to know and admit the truth about ourselves—the help of God and another human being. Only by discussing ourselves, holding back nothing, only by being willing to take advice and accept direction could we set foot on the road to straight thinking, solid honesty, and genuine humility....

Until we actually sit down and talk aloud about what we have so long hidden, our willingness to clean house is still largely theoretical. When we are honest with another person, it confirms that we have been honest with ourselves and with God. The second difficulty is this: what comes to us alone may be garbled by our own rationalization and wishful thinking. The benefit of talking to another person is that we can get his direct comment and counsel on our situation and there can be no doubt in our minds what that advice is. Going it alone in spiritual matters is dangerous. How many times have we heard well-intentioned people claim the guidance of God when it was all too plain that they were sorely mistaken. Lacking both practice and humility, they had deluded themselves and were able to justify the most arrant nonsense on the ground that this was what God had told them. It is worth noting that people of very high spiritual development almost always insist on checking with friends or spiritual advisors the guidance they feel they have received from God. Surely, then, a novice ought not lay himself open to the chance of making foolish, perhaps tragic, blunders in this fashion. While the comment or advice of others may be by no means infallible, it is likely to be far more specific than any direct guidance we may receive while we are still so inexperienced in establishing contact with a Power greater than ourselves....

Provided you hold nothing back, your sense of relief will mount from minute to minute. The dammed-up emotions of years break out of their confinement, and miraculously vanish as soon as they are exposed. As the pain subsides, a healing tranquility takes its place. And when humility and serenity are so combined, something else of great moment is apt to occur. Many an A.A., once agnostic or atheist, tells us that it was during this stage of Step Five that he first actually felt the presence of God. And even those who had faith already often become conscious of God as they never were before.

This feeling of being at one with God and man, this emerging from isolation through the open and honest sharing of our terrible burden of guilt....

The experience of A.A. reminds us of an opinion of Saint Thomas to be found in his *Summa Theologica* (Suppl. Q. 8, A. 2). The Angelic Doctor teaches that if a person is in an extreme necessity (e.g., dying) and a priest is not to be had, a man has much to gain by confessing his sins to another; for even though the other, not being a priest, is unable to give absolution, the penitent is thereby more assured of the forgiveness of the Father.[2]

It is well to confess weekly or twice a month. In the absence of mortal sin, this is a confession of devotion. Then the preparation should ordinarily last no longer than five minutes (especially in the case of those who are meticulous or inclined to scrupulosity), with the emphasis on acts of contrition. The principal venial sins are noted, and those may be chosen for confession which were the more voluntary, which touch more nearly on tendencies to mortal sin, or which are hardest to reveal. To make sure that there is "sufficient matter" for the validity of the sacrament, Catholics are taught to add to venial sins confessed some sin of the past, in general terms, for which they arouse true contrition: "In my past life I have committed sins against the virtue of charity (or humility, or purity, etc.), for which I am sorry."

Acts of prayer and contrition, such as are made in mental and vocal prayer, in the use of sacramentals (as holy water), and especially in the reception of holy Communion, bring forgiveness of sins. Nevertheless, the graces of the sacrament of Penance are unique and have a special healing value.

---

[2] A layman, Mr. Thomas Arthur, who generously gave his services in the typing of this book, when he came to this page recalled a significant incident. During World War II, an American Catholic soldier, awaiting the signal for an action in which he would be killed, was bemoaning the lack of a priest to whom he could make his confession. A Protestant fellow-soldier, to quiet him, said that in the absence of a priest, he would listen to his account of his sins. He did. The sequel to the story is no less interesting. This Protestant considered it his duty to tell these sins, which he had retained in memory for years, to a priest. Finally one night he reviewed them and the next day approached a priest and told him the story, but when he came to narrate the sins he could not bring them back to mind. The priest sent him away reassured that all was well.

18 Vocations:
Marriage, The Single State,
The Consecrated Single State

Many are called by the Father to the priesthood or to the religious life. But many are called by Him to be lay people. This is also a vocation in the Church, a vocation consecrated by the sacraments of Baptism, Confirmation and the Eucharist. Lay people witness to Christ by their example and fidelity to the duties of their state of life, by their Christ-like love. They help to change the world by their prayer, example and good actions. They are also called to transform the temporal structures of the world, so that it may more reflect the goodness of the Father and His justice and peace. They may be of more help to others than they realize. During the course of their lives, they will be in a position to assist souls whom priests and religious cannot reach and who, perhaps, might not be saved but for them.

Social usefulness is a factor to be considered in the choice of employment; it contributes more to the real happiness of the lay person than higher pay or the greater honor or reputation that might attach to other work. The ultimate purpose of our existence, and hence also of our work, is to know, love and serve God in this life and to be happy with Him forever. We may fulfill this purpose in an employment that serves as a means of self-support, and this is a good and sufficient motive for working.

Other factors of importance in choosing an occupation, besides its social utility, are one's aptitudes, interests and opportunities. In some places Catholic (more often, non-Catholic) vocational guidance is available.

Whatever one's work, it begins to be socially useful and helpful for the sanctification of oneself and others when it is accomplished well with a pure intention, in union with the intentions and merits of Jesus. Fidelity to the duties of one's state of life from a supernatural motive leads to sanctity, satisfies for one's own sins and the sins of others, and constitutes a continuous petition to the Father for grace. Works not good in themselves, nor evil in themselves, are made good by a good intention. Our good works have a satisfactory and impetratory value, that is, a value as petition. And if we wish to greatly increase the value of these works and of our lives, we can consecrate them to Mary, turning over to her their satisfactory and impetratory value to dispose of as she pleases for the welfare of souls living on earth or in Purgatory, and counting ourselves and all that we have as hers. Then she will increase the value of our lives, preserve our virtues and merits, obtain for us perseverance, and unite us more fully and intimately to her Son, Jesus.

MARRIAGE BETWEEN baptized Christians is a holy state and a great sacrament; Jesus becomes the cornerstone of the newly-founded family. Married persons need His help and the graces of the sacrament in order to bear well the burdens of the married state and to sanctify themselves in it.

Most important for the sanctification of this state is the right choice of a partner. Upon this choice depends the welfare of one's children; one's entire future is affected, including the conditions under which one's spiritual life will be lived. These conditions may be favorable or unfavorable to one's salvation and sanctification. Marriages entered into too young (e.g., in the teens), or too emotionally, are apt to end unhappily; marriages entered into at a more mature age and with prudent deliberation, with a careful weighing of faults, virtues and compatibility, are apt to be more happy. True love always has a basis in the intelligence and is quietly reasonable. In a partner those qualities which reason discerns and approves as the basis of its love will still be there after the wedding and even when the illusions of emotional love are shattered by the frictions of married life.

Spiritual excellence, solid devotion joined with good character and common sense, is of first importance. A happy marriage joins two persons in spirit first and above all. Such a union in spirit is hindered when the parties differ in faith, hence the Church's motherly attitude toward mixed marriages. In these, there is always some danger of loss of faith to the partner and to the children. A common background, common interests and congeniality, a certain closeness of age, also help to make for a happy marriage.

Besides noting the positive presence of virtue, of the spirit of humility, sincerity and selfless devotedness, it is well for prospective partners to judge whether notable defects and bad habits are absent.

Such notable defects as endanger the happiness of a marriage are heavy drinking and alcoholism; marked irascibility or anger; excessive vanity and pride, slothfulness and immaturity with the inability to assume and fulfill responsibilities. A sense of infallibility together with an unwillingness to acknowledge and correct defects; intolerance of the opinions of others, are manifestations of pride that threaten the happiness of common life in marriage, as they are also threats to happiness in the religious state.

Psychological and emotional maturity are not usually attained in this country before the age of twenty-four in men and twenty-two in women. This maturity supposes sound judgment and a habitual good will with some adaptability and consistency in willed actions. The good character of the mature person is the effect of repeated right willing, of overcoming rather than yielding to the unreasonable tendencies of the emotions even under difficulties and strain; this is the source of stability and constancy.

Some persons, for emotional reasons having to do with their personality development, have a deep-seated conflict concerning marriage. For example, some are unable to accept the sex act as an expression of spiritual love and unity: they wish to separate sexual gratification from the deep love and respect they feel for the person of their choice. These persons may require counselling before marriage, especially if there are such indications as a depressive or markedly neurotic reaction when the decision to marry is taken or as the date of the marriage approaches; otherwise marriage, pregnancy, birth of a child, etc. may be the occasion of a depression or mental disorder. The same may be said about those with homosexual tendencies: before entering a marriage, the sex tendency toward the person they intend to marry should persistently and markedly predominate over the homosexual tendency, and the ability to prevent expression of the latter in act must be proven; otherwise they will not have a reasonable assurance that they have sufficient aptitude for marriage, that is, for a happy marriage.

Sometimes persons with such a conscious or unconscious conflict feel attracted to a religious life, and actually enter religion or a seminary when they are really seeking to avoid certain aspects of married life for which they are not psychologically prepared. Resolution of the conflict, sometimes through counselling, would seem to be the proper procedure. The unsuitability of these persons for the clerical or religious life may be evidenced by their depressive or neurotic tendencies, and the lack of a true calling by their utilization of such a vocation as an escape. Supernatural discretion as well as psychological insight is required in judging these cases.

A man would do well to have a certain economic ability, proven before marriage, and reflected in constancy of employment and a sufficient salary if not also savings. A woman, even is she has a career, should have the ability to care for a household and for children together with a willingness to have them and raise them. Both should be capable of a deep attachment to another evidenced by deeds of sacrifice for another's welfare; this is often shown by a mature and selfless courtesy, respect and love toward parents manifested in the home, and is opposed to neurotic self-centeredness and immature dependence. Both should prepare for marriage by chastity, which is an important foundation, and which, maintained throughout courtship, makes for stability in marriage.

What most secures the happiness of marriage and brings to other aptitudes their right development and balance is a true interior life that expresses itself in a sincere and constant supernatural devotion to Jesus and His Church, its doctrine, laws and sanctifying practices, and a true and sincere fraternal love. To fulfill one's nature, one needs to be subject to the Most High. Nevertheless the balanced temperament and good judgment of the parties is very important.

Those seeking matrimony should strive to know the Father's will and to submit themselves to it.

Some persons remain in the single state because they do not believe themselves to possess the qualities necessary for a happy married life; others because they do not find a suitable partner. Some perfectionist types are never satisfied with the persons they meet, and perhaps this is just as well both for them and the other party; but if they can moderate this tendency, so often rooted in unconscious pride, they will be more suited for marriage and more apt to find a good mate.

When a woman prudently doubts whether she should accept or reject matrimonial prospects, she is apt to have regrets either way: if she remains single, for her failure to take the opportunities that presented themselves; if she marries, for having done so rashly. If her decision to reject her last opportunity is prudent, it seems right that she have no regrets, but rather that she rejoice in the special opportunities for sanctification that are hers. Then in eternity she will be able to congratulate herself.

The advice to marry is sometimes wise and appropriate, and encourages those who have a vocation to the married state to overcome their selfishness, their undue timidity, hesitancy and desire for freedom from responsibilities. The single state is not superior to the married state unless it is chosen for the love of God, unless it is a single life in which virginity or perfect chastity is given to the Father.

Happiness in marriage, then, depends on the right choice of a partner. But it also depends on the right understanding of its purpose. Marriage is a blending or union of two lives, of two hearts, of two spirits, expressed by a union in the flesh, which flowers in the blessing of new life. The marriage covenant includes a certain right regarding the partner's body; the use of this right is union in the flesh; the end or purpose of this Union is the intimate loving gift of each to the other, and to the child that may naturally result from it.

Couples entering marriage with a genuine understanding of marriage will be prepared for the happiness that is proper to this state. Their attitude toward each other and toward their children will be one of intelligent and loving acceptance. This is exactly what is needed for the right development of the temperament and character of the child and for its mental health. The rejection of one of the purposes of marriage by so many who enter into this state contributes to the great increase in mental disease. The rejection of the procreative purpose of marriage makes a couple more self-centered.

The indissolubility of the marriage bond—the exclusion of divorce—confirms and strengthens the partners to a marriage, and helps them to overcome the temptations to inconstancy. Thus they are more secure in their mutual love and can give their united love to their children. It is evident that the violation by divorce of the natural moral law (and of the Catholic teaching which upholds it) increases the insecurity of the children of the modern home and the incidence of mental disorders and of delinquency, and seems to be an important factor in the disorders of contemporary society, both with respect to adults and children.

MARRIAGE CAUSES a blending of two lives and hearts which is most perfect when both are seeking union with God. Pope Pius XI brings out the purpose of marriage to render mutual help in advancing to Christian perfection in these words of his encyclical "On Christian Marriage":

> The love, then, of which we are speaking ... must have as its primary purpose that man and wife help each other day by day in forming and perfecting themselves in the interior life, so that through their partnership in life they may advance ever more and more in virtue.... For all men of every condition, in whatever honorable walk of life they may be, can and ought to imitate that most perfect example of holiness placed before man by God, namely Christ Our Lord, and by God's grace to arrive at the summit of perfection....

Marriages of persons with good sense and emotional balance who are dedicated to authentic love, and are seeking true Christian perfection, are blessings not only for the parents and their children, but also for the Church and society. Their children have a head-start to becoming good citizens of Heaven and earth.

When the parents are united in seeking Christian perfection they are wonderfully helped in directing their children. Such direction requires deep respect for the individuality and personality of the child, and an expression of parental love which does not smother but guides the child, teaching and helping it to become self-controlled and self-determining: a responsible person. Correct principles are communicated to the child's mind by education (appropriate use of concise moral sayings is effective) and by example. A peaceful vigilance over the child removes occasions of sin and scandal; for parents must ever remember that "man is prone to evil from his youth," and readily learns what is most harmful to himself. Children approaching the age of reason must be taught to practice charity, yielding to one another, and to deny themselves in little things for the love of Jesus, to please Him and to obtain the heavenly reward. Suitable instructional and religious books may be obtained for them. Care must be taken to keep from them such comic books and TV shows as incite to vice; the strong influence of the former in promoting delinquency has been shown by the psychiatrist Dr. Frederic Wertham of New York City.

Parents have a serious obligation to ensure the Catholic education of their children. Children rooted in truth and virtue from childhood by the love, example and training of their parents as well as by a Catholic education, are prepared to pass more securely through the storms of adolescence and to attain a mature Christian adulthood.

Marriage requires an adjustment of two persons to a common life. The husband must use his authority in the home reasonably and lovingly; the woman, the mistress of the household, must preserve unity with her husband by her obedience in all that is in harmony with her dignity as wife (Pius XI, "On Christian Marriage"). And as John Paul II has said, each should be willingly subject to the other in imitation of Christ. They are called to a relation of complementarity.

From the grace of the sacrament will come the strength to persevere in a spiritual life and in the trials connected with marriage with courage and gladness. As in the spiritual life, the time of consolation and of emotional glow is apt to be followed by dryness. Then the continued acknowledgment of each other's love and excellences, and the union of wills fostered from the start, lead to an increase in devotion, more in the will now than in the sensible emotions. Thus love is purified, strengthened and rendered more meritorious.

What of those who find themselves in a marriage which is not altogether, or not at all, happy? By embracing the spiritual life seriously they will find the grace they need to bear their lot. Their first object should be to know themselves and to seek to remove whatever obstacles to the happiness of their marriage arise from themselves. Since the spiritual life is a transformation into Christ, it requires self-knowledge, the acknowledgment of one's faults, and the determined effort to correct them with the help of God's grace. The first faults to seek to correct, after mortal sin has been eliminated, are those that provoke, irritate, burden or disturb one's partner, or which jeopardize the happiness of one's marriage. To acknowledge one's faults (even to oneself) when both are at fault and long-standing friction exists, may require much grace and courage: it is very pleasing to Christ Who rewards humility.

What cannot be changed must be borne with supernatural resignation, with the realization that the cross works purification and sanctification for those who bear it willingly, and Redemption of others. To bear the cross generously is to find one's happiness in God. Prudent decisions may help to lighten the cross; the consultation with one's parish priest or confessor may be of advantage. Marriage counselling may be helpful. When a union is spiritually or physically gravely injurious to one of the partners or their children separation is warranted.

Married persons must exercise their charity first of all toward each other. Where one embraces the spiritual life without the other, he or she must be careful that this devotion to God results in a devotion and tactful charity toward his partner. Those who are married must make sacrifices for one another's welfare; this is a large part of their way to sanctity.[1]

·   ·   ·

[1] Of value to married persons or those contemplating marriage may be the Cana and Pre-Cana courses of instruction.

THERE ARE many persons who do not wish to embrace the clerical or religious life on the one hand or the married state on the other. Perhaps they are not suited for these states of life; perhaps they are lacking in the requisite qualifications. They may need a greater degree of freedom and flexibility of life than is possible in these vocations. Or they may lack selflessness, and in this case, perhaps with an intensification of their spiritual life and the practice of charity, they may find themselves drawn to one of these other forms of life for which they may have the basic aptitudes.

But there will always be single persons living in the world, and many of these are destined by the Father to remain single. All single persons may use their freedom for their spiritual advancement, for the sanctification of their ordinary duties, and for charitable activity. Each state of life has its advantages as well as its special burdens, and spiritual success and contentment require that we make use of the advantages to sustain the burdens.

As the love of the Father grows in single persons, it fructifies all they do, and they become helpful to others by their merits, example, prayer and the good works that love prompts them to perform. In this way of life, a socially useful occupation (see the beginning of this chapter) and true spiritual friendships are sustaining forces. Sometimes such friends are found in Catholic groups and associations.

The dedicated single state is a vocation in the world to which many single persons may aspire. Perfect chastity, the voluntary renunciation of marriage and of deliberate sex pleasure may be undertaken by the layman. When this renunciation is upheld by a perpetual vow for the love of God it becomes a consecration of the entire person to the Most High. "The evangelical counsel of chastity embraced for the sake of the Kingdom of heaven, is a sign of the world to come, and a source of greater fruitfulness in an undivided heart" (Can. 599). Incidentally, perfect chastity may be given to God by those who have lost their virginity by one or more fully deliberate grave sins but who have repented them. "Through their pledge to follow Christ more closely, virgins are consecrated to God, mystically espoused to Christ and dedicated to the service of the Church, when the diocesan Bishop consecrates them according to the approved liturgical rite" (Can. 604).

Our Lord counselled perfect chastity: "Let him accept this teaching who can" (Matthew 19:12 NAB). Saint Paul, in his turn, advises those who are married to remain married and those who are single to remain single (1 Corinthians 7:7-8, 27, 39-40). He wishes the single to be spared the afflictions of married life and to be free to devote themselves singleheartedly to the love of God, provided they have the gift to remain single.

Vatican Council II teaches that

the holiness of the Church is also fostered in a special way by the observance of the manifold counsels proposed in the Gospel by our Lord to His disciples. Outstanding among them is that precious gift of divine grace which the Father gives to some (cf. Matthew 19:11; 1 Corinthians 7:7) so that by virginity, or celibacy, they can more easily devote their entire selves to God alone with undivided heart (cf. 1 Corinthians 7:32-34). This total continence embraced on behalf of the kingdom of heaven has always been held in particular honor by the Church as being a sign of charity and stimulus towards it, as well as a unique foundation of spiritual fertility in the world (Constitution on the Church, No. 42).

Pope Pius XII said, in his encyclical letter of March 25, 1954, "On Holy Virginity,"[2] "This doctrine of the excellence of virginity and of celibacy and of their superiority over the married state was, as we have already said, revealed by our Divine Redeemer and by the Apostle of the Gentiles; so too, it was solemnly defined as a dogma of divine faith by the holy Council of Trent." Nevertheless this does not mean that a married person may not exceed consecrated persons in charity and Christian perfection. Saint John of the Cross says: "In the evening of life we shall be judged by love alone." Love alone determines one's eternal intimacy with Jesus and the Father, one's place in Heaven.

Pius XII explained to us the purpose of Christian virginity and perfect chastity in the same letter: "This then is the primary purpose, this is the central idea of Christian virginity: to aim only at the divine, to turn thereto the whole mind and soul; to want to please God in everything, to think of Him continually, to consecrate body and soul completely to Him."

[2] Obtainable from the U.S. Catholic Council, 1312 Massachusetts Ave., N.W., Washington, DC 20009.

The taking of the obligation of perpetual perfect chastity is a kind of spiritual marriage by which the soul is wedded to Christ; it permits the person to dedicate all his or her energies either to Christ directly or to Christ in his or her neighbors. It is an imitation of the virginity of Christ, of Mary and of Saint Joseph. It offers great advantages, including a drastic and effective means of curtailing the tendencies of the lower faculties, which, if given a lawful liberty, may go further and involve one in dishonorable actions. In other words, the total abstinence of perfect chastity is, for many, easier to maintain than the partial abstinence of marriage.

The vow of perfect chastity adds to the observance of chastity the merit of the virtue of religion. It seems that it should be made only by those whose experience shows them they can keep it, and upon the advice of a prudent confessor and for a limited period such as six months or one year. It may then be renewed periodically for several years. Before the perpetual vow is taken, one should have secure knowledge that one is called to the single state and can maintain the life of perfect chastity, as well as prudent counsel from those skilled in vocational guidance and sympathetic to the ideal of vowed chastity. Those who take this vow should nevertheless have a clear appreciation of the married state which they are foregoing.

To fulfill a vow of perfect chastity while living in the world requires fidelity to its spirit: singleness of heart in seeking God in the midst of the duties of one's state of life. Important means to this end are daily assistance at the Sacrifice of the Mass and the daily partaking of the Bread of Life, devotion to the Most Pure Heart of Mary (especially the perfect devotion of Saint Louis Grignion de Montfort), punctual fidelity to the duties of one's state of life, prompt flight from the occasions of sin, prompt elevation of the mind and heart to God in the time of temptation, a quiet habitual watchfulness over the senses (modesty of the eyes, ears, tongue, touch—"the prudence of chastity"), avoidance of idleness and questionable companionships: in general an integral spiritual program (see Chapter 35).

Pius XII teaches in the above-mentioned encyclical:

It is abundantly clear that with this warning ("if thy right eye scandalize thee, pluck it out") our Savior demands of us above all that we never consent to any sin, even internally, and that we steadfastly remove far from us anything that can even slightly tarnish the beautiful virtue of purity. In this matter no diligence, no severity can be considered exaggerated. If ill health or other reasons do not allow one heavier corporal austerities, yet they never free one from vigilance and internal self-control.

And:

We can more easily struggle against and repress the wiles of evil and the enticements of the passions if we do not struggle directly against them, but rather flee from them as best we may. For the preserving of chastity, according to the teaching of Jerome, flight is more effective that open warfare: "Therefore I flee, lest I be overcome." Flight must be understood in this sense, that not only do we diligently avoid occasions of sin, but especially that in struggles of this kind we lift our minds and hearts to God, intent above all on Him to Whom we have vowed our virginity.

MANY LAY PERSONS wish to devote their energies immediately to the cause of Christ and to the welfare of souls.

In virtue of the lay person's incorporation in Christ and the Church by the sacraments of Baptism, Confirmation and the Eucharist, the lay person shares in the priestly, prophetic and royal office of Christ, in the mission of the Church and in its apostolate. As lay persons are immersed in secular society, they are called to bring to it the light and life of Christ in word, deed, example and prayer. They are called to penetrate and perfect the temporal order in the spirit of the Gospel. Their temporal activity can be a witness to Christ and promote the salvation of persons (Vatican II, Decree on the Apostolate of the Laity, No. 2).

The first orbit is the lay person's own family: to be a better father, mother, wife, husband, son, daughter. The basic unit of society on which its renewal depends is the family. Then come the duties which accrue to one in one's work: to be a better worker. Then the social, political and economic orders need to be perfected according to their own principles and in accordance with the light of Christ and His Holy Spirit.

THE THIRD ORDERS are associations of laymen (secular priests are admitted too) living in the world and seeking perfection in the spirit of the Order to which they are attached, and in accordance with an approved Rule of life. There are Third Order Augustinians, Carmelites, Dominicans, Franciscans, Premonstratensians, Servites, and Trinitarians, and the Oblates of Saint Benedict who correspond to the Third Order.

The Legionaries of Christ, an excellent and rapidly growing religious congregation, aims to transform all levels of society and trains lay persons to work parallel to their priests.

Opus Dei is an institute of priests, and lay people (men and women), which also seeks the transformation of society. It is made up of numeraries who take the vows of obedience, chastity, and poverty, and of supernumeraries and associates who do not.

The Sodality of Our Lady is for those truly seeking perfection.

The Legion of Mary is an excellently organized and inspired form of Catholic Action which promotes the sanctification of its members and directs their apostolic work in the spirit of the true devotion of Saint Louis Grignion de Montfort.

The Saint Vincent de Paul Society is an association of Christian men, who serve the poor, sick and unemployed of the parish.

Those interested in the lay apostolate will find it profitable to read the "Decree on the Apostolate of the Laity" in the Documents of Vatican II, as well as associated passages on the laity in other documents of Vatican II.

A new form of consecrated single life in the world is that provided by the secular institutes. This is a canonically established state of perfection for laymen and secular priests which has as its purpose the sanctification of its members in the world by the practice of evangelical counsels of Christ, poverty, perfect chastity and obedience. Its members live in the world and are not religious. They bind themselves under pain of sin to the practice of the counsels, after undergoing a novitiate. Each institute has its special end; in general these institutes have the purpose of penetrating society and culture with a new Christian spirit. Married persons may become associate members.

Secular Institutes are defined by the new Code of Canon Law as follows: "A secular institute is an institute of consecrated life in which Christ's faithful, living in the world, strive for the perfection of charity and endeavor to contribute to the sanctification of the world, especially from within" (Can. 710). Again it says of them: "Members are to live their lives in the ordinary conditions of the world, either alone, in their families or in fraternal groups, in accordance with the constitutions" (Can. 714).

Group study of, and group sharing on, the Scriptures have helped to form spiritual and apostolic Christians.

The Charismatic Renewal has been of help to many through its prayer groups and covenant communities. This movement has brought a new awareness of the Holy Spirit, the third person of the Trinity, and of His Gifts. It is of importance to the development of this movement that the greatest gift of all, charity, be most sought and practiced, and that among the means, besides group prayer, daily personal prayer and spiritual reading, and the other means of pursuing personal holiness recommended in this book be employed. Chapter 20 is devoted to the Charismatic Renewal.

19 Vocations: The Priesthood & The Religious State

In the Apostolic Constitution *Sedes Sapientiae* of May 31, 1956, Pope Pius XII declared:

> It is truly a great blessing of divine Providence that down through the centuries, Christ the Redeemer has beckoned to souls, the object of His predilection, with an interior and, as it were, mystical word, addressing to them the same invitation which He had addressed by word of mouth to the young man inquiring about eternal life: "Come, follow Me."...
>
> To begin with, We would have everyone know that the foundation of every life, be it religious or be it sacerdotal and apostolic, which we call a divine vocation, is composed of a twofold element which is to all intents and purposes essential: one calling is divine; the other, ecclesiastical. With regard to the first, it must be said that

the call from God is so necessary to embrace the religious or priestly state that, if it be lacking, then the very foundation on which the whole edifice rests is lacking....

For he whom God does not call is neither guided nor aided by His grace....

On the other hand, to proceed to the other element of the religious and priestly vocation, the Roman catechism teaches that "they are said to be called by God who are called by the lawful ministers of the Church."

Far from contradicting what we have already said concerning the divine vocation, actually this is closely connected with it. For the vocation to the religious and clerical state—being given so as to destine someone publicly to lead a holy life and to exercise a hierarchical ministry in the Church—must be authoritatively approved, accepted, and governed by Superiors who are themselves hierarchical and to whom God has entrusted the government of the Church.

These are to be observed by all those whose task it is to recruit and examine vocations of this type. Accordingly, they must never force anyone in any way at all to the priesthood or the religious state, nor invite or admit anyone who actually shows no true signs of a divine vocation, nor raise to the clerical office someone who proves to have been divinely called only to the religious vocation; and as for those who have received this divine gift as well, they must not pressurize them or steer them wrongly to the secular clergy. Finally, they must not rule out any candidate for the priesthood, if it is recognized by certain signs that he actually has a divine vocation....

On the other hand, everyone understands that the germs of a vocation as well as the qualities required, from the moment of their existence have need of education and formation in order for them to develop and mature. Nothing as a matter of fact, appears to be perfect in the first instant of its birth; rather perfection is gradually acquired, by degrees.

Likewise "Priestly Formation" of Vatican II says:

For God properly endows and aids with His grace those men divinely chosen to share in Christ's hierarchical priesthood. To the lawful ministers of the Church He confides the work of calling proven candidates whose fitness has been acknowledged and who seek so exalted an office with the right intention and freedom. (No. 2)

MANY PERSONS who are attracted to union with God consider this attraction a divine call to the religious state or to the priesthood. This is not always the case; they may only be experiencing a call to union with God in the lay state. This is certain when they do not have the aptitude or the health, the temperament or the mental stability to bear the burdens of the religious life or of the priesthood. But others who have such aptitude and find in the Father sufficient courage and generosity to make the sacrifice that He is calling them to make in the religious life, will find in that life the hundredfold of joy and peace. In the religious life, as Saint Bernard says, the soul makes progress more rapidly, walks more securely, falls more rarely, rises more speedily and attains (other things being equal) to a higher degree of charity. This life removes obstacles to union with the Father, that is, to perfect charity, by the practice of the counsels of Christ: poverty removes solicitude about material things, perfect chastity removes the concerns consequent upon married life, and obedience removes the obstacles of pride and self-will.

The priesthood is open to those called by the Father, who have the aptitude and the right intention, who are not debarred by canonical impediments, and who are accepted by ecclesiastical authority. The sacrament of Holy Orders completes the work of the sacraments of Baptism and Confirmation in configuring the soul to Christ by the indelible character which it imprints. The priest is a mediator between God and man in the things that pertain to God; he is ordained for the welfare of souls. His own salvation depends upon his fidelity to the souls for whose sake he was ordained.

The priest offers the Sacrifice of the Mass in union with Christ Who is the principal priest of each Mass. With Christ, he also offers himself as a victim. His daily life is a fulfillment of his daily Mass. Above all others, he must lead a life of prayer and penance, of virtue and mortification. His increasing intimacy with Jesus and Mary will make the sacramental grace of Holy Orders more fruitful, so that he can perform more worthily the holy tasks of his ministry. The priesthood lived in fidelity to the grace of Holy Orders is a way to abundant sanctification, the happiest life on earth.

The priest in the contemplative religious orders fulfills his ministry to souls by offering the Holy Sacrifice of the Mass, by participating in the liturgical chanting of the Divine Office, and by a life of prayer and sacrifice in fidelity to his religious obligations. His life resembles at times that of Jesus on the Cross, at times that of Jesus risen and ascended to the right hand of the Father. With Jesus, he is on the cross of loneliness, darkness, trials, temptations, aridity. This is the most fruitful work that man can do and to it all, priests in particular, are called at times. The endurance of these trials comforts the Heart of Christ and obtains grace for souls. Less often, the priest is with Jesus risen and at the right hand of the Father, partaking of His peace, joy and serenity in abundant measure while all things on earth have faded out of sight and He offers an oblation of pure love and adoration to the Father. With Jesus, he is a mediator between God and man; his adoration, worship and love obtain plentiful graces for other priests, religious and laymen. Indeed, Pope Pius XI said of the contemplative religious, in the Apostolic Constitution *Umbratilem*, that

> they who assiduously fulfill the duty of prayer and penance contribute much more to the increase of the Church and the welfare of mankind than those who labor in tilling the Master's field.

And the document on the religious life of Vatican II says of "members of those communities which are totally dedicated to contemplation":

> They brighten God's people ... By their example they motivate this people; by imparting a hidden apostolic fruitfulness, they make this people grow ... their withdrawal from the world and the practice of their contemplative life should be maintained at their holiest (Decree on the Appropriate Renewal of the Religious Life, No. 7).

The life of the contemplative nun is like that of the contemplative priest. As Saint Thérèse says, she has the place of the heart in the Mystical Body of Christ. Her intercessory and meritorious love propels the life-giving and nourishing blood of grace throughout the Body of Christ—to the Holy Father, the bishops, priests, religious, and the laity. She has chosen the better part and is truly the daughter of Mary and the spouse of Christ.[1]

---

[1] An excellent insight into this vocation may be gained by reading *My Beloved* by Sister Catherine Thomas, O.C.D. (N.Y.: McGraw-Hill, 1955).

All Christ's faithful are called to the same holiness. But those who are members of institutes of consecrated life are called to union with Christ by a new consecration added to that of their baptism, confirmation and to their participation in the Eucharist. The institutes of consecrated life include secular institutes which have been mentioned already, and the religious life, which is distinguished by a certain separation from the world proper to the character and purpose of each institute.

ACTIVE RELIGIOUS (including priests, brothers and sisters) are called to the same heights of holiness as are the contemplative religious. They have a special obligation of perfection resulting from their religious state. By fidelity to the rule and spirit of their Institute and to the activities which fulfill its special end, they advance in charity and union with the Father. Prayer and spiritual reading, the daily reception of the Sacrament of Love, and the frequent reception of the sacrament of Reconciliation lead to a deepening spiritual life. This deepening often shows itself in an attraction to prayer, silence and solitude, together with a painful awareness of the inner and exterior obstacles to union with the Father. This they may mistake for a call to the purely contemplative form of life while in reality it is usually but a manifestation of the action of the Father that is going on in their souls. If they are faithful to their duties and obedience, to their spiritual exercises, recollection and detachment, their souls will be purified and they will attain to a deeper interior life and eventually to the perfection to which they are called in their Institute.

THE APOSTOLIC LIFE of the secular priest leads to the perfection of contemplation, too. The perfect fulfillment of the apostolic life comes through the overflow of the priest's own contemplative life; of this truth the holy Curé of Ars is a glorious example. The apostolic life, Saint Thomas teaches, is not less than the contemplative life, but *adds* to it the giving to others of the fruits of one's own contemplation. The loneliness sometimes experienced by secular priests is a divinely appointed means for the development of the spiritual life and the detachment so necessary to companionship with Jesus and Mary.

The external ministry of the secular priest, as that of the religious priest and others engaged in external good works, increases charity, exercises the moral virtues, purifies the soul, and prepares it for increasing union with God in prayer. In order that his ministry should have these effects, the apostle must maintain a spirit of recollection and purity of intention (these go together: we must work *with* Christ, if we are to truly work *for* Him); he must mortify his temperament which tends to introduce many imperfections and faults into his conduct, and remain faithful to daily mental prayer, visits to the Blessed Sacrament, spiritual reading and examen. For him it is important to retire early, insofar as this is possible, so that he may have his period of mental prayer before his daily Mass.

The priest with active ministry is ordained for the salvation of other souls besides those to whom he ministers. He offers the daily Mass for the salvation of the entire world and for the welfare of the entire Church; and for these ends he daily recites his Divine Office, as well as for those to whose service he is assigned.

He is called to comfort the Heart of the Savior for the sins of others, especially of those he serves, and from this Heart he daily draws the light and strength he needs in his daily duties. To this divine Heart and to the heart of the Father he commits all his anxieties, including those of the souls he is charged to help and guide.

THE DIOCESAN SEMINARIAN finds a precious opportunity for advancing in holiness in the rules of his seminary when he accepts them as the will of the Father manifested through due ecclesiastical authority. A supernatural obedience based on faith in Christ speaking through his superiors prepares the seminarian for *supernatural* obedience to his superiors after he has become a priest, and to see in their disposition of his services (in his assignments and in the circumstances of sacerdotal life) the Father's will. The supernatural, loyal, uncritical adherence to their Bishop by his priests, rallying around him because they see by faith Christ's authority in him and Christ's will in his, is essential for their sanctification (as well as for the accomplishment of the Father's will in the diocese). For it is by obedience that Christ is followed by His priests as well as by His religious and the laity.

In the seminary there should be a schedule of spiritual exercises, and ascetical and mystical teaching from which the seminarian must abstract those principles needed for his own spiritual advancement, as well as for the guidance of others. After ordination and assignment to the ministry, he grows through his priestly activity and by adhering faithfully to daily mental prayer, spiritual reading, and other spiritual exercises. Helpful too is his fidelity to the other resolutions that he has prudently formed in the seminary. He must know how to adapt them to the exigencies of his priestly life, in order to safeguard the continual growth in holiness so necessary for the fruitful accomplishment of his pastoral charge. A due measure of daily spiritual exercises is the salt that preserves the spirit of the secular priest.

Progress in prayer means a deepening friendship with Christ, and manifests itself in a more dedicated service of Him in others. Such service in turn leads to further progress in prayer. Thus friendship with Christ extends more and more through the priest's life which becomes more simply a life of love—of Him and His people, and of the Father. This love is basically a union of wills, our will and His, our will seeking to do His will, His will loving and enabling us. This is true for all persons, but applies in a special way to the priest, who is another Christ, through whom Christ teaches, sanctifies and leads His people.

Part Four:

A
Contemporary
Prayer
Movement

20 The Charismatic Renewal

The Charismatic Renewal is an important movement in the world and the Church, about which anyone engaging in spiritual practice should have some knowledge. This movement provides important insight into certain aspects of the spiritual life.

I will therefore present the positive values in the Renewal, its promise for the Church, the threats to its growth, and its needs, from the viewpoint of the Christian tradition, which is set forth in this book. This may be useful to both those who are in the Charismatic Renewal and those who are not.

The Charismatic Renewal, like the appearances of Mary at Lourdes and Fatima, may be seen as a response of the Father to an age which has tried to separate itself from Him in its personal life, in public life, in philosophy, the arts, and all other phases of endeavor. Through these interventions, He declares to His sons and daughters that He will not be separated from His creation. He can interpose in human affairs whether they like it or not. True, He does not interfere with the human will, which He has made free, but He exercises His power in fresh initiatives of love and mercy and then relates in a special way with those who acknowledge Him and are ready to receive Him.

The Charismatic Renewal seems to be such a fresh initiative of love and mercy. It is a manifestation of the third person of the Trinity, the Holy Spirit. Through the Charismatic Renewal, He has poured out in ample measure His gifts of revelation, prophecy, teaching, healings and tongues (cf. 1 Corinthians 13)—to an extent unknown, some believe, since the time of the early Church.

In an ideal charismatic prayer group meeting, the faith in Jesus and love of Jesus and of each other is enkindled by the Spirit. His presence is manifested by the charismatic gifts. Members respond in praise, sometimes in tongues, sometimes in song, and minister to each other in prophecy, teaching, and healing as well as in counsel, instruction and other forms of mutual help. It is only fair to say that charismatic gifts are waning in prayer groups in this country.

The charismatic gifts are different from the sanctifying gifts of the Spirit, which also manifest the presence of Jesus and of His Spirit. The sanctifying gifts are wisdom, understanding, knowledge, counsel, piety, fortitude, and fear of the Lord.

Since the charismatic gifts are ministries given for the building up of the body of Christ, their presence throughout the Church would be useful for its well-being. The ministries of the laity who constitute the bulk of the charismatic renewal belong to the organic structure of the Church and flow directly from their union with the Lord in faith and love, which is the foundation of all ministry.

Vatican Council II's "Decree on the Apostolate of the Laity" says:

> The Laity derive the right and duty with respect to the apostolate from their union with Christ their Head. Incorporated into Christ's Mystical Body through Baptism and strengthened by the power of the Holy Spirit through Confirmation, they are assigned to the apostolate by the Lord Himself. (No. 3)

It is the responsibility of pastors to discern the "true nature and proper use of these gifts, not in order to extinguish the Spirit, but to test all things and hold fast to what is good (cf. 1 Thessalonians 5:12, 19, 21)" (No. 3). When pastors throughout the Church do this, the Charismatic Renewal and the entire Church will prosper.

The Charismatic Renewal is not homogeneous, it takes different forms, and it is in different stages of development in different parts of the world. It has been characterized as the free association of Christians forming self-governing groups which meet for a form of prayer, chiefly of praise, which is spontaneous, informal, and makes use of the body. Such bodily activity includes the raising of hands (a biblical gesture of prayer), handclapping (mentioned as a form of praise in the psalms), the laying on of hands, rhythmical singing and chanting.

As the noted theologian Yves Congar, O.P. remarks in his evaluation of the Renewal (*I Believe in the Holy Spirit*, Vol. II, 1980), to persons repelled by what seems to them to be excessive organization, cerebral religion, inhibition in worship, and suppression of individual initiative in the churches, this type of individual and communal freedom is attractive. Moreover, the Renewal involves people in active worship.

But the Charismatic Renewal is more than this. It is a movement to bring Christians through the power of the Holy Spirit into a personal living relationship with Jesus their Lord, and to nourish this relationship through meetings in which they praise and love Him.

The freedom in form, the shared personal conviction in Jesus as Lord, the love among the members, and the welcome extended to newcomers who are readily incorporated into the group, make prayer groups an effective form of Christian evangelization. Such prayer groups show promise for parish renewal. This promise is realized where members of prayer groups enter with fervor into the sacramental life of their parishes, particularly in the daily participation and reception of the Eucharist and in the frequent reception of the sacrament of Penance, and where they make themselves available for parish ministries, and participate in parish activities. It is through incorporation in the parish that Christians and prayer groups find a balanced vitality, blessed by the Father, Who is not a God of confusion. Prayer groups are not an elite group in the Church, or a structure parallel to the Church, but need to be structurally united to the local Church, whose communal life takes place in the parish. A parish priest should be associated with the parish group.

A further contribution of the Charismatic Renewal is its emphasis on the importance of the charismata, free gifts of grace given by the Father for the building up of the Church which promote a lively experienced faith. From among the charismata, Paul emphasizes prophecy, which is akin to teaching. Both are ways of conveying the Gospel message, the truths of Revelation, but prophecy is God giving a message to His people which is always in accord with the doctrine of the Church. Teaching is also important; by it the faithful are built up in the truths of the faith, and in the spiritual path to God. The charism of teaching is not merely a natural facility or endowment, nor does it rule out the value of study and scholarship, but it is teaching under the direct influence of the Holy Spirit, and therefore in the power of the Spirit. Such teaching goes to the hearts of the listeners, and is much needed.

Contemporary scholarship downplays revelations and prophecies. Father Tavard in an article "The Christology of the Mystics" (*Theological Studies*, Vol. 42, No. 4, Dec. 1981, p. 561), recommends to theologians that they take into account the knowledge of Christ of the mystics as a source of reflection, in order to redress an imbalance in present day scholarship. Similarly, reflection on the phenomena of mysticism in the saints of the Church would bring some balance into the naturalistic tendency inherent in science which intrudes into some contemporary scripture scholarship. In the lives of the saints verifiable revelations, prophecies, and miraculous events have occurred. Yet when such events are related in Scripture, some scholars tend to assign a merely natural explanation, which is not always reasonable.

In the Charismatic Renewal revelation, prophecy, miracles, and healings (together with the other charismata listed in Scripture) are acknowledged as phenomena which actually occur, as phenomena which have the Holy Spirit as their author in a genuine sense, which are truly supernatural and not explainable as merely natural phenomena. Of course discernment is necessary to distinguish the authentic from the inauthentic, and credulity has to be avoided. No doubt many of the supposed charismata occurring in the Charismatic

Renewal are not genuine. It is particularly the role of priests associated with the Charismatic Renewal as vicars and liaison officers, spiritual directors, and parish priests, to practice this discernment without quenching the Spirit (Constitution on the Church of Vatican Council II, No. 12). But it is also the function of prayer group leaders, who need to be properly instructed to fulfill their responsibilities.

Catholic spirituality has been wary for good reason of those special graces which it calls extraordinary, as have some non-Catholic spiritual traditions. It is important for all those interested in spiritual practice to share this attitude, but without excess or undue skepticism. Extraordinary phenomena in the spiritual life are a fertile source of illusion, of misplaced interest and curiosity, and easily become a detour on the way to the Father. Persons who open themselves to the desire for these things may easily be misled from a primary orientation to the seeking of the Father and the Father's will in faith and genuine love, and with fidelity to the duties of their state of life. While the Father remains sovereignly free and can give these extraordinary graces according to His own will and purpose, and in particular to build up the Church as Vatican II teaches, they do require discernment, and call for wisdom in their use.

While there is a discernment which is itself a charismatic gift, there is also an instinct for discernment which is associated with the sanctifying gifts of the Spirit (and of course common sense is very helpful!). And then there is a discernment which comes from a knowledge of sound Catholic theology.

For the charismatic gifts to flourish in the Church personal holiness must be sought. Personal holiness increases faith, hope and love, by which the person is immediately united with God. As personal holiness is pursued, the sanctifying gifts of the Holy Spirit, wisdom, understanding, knowledge, counsel, fortitude, piety, and the fear of the Lord (reverence) become more active. These gifts perfect faith and charity and make faith more experiential. It is this faith which Paul expresses when he says: "I know Whom I have believed!" They make love more powerful. I refer the reader to Chapter 32 on the degrees of the spiritual life which explains how in the process of sanctification the Spirit becomes more active in the person through His sanctifying gifts.

These sanctifying gifts of the Holy Spirit are a tremendous resource for ministering to others. They change a person from a functionary to a living witness, to a servant of the Spirit. Without them, the charismatic gifts could not be properly and advantageously used.

Now it seems that the Father's purpose in pouring forth His gifts in the Charismatic Renewal has been to attract people to a genuine love of Jesus and of each other and to an awareness of the Holy Spirit. God's greatest gift is Himself. The Father gives Himself to us in giving us the Holy Spirit and the charity which the Holy Spirit pours forth in our hearts (Romans 5:5). This charity, as I have said, is perfected by the sanctifying gifts of the Spirit. Jesus says: "What father among you will give his son a snake if he asks for a fish, or hand him a scorpion if he asks for an egg? If you, with all your sins, know how to give your children good things, how much more will the heavenly Father give the Holy Spirit to those who ask Him?" (Luke 11:10-13 NAB).

The Holy Spirit has been given to us in Baptism and in Confirmation. The Charismatic Renewal offers us, as does the Christian spiritual life in all its forms, an opportunity to renew, with conscious awareness, the dedication to a personal relationship with Jesus which is implicit in Baptism and in Confirmation.

Members of the Charismatic Renewal recognize that besides Scripture and the sacraments (to which the Holy Spirit imparts an attraction), times of personal prayer during the day are necessary to maintain contact with the Holy Spirit, and to remain under His influence.

In other words, attendance at prayer meetings, good in itself, is not sufficient to grow in love, but spiritual practice as understood in the Catholic tradition is essential. Personal prayer and the striving for personal holiness, with the means which the Christian tradition puts at our disposal, is needed.

I have mentioned that one of the appealing features of the Charismatic Renewal is that it consists in spontaneous self-governing groups. Early in this movement, the U.S. Bishops encouraged priests to become associated with it. While lay persons are usually leaders of the groups, frequently, and certainly optimally, a priest has responsibility as a spiritual advisor for each group, which should remain under the control of the pastor. A free and loving submission to ecclesiastical authority is a gift of the Spirit. It is the hallmark of holiness and a necessity for those who are striving for holiness. It is a check on ill-advised adventures and activities. It is customary for a diocese to have a priest as liaison for the prayer groups of the diocese, and this function can be imparted by the Bishop to a vicar for charismatic groups.

While prayer groups extend fellowship to those who have mental difficulties or personality disorders, this beautiful charity should not lead to the disruption of the group's prayer. Group leaders, with the assistance of a priest, need to discern disturbing activities promptly, including disruptive sharing, personal displays, erroneous teaching, and false prophecy, and the persons involved should gently but firmly and privately be directed to control such behavior and not to impose it on the group.

Wise discernment on the part of leaders and spiritual directors, supported by the good sense of the group, is needed so that the different gifts of the Spirit present in the group will serve to deepen the spiritual life of each member and thus build up the body of Christ. All exaggerations or lack of good judgment in the use of any of the gifts, and all imitations of the gifts, especially in the areas of prophecy, tongue-speaking, healing, resting in the Spirit, visions, locutions, etc., should be matters of deep concern and prudent and firm action on the part of those in leadership. Leaders must constantly stress the importance of attending to the Giver of the gifts rather than to the gifts. Praise, which is the group's response to the Lord in its midst and which brings blessings upon the group, should not be displaced by sharing.

As is true in all spiritual practice, the goal of every charismatic community and prayer group should be, in addition to the praise and worship of the Trinity, the personal growth in holiness of each member through deeper participation in the sacramental life of the Church, personal daily prayer and spiritual reading, and the practice of charity. Charity is exercised first of all in the fulfillment of the duties of one's state in life, but also in concern for one's neighbor and for the Church, particularly the local Church, and for society. It is only by keeping this goal in mind and making use of the appropriate means, that the human weaknesses of pride, jealousy and ambition, with their attendant vices of quarrelling, disputes, and back-biting, mentioned by Saint Paul as present in the early Christian churches, and which have so often plagued movements in the Church, can be overcome, so that the Spirit of love and truth may prevail. Discernment and the striving for personal holiness, for becoming a better person, are necessary to overcome the works of the flesh, so that the fruits of the Spirit may ripen (Galatians 5:16-26). "Since the Spirit is our life, let us be directed by the Spirit. We must stop being conceited, provocative and jealous."

The graces sought and obtained in prayer groups (and in Life in the Spirit seminars) should tend towards establishing the life of charity, which is the life of the Spirit, in the lives and hearts of each and all.

It is apparent then, that the classical Christian spiritual tradition, with its advice regarding the path to the Father can be in fruitful dialogue with the Charismatic Renewal to the benefit of both.

CARDINAL SUENENS of Belgium, at the Fifth International Charismatic Leaders Conference in Rome in 1984, shared his conviction and "dreams" about the Charismatic Renewal, which are valuable for all interested in pursuing a spiritual life:

1. That the name be clarified and changed to "Catholic Pentecostal Renewal," since "charismatic" is too narrow. He noted that the stirring up of the charismatic gifts, while an important aspect of the renewal, is only one aspect. The Spirit, through the graces of Pentecost, is revivifying all aspects of Catholic life and the name "Pentecostal," the Cardinal suggested, focuses on this broader renewal of the Spirit.

2. That we be rooted in the sacramental life of the Church (this is what Paul VI asked in 1975 and John Paul II in 1981, as well as again at the Fifth International Conference in 1984), realizing that we "became a Christian" when we were claimed by Christ in Baptism and that our charismatic experience is an appropriation or release of the sacramental graces in one's life. The Cardinal stated his conviction that the Charismatic Renewal would be strong or weak according to the place given to the sacraments, especially the Eucharist.

3. That we be very much part of the local church, in close contact with the local Bishop, so that we can hear his concerns for the local church and cooperate with him in working for renewal, for it is in the local church that the community of Christ's followers is built up.

4. That we be rooted in the apostolic faith of the Church, holding to that which is guaranteed by the Apostles and their successors, and not going by private revelations, apparitions, visions and prophecies. He recommended following the lead of the local Bishop in whose diocese such phenomena are reported.

5. That we be rooted in the apostolic life of the Church, sharing our gifts with all, for the sake of the Lordship of Jesus Christ, bearing witness to Him by our words, actions and works of mercy.

AT THIS SAME Fifth International Charismatic Leaders Conference in Rome, John Paul II gave an important message on April 30th which confirms what has been said in this chapter and in Cardinal Suenens' talk:

With all my heart I welcome you to Rome, in the joy of the Risen Christ. Your meeting in Rome, at the center of the Church, comes at the time when she is giving thanks to the Father of our Lord Jesus Christ for the Sacrifice of His Son and for the action of the Holy Spirit, which fills her with new life.

As I said in my Easter message, the Holy Door of the Jubilee Year of the Redemption has now been closed, but we must keep remembering that at Easter the door of Christ's tomb was opened once and for all. He Who is the Resurrection and the Life knows nothing of closed doors, for He has conquered sin and death. Yet because of human freedom, many doors do not open to Him. And for this reason I ask you, and all the members of the Charismatic Renewal, to continue to cry aloud to the world with me: Open the doors to the Redeemer!

The Church's mission is to proclaim Christ to the world. And you share effectively in this mission insofar as your groups and communities are rooted in the local churches, in your dioceses and parishes.

The Jubilee Year of the Redemption has brought us back to the source, to the "heart of the Church," the only source that can nourish our Christian life. It has enabled the People of God throughout the world to rediscover the importance of the sacraments, notably the sacraments of Penance and the Eucharist. Because they are the full enactment of the word of God, they are the most precious gifts that He has given us in His Son, Our Lord Jesus Christ.

I am particularly pleased that you are concentrating on the sacraments in your reflections. This is of the greatest significance, for all your spiritual strivings must be directed to *a personal encounter* of each individual with the Lord, in the community of the Church, which through the power of the Holy Spirit is herself the great sacrament of salvation.

Real openness to the Holy Spirit as He vivifies and guides the Church helps you *to live in union with the Lord Jesus*. It is your strength and your special treasure, and you are striving to exercise it in different ways. But this gift from God is also a fragile treasure and one which you must take special care of. It is for this reason that your international meeting at the center of the Church, at a time so strongly marked by the Jubilee of the Redemption, can be of decisive importance for the whole Catholic Charismatic Renewal.

I would interpret your presence here, and your choice of themes for your discussions, as a decision to return to the sources: *to center your whole lives on the encounter with the Redeemer in His sacraments*. It is precisely the openness of the human heart to the sacramental grace that God offers you in the Church which enables you to meet Christ in a real and lasting way, to respond to His loving command: "Remain in My Love" (John 15:9).

I mentioned the fact that you are rooted in your local churches. And the Church herself as a sacramental reality communicates the grace of the sacraments through the ministry of priests in the local churches. It is at the sacramental heart of the Church, and at the sacramental heart of your local churches, that your life as baptized and confirmed Christians can be ceaselessly renewed—that life which in the power of the Spirit makes you witnesses to Christ the Redeemer.

Soon we shall celebrate Pentecost. In the midst of the Apostles there is Mary, the one who accepted the Holy Spirit's greatest gift: the life of Jesus. May she who thus became the Mother of the Church be in a special way your Mother and the Model of renewal in the Church. Let us entrust to her our lives, our commitment, and our desire to grow in the love of Jesus Christ and in fidelity to His holy Church.[1]

---

[1] Emphases added.

Part Five:

Progress
in the Life
of Happiness

21

Divine Adoption
& The Theological Virtues

When the Wisdom of the Father wed human nature, He raised human nature to a dignity unimaginable. By the God-Man's bloody death upon the Cross, all mankind was redeemed and called to possess through grace the dignity which the Son of God possesses by nature. Christ established the Church and the sacraments through which this grace could be conferred upon those who would accept it. What the Son is by nature, we are by grace; we become the partakers of the divine nature (2 Peter 1:4). He is the only-begotten Son, the first-born; we are His brothers and sisters, sons and daughters of the Father.

As the rational life is perfect only in the mature person, so the spiritual life is perfect only in the mature Christian. The spiritual life is perfect when the Christian thinks, acts and suffers not only according to the rational principle of his or her nature, but also and especially according to the divine principle by which the Christian is an adopted child of God. "All who are led by the Spirit of God are sons of God" (Romans 8:14 NAB). Christian perfection implies the full development of the gifts of the Holy Spirit, by which the purified soul is moved by the Spirit in its acts and operations.

To move oneself freely by one's own natural rational principle is good; to move oneself by this rational principle enlightened by infused faith and enlivened by charity is better; to be moved by a divine principle, by the Holy Spirit, acting through His gifts, is best, and leads to a higher perfection, since what is done by God is more perfect than what is done by man (S.T. I-II, Q. 68, A. 1).

To reach this full development, the Christian must subject the lower nature to reason and reason to faith and divine inspiration. One must mortify and detach oneself, practice the infused theological and moral virtues by prayer and good works, and one must be purified by divine action.

The most intimate and highest purpose of the religious state is to help humans on to this perfection, to which they are led by the Father in all their acts. This is the highest reason for poverty and obedience, which foster in the religious a mature dependence on the divine authority embodied in other persons; this, in turn, facilitates a child-like dependence on the indwelling Holy Spirit.

In this light we appreciate the implications of spiritual childhood as taught and exemplified by Saint Thérèse of Lisieux. Perfect docility to the inspirations of the Holy Spirit leads to the fulfillment of the highest potentialities of sanctifying grace and of the divine adoption in this life, in preparation for their ultimate fulfillment in Heaven. This is true maturity and adulthood.

SANCTIFYING GRACE resides in the essence of the soul, perfecting and completing it. From it proceed the infused virtues and the gifts through which supernatural actions are performed. It is the activity of these infused virtues and gifts which makes our life spiritual and divine and Christlike. For sanctifying grace, the virtues and gifts come from the Heart of Christ and are a participation in the inner life of His

Heart; and by them our heart lives in His and communicates intimately with His.

The theological virtues, faith, hope and charity, have God as their object and unite us directly to Him; they are especially exercised in prayer. Faith was present in the Most Pure Heart of Mary in an exceedingly high degree, but not in the Sacred Heart of Jesus, because His soul from its first moment had the beatific vision, and vision is sight. Faith believes what it does not see, but faith is not unreasonable. It is not unreasonable to believe God, Who is Truth Itself and can neither deceive nor be deceived. What He tells us we can believe with absolute certitude. And since the Son of God has confided the truths that He has brought to earth to a Church made infallible by the Holy Spirit Who is present in it, we can believe with the same absolute certitude the truths that this Church declares are divinely revealed. Indeed it is Jesus in her Who teaches us these truths through His Holy Spirit.

The safeguard of infallibility pertains both to the extraordinary and ordinary teaching of the Church. The extraordinary teachings are the dogmas concerning faith and morals solemnly defined by the Pope speaking as the Vicar of Christ, that is, *ex cathedra*. Sometimes these definitions are declared infallibly by a council of the Church, but always in union with the Pope. The ordinary teaching of the Church is her universal teaching. It is upon this teaching that catechisms and books of religious instruction are based, or should be based.

The *imprimatur* of the bishop is his assurance, founded on the approbation (*nihil obstat*) of the censor to whom he has deputed the examination of the book to which it is affixed, that it contains nothing contrary to faith and morals. Of course this is not an infallible decree. The Catholic should appreciate the vigilance of the Church in its censorship. The new Code of Canon Law states that: "In order to safeguard the integrity of faith and morals, pastors of the Church have the duty and the right to ensure that in writings or in the use of the means of social communication there should be no ill effect on the faith and morals of Christ's faithful. They also have the duty and the right to demand that where writings of the faithful touch upon matters of faith and morals, these be submitted to their judgment. Moreover, they have the duty and the right to condemn writings which harm true faith or good morals" (Can. 823). Loss, or at least impairment, of faith sometimes follows imprudent reading. We cannot strengthen our faith at the same time that we are injuring it; and it may be injured if we expose ourselves rashly to error.

Faith is precious because it is the beginning of everlasting life. What we now hold by faith, then we shall see; the only way to know now the truths that surpass human reason, the mysteries, is by faith. This faith, this knowledge of God, enlivened by love, and stemming from sanctifying grace, is our participation in the divine nature. Christ is the divine Truth, and this Truth we hold securely and firmly by living faith; He is in us by our faith and we are united to Him by faith. Hence the sublimity of this virtue.

One of the teachings most insisted upon in the Gospel is the importance of faith. In many beautiful incidents of His life Our Lord made clear the value which faith has in His eyes. Thus when He, Peter and John were returning from the Mount of Transfiguration, He met the father of the epileptic boy possessed by an evil spirit. The father begged Him for a cure for his son, saying: "If You can do anything to help us..." Christ immediately drew attention to the limitations of the father's faith, saying: "If you can? Everything is possible for anyone who has faith" (Mark 9:22). The poor father strove to rise to the occasion, exposing his difficulty to Jesus, "crying out, with tears: I do believe, Lord; help my unbelief." How beautiful the candor of this father! He believed that Jesus had the power of God but his belief was imperfect; in his heart he wavered. With all simplicity he acknowledged the imperfection of his faith while applying in petition to Him Who can make faith perfect. We can often beg Our Lord for an increase of faith, and when we find that our faith is mixed with a measure of unbelief then we should ask Him to remove our unbelief. With the father of the Gospel, we may cry out to Jesus; "Lord, I believe, help my unbelief."

A touching evidence of faith in Him, which Christ instantaneously rewarded with a cure, was the faith of the woman afflicted for twelve years with a flow of blood, who said in her heart: "If only I can touch his cloak, I shall get well" (Matthew 9:21 NAB). Our Lord turned to her, very much pleased with her faith, saying: "Daughter, your faith has restored you to health." Again to another suppliant He said: "Be it done according to your faith." To the alien woman of Canaan, who, by faith, accepted with serenity the stern reply of Jesus, "It is not right to take the children's food and throw it to the dogs," and who took up the analogy in humility saying, "Please, Lord, even the dogs eat the scraps that fall from the table of their masters," Jesus responded with joy: "Woman, you have great faith, let your wish be granted" (Matthew 15:26-28).

In His lifetime Our Lord worked many cures which manifested the loving desire of His heart to heal all diseases. The physical maladies cured by His divine power were visible, but they moved to pity the heart of Jesus less than the invisible spiritual ills which He had come to earth to heal. Faith made the bodies of the afflicted well; faith purifies our souls and makes them whole. This especially is the cure that Jesus wishes us to ask of Him. "O Lord, that I may see"—that the blindness of my soul which hides from me the beautiful destiny that is mine, may be cured. "Lord, that I may walk"—that the paralysis of soul, that the apathy and spiritual sloth which prevent me from embracing the means to my eternal end, may be overcome. We must cry out throughout our life until the process of our justification is complete, until we have passed from this life to a better one.

The object of our prayer should be, primarily, growth in the knowledge and love of God. Temporal things can, and sometimes should, be the object of our prayer. But our happiness comes not through the entire fulfillment of our own will but through its renunciation; the spiritual life is not a means of getting our way with God. We need have no undue solicitude about temporal things if we are truly seeking God, for as Our Lord said: "Seek first His kingship over you, His way of holiness, and all these (temporal) things will be given you besides" (Matthew 6:33 NAB).

As regards temporal things, we often do not know what is good for us. We desire those things that are harmful to our souls and do not appreciate the Father's wisdom and mercy in depriving us of them. The trials that He permits are often of much greater value to us in increasing our true happiness and preserving us from evil than the temporal things upon which our hearts are unduly set. Nevertheless the Father did create temporal goods for our use and enjoyment and He invites us to share our enjoyment of them with Him, as He shares our pleasure in them with us.

Jesus demanded faith of those who came to Him for cures. He demands faith of all for salvation: "He who believes and is baptized will be saved, he who does not believe will be condemned" (Mark 16:16). But He demanded greater faith from His disciples. Thus before His Ascension "He showed Himself to the Eleven while they were at table, and He reproached them for their incredulity and obstinacy, because they had refused to believe those who had seen Him after He had risen" (Mark 16:14). They should have been prompt to believe His witnesses after He Himself had told them that He would rise on the third day. So also Peter in his great faith in Christ walked upon the waters to Him, but seeing the wind strong, and considering the raging sea, began to fear and to sink, yet still believing in Christ, turned to Him and cried out: "Lord, save me!" Jesus, taking him by the hand, said: "Man of little faith, why did you doubt?" (Matthew 14:29-31). Thus Our Lord taught those who follow Him to have great and unwavering faith; He wants them to have the faith which moves mountains.

Jesus wishes us to beg Him most earnestly and confidently for the graces we need for our salvation and sanctification. He said: "Ask, and you will receive. Seek, and you will find. Knock, and it will be opened to you. For the one who asks, receives. The one who seeks, finds. The one who knocks, enters" (Matthew 7:7-8 NAB). His teaching not only contains clear promises and explains how we ought to ask, but also tells us for what we should ask: "What father among you will give his son a snake if he asks for a fish, or hand him a scorpion if he asks for an egg? If you, with all your sins, know how to give your children good things, how much more will the heavenly Father give the Holy Spirit to those who ask Him" (Luke 11:11-13 NAB).

So, then, it is the good Spirit which is the good gift for which we should ask. And if the Father has given His Spirit to us, what does He wish but that we live in the Spirit and grow in the Spirit? What is more important to us than this? Therefore, it is the love of the Father, and an increase of the love of the Father, that we should desire most and pray for most earnestly and continuously.

Faith as it existed in Mary was most powerful. Her faith was a belief in the Father's truth, to which she always adhered, and through which she was united to Him always. In her this faith was more or less constantly actual. All the truths in her resplendently clear intelligence were ordered in accordance with this highest and most certain knowledge of faith. Mary scorned as nothing whatever was contrary to her faith, and while she gave due attention to temporal things, her mind penetrated through and beyond them to infinite reality. Mary's faith in Jesus was firm, secure and constant; it did not waver when confronted with difficulties. She knew that Jesus was God when she ministered to His infant needs; when, at the age of twelve, He was lost for three days; when the high priest of the nation condemned Him to death as a blasphemer; when the Roman executioners hung Him upon the gibbet of the Cross; and when she received Him from the hands of Saint John in the sacrament of the Altar. Her heart was a faithful heart upon which Jesus could rely come what might. It is in Mary's company that our faith will come to resemble hers and to partake of its splendor.

22 Faith:
Our Foundation

Our day has seen the defamation of faith in the name of reason and the defamation of reason in the name of the senses. Rationalism has opposed faith, and materialism has opposed faith and rationality.

All our natural knowledge comes through the senses, through which we know the appearances of things. It is our reason which penetrates through these appearances to the nature of the things we sense. This element of reason makes perception something more than sensation. With eyes and nose we sense the round, red, sweet-smelling; our reason, working together with our senses, perceives the apple. Reason, then, is a power by which we penetrate through the accidents of things to their essential reality.

160

The perfection of reason is present in the perennial philosophy which expresses formally the truths concerning reality that it adduces mediately or immediately from the senses. The perennial philosophy, therefore, strengthens human rationality, purifies intelligence from the errors of false reasoning and from false opinions and illusions. That all may have the benefits of philosophy insofar as it is needful, the Father included in His Revelation certain truths of reason, such as those concerning His existence and providence and the immortality and spirituality of the soul.

Whereas reason penetrates to the natural reality of things, faith penetrates still further to the divine reality that sustains their being. Just as reason, without disturbing the action of the senses, completes them, so faith, without disturbing the action of right reason, completes it. Faith is necessary for an entire and integrated sense of reality, including human nature and human happiness. Reason, indeed, leads us to the knowledge of the existence of God, and teaches us that our happiness must consist in the highest activity of our highest power directed toward its highest object, i.e. the activity of contemplation of God. So Aristotle rightly reasoned (*Nicomachean Ethics*, Book X, especially Chapter 7). But what the human reason and the most enlightened philosophical inquiry could attain at the end of years of research and the culmination of a remarkable succession of wonderful minds (Socrates, Plato, Aristotle) is only a fragment of the truth to which faith penetrates, having as its object the revelation of God concerning Himself, our destiny and the means thereto, and the supernatural order that He instituted and by which He has reconstituted fallen human nature.

Modern science continues to add much to the knowledge given us by philosophy and faith. Its scope is restricted by its self-imposed limitation to sense-knowledge. Its findings need to be corrected by right reason, and are subject to the order of philosophy, which in turn must respect all that is true in science. The conjecture of scientists, when they draw conclusions transcending the limits of their science, must be subjected not only to right reason but even more to faith which attains to the most certain knowledge, having as its object God Himself, as He knows Himself and reveals Himself to us. Science, philosophy and faith, therefore, should exist in harmonious order, giving to our minds a growing knowledge of reality in which the order of values, natural and supernatural, is preserved.

What becomes of scientists and philosophers who do not become saints? The saint, who is not a scientist or philosopher, will possess all truth. Saint Paul glories in knowing but Jesus Christ and Him crucified. Science and philosophy perfect reason but they do not perfect the whole person; sanctity heals and perfects the whole person. The person without faith is like an empty vessel; the person with living faith is a vessel containing very precious wine.

Faith heals the ignorance and errors of reason by illuminating it from above. In Revelation God communicates to us not only supernatural truths but also truths of the natural order to insure to all sufficient enlightenment for their needs on the way to happiness. People need light and guidance from their earliest years, which true faith provides. Materialistic scientists, on the other hand, by their unbelief and false philosophical doctrine, impair and blunt their intelligence and make themselves incapable of knowing reality as it is in its fullness; and even as it can be known by right reason. Hence their opposition to true philosophy.

Once faith has been given to a person he can exercise it at will, grace always assisting him in its exercise. Faith is placed in the keeping of our own will. It is our part to defend it, to reject all that is contrary to it, to make strong acts of faith, determinations of our will by which we accept fully all that God teaches us through His holy Church.

For those who possess it, faith itself is its own testimony. We experience a firm certitude by which we adhere to revealed truths despite the fact that they are beyond the proof of reason. It is by faith that we know God as our end and Ideal, as our eternal happiness, and by which we know the means that lead to Him. It is faith that makes us order our days in such a way as to attain our Ideal and end. It is faith that leads us to value prayer and spiritual reading, the Holy Sacrifice of the Mass and Holy Communion, the practice of virtue, mortification and sacrifice. And through these exercises faith grows, and the love of Jesus is rooted more deeply in our hearts and lives.

Difficulties in connection with the faith may occur to some according to their particular mentality and temperament. In times of stress and strain, when these difficulties come in the form of temptations against faith, we must treat them as temptations and make acts of faith, assuring Our Lord that we will honor His testimony with our belief. As Simon Peter said when Our Lord asked His Apostles, "Do you want to leave Me too?": "Lord to whom shall we go? You have the words of eternal life" (John 6:67-68 NAB). Jesus is the divine Truth and what truth can be more true than Truth? By what truth can we disprove the truth of Truth? Any statements which are truly contradictory to the truths of faith are most certainly false by that very fact. No matter how convincing an array of evidence against the faith may seem, we need experience no concern or trouble, for we know Whom we have believed. When we properly put aside reading or turn from talk that is contrary to our faith, this is not a sign of weakness of faith any more than the refusal to listen to the besmirching of one's mother's name is a sign of doubt concerning her honor. Furthermore the faith is precious and we cannot presume upon ourselves to keep it. We trust in God's grace, which has given us the faith, for its preservation; hence, we do not tempt God by exposing our faith needlessly. An eminent professor refused to read a book whose orthodoxy was questionable saying: "My faith is too precious."

THE GIFT OF UNDERSTANDING makes the soul ready for the enlightenment of the Holy Spirit Who acts in the soul through the gifts whenever He wills. By His action He often enlightens our faith so that it penetrates its object. Thus at times, enlightened by the Holy Spirit and strengthened by the luminous certitude which He imparts, our faith touches Jesus. We are as assured of His presence as if He stood before us. At other times, words we read or hear are illuminated so that our understanding searches the deep mysteries of God. Thus as we go on in our life of faith, many of our difficulties are resolved through the action of the infused virtue of faith and the gift of understanding. Study, common sense and reason resolve other difficulties, for while faith cannot be proved by reason since it is above reason, yet all arguments against faith can be disproved by reason. At the time of temptation we should, indeed, set aside the "doubt," but at other times we can turn to it to resolve it in the spirit of humble, prayerful inquiry, or we may seek the solution from a sufficiently learned and sound priest. It is a difficulty and not a doubt so long as we adhere to our faith (which we do by making an act of faith), for as Cardinal Newman said, "A thousand difficulties do not make one doubt."

FAITH PLAYS a very important role in the balancing of our powers, in securing mental health, in preparing us for happiness and in lighting up the ideal we need for a happy and fruitful life.

While the will in a sense is the "master" faculty, it is blind and needs the intellect to lead it. The intellect in its turn can only operate intelligently in the practical order after it has possessed itself of truth.

Hence the possession of truth is the most important foundation of our personal life, and this foundational truth must bear the stamp of certitude. Such truth is difficult to obtain, and in the ordinary course of events would be attained only by a few. The extraordinary and supernatural avenue of divine Revelation, however, comes to the rescue, making available to all this precious stuff of truth out of which they can then fashion the fabric of their lives and happiness.

It does indeed matter *that* we believe, and also *what* we believe. One who knows oneself to be possessed of the truth is able to elicit the full strength of that marvelous energy, the will. Such a one can overcome the contrariness of human nature, the interior opposition and discord existing in all, that tosses many about, because they have no clear and intense light on the true goal of life and are unable to exercise the power of their will in a sustained and consistent way toward a worthwhile and attractive goal.

Without a purpose in life we cannot be happy. The purpose of our lives must be founded in truth and goodness, suited to us, realizable, and worthy of our entire dedication and striving. The absence of such a purpose leads to a life subject to crises or to a shiftless, bored and discouraged life. Tension, sadness, unhappiness, misguided activity result from an ideal which is not founded in truth and goodness, or which does not answer to the need of the entirety of the person, or which is not realizable.

Dr. C.G. Jung, the founder of a modern school of psychology, has pointed out that in his patients (most of whom were over thirty-five), unhappiness, mental conflict and mental disease come from the lack of a religious purpose in life. Many of his patients were successful but once they had succeeded, they found that the goal for which they had striven and which they had achieved was not such as to make them happy; it was not sufficient. In each case, he asserts, the true solution was to be found only in a religious outlook on life. Only God can *provide* and *be* a fully satisfactory ideal and purpose for humans. And that is so because our ideal, our purpose, is our end, and only God is our true last end. We may indeed have an unconscious, as well as conscious, ideal. But the former can be brought into harmony with the latter, strengthening our mental health, relieving tension and false direction of energy—by prayer and spiritual reading which reshape the unconscious as faith penetrates more and more deeply, and as humility and self-knowledge increase.

It is faith that proposes to us this purpose and ideal as It is, and as It is attainable. Through the Incarnation, God has made His infinite beauty and attractiveness, His mercy, goodness and wisdom sensible to us. In Jesus we find God-made-visible. Thus we have an Ideal, a model, at once boundless in its infinity and concrete in its incarnate representation. This is an Ideal that moves our human nature to its totality, in its intelligence, will and senses; an Ideal that we can keep present to ourselves at all times to encourage ourselves to suitable activity.

We can take Jesus under various aspects (His "mysteries") as our Model: as a child in His dependence on Mary; as a worker, citizen and member of the Holy Family in His hidden life; as a teacher and warrior of truth in His public life; as a victorious sufferer in the mental anguish of the garden of Gethsemane and in the afflictions of His Passion. And we can take Him as our Model as living within us by His grace, as our Lord and King, our Love, our Friend, our Brother. Thus we can assimilate and supernaturalize our personal ideal according to our particular attraction. We do not aim at "copying" in a material fashion the states and doings of Jesus, but of making our own His inner dispositions, of living in accordance with the light that shines from His example—*under* the circumstances and *with* the temperament, talents and ability, and *in* the vocations which are given *us*. In brief, we aim at being supernaturally ourselves.

Our faith shows us that this Ideal is attainable, for we are united to Christ by sanctifying grace and grow in His likeness and are transformed into Him by the growth and perfection of charity. Finally, all our actions and sufferings, all our circumstances and conditions can assist us in attaining this Ideal.

This Ideal, which is Reality Itself, which is truth and love, lives within us, the source of our life and being, of our understanding and love, and also their end and object. God is within our souls, present in our wills, communicating to them energy and strength. In trouble and tribulation, in tempest and trial, He is there, within, powerful to help us. And then in moments of leisure, *we may unite ourselves interiorly with Him, losing ourselves in His love.*

It is through the Most Pure Heart of Mary that we may most intimately unite ourselves to Jesus. By making her, the Mother of God, the seat of wisdom, our Queen, we shall be enabled to make Him more effectively our King. When we make Him to reign in our hearts, then we shall be indeed free, secure, happy and full of peace and joy.

We cannot be too grateful for the gift of faith which Christ has given us; we should make it the foundation of our lives. Jesus said: "Anyone who hears My words and puts them into practice is like the wise man who built his house on rock. When the rainy season set in, the torrents came and the winds blew and buffeted his house. It did not collapse; it had been solidly set on rock. Anyone who hears My words but does not put them into practice is like the foolish man who built his house on sandy ground. The rains fell, the torrents came, the winds blew and lashed against his house. It collapsed under all this and was completely ruined" (Matthew 7:24-27 NAB).

23 Hope: Our Anchor

Faith leads to hope and hope to charity; without charity, faith and hope are dead. Faith and hope remain in the person who commits mortal sin and has lost charity, but has not sinned against these two virtues. With their help and with actual grace such a person may rise quickly from his fall, and when he or she does the spiritual organism, whose principle is sanctifying grace, revives together with his or her merits. This means that the Father, the Son, and the Holy Spirit will return to make their dwelling place in him or her. If his contrition is sufficiently intense, he will at once resume that degree of virtue which he had when he fell, and even a higher degree.

Hope is a glorious virtue which makes the soul radiant and strong. It is too often forgotten, although in our times it is urgently needed.

Like faith, hope has God Himself as its object. Hope hopes for God and hopes in God. It is an act of will by which the soul expects to attain to its eternal happiness and this expectation is characterized by certainty, which, however, is not absolute (S.T. II-II, Q. 18, A. 4). By hope we expect from God both the attainment of our end and the means thereto.

Its foundation is the omnipotence and mercy of God and the promises and merits of Christ, not our own ability or resources. Christ has opened Heaven to us; His merits are sufficient for us. The goodness of God is so great that He commands us not to despair; indeed He makes despair a mortal sin. We are obliged to hope; we are obliged to expect the divine power and goodness to lead us safely and securely to eternal life. It is of faith that, "As I live, says the Lord GOD, I swear I take no pleasure in the death of the wicked man, but rather in the wicked man's conversion, that he may live" (Ezekiel 33:11 NAB).

At the same time we are warned against the sin of presumption. Whereas despair causes us to cease to hope that we can attain to Heaven, presumption leads us to expect to attain Heaven without taking the means. It says: God is so merciful that He will save me without my repentance. We ought to have a certainty of attaining Heaven but it should be combined with a resolution to take all the means that are necessary to get there. Our Lord told us what these are: "If you will have eternal life," He said, "keep the commandments." That is all. We must avoid mortal sin and practice the twofold virtue of charity: love of God and love of neighbor, which sum up all the commandments. He who dies in the state of grace is saved.

Hope is founded on the omnipotence and goodness of God. Its excess, presumption, is eliminated by the remembrance of the justice of God. God can act either through His mercy or His justice, but as He said to Sister Benigna Consolata of the Visitation Order: "The door of My mercy is always ajar. A touch will open it. The door of My justice is locked. It must be broken into." There is no ground for despair for anyone on the face of the earth, for all sins have been expiated by Christ Who wills the salvation of all, Who loves all, and Whose mercy is seeking all.

Divine mercy is called forth by human misery. The Father leaps with joy, as it were, when the sinner humbles himself sincerely in contrition before Him. As the father went out to meet his prodigal son, the Father hastens to justify the sinner. The publican prayed: "O God, be merciful to me, a sinner." "This man," said our Lord, "went home from the temple justified ... he who humbles himself shall be exalted" (Luke 18:13-14 NAB). "A heart contrite and humbled, O God, You will not spurn" (Psalm 51:19 NAB).

Mercy is an attribute which regards the needs of others; faults and sins represent needs. They can be punished, and thus brought back into the order of justice; or forgiven, and the virtues which are wanting supplied. The Father loves to act through His attribute of mercy, and this attribute we must recall frequently throughout our mortal life, weak and sinful as we are.

It is not, then, in our merits that we trust, but in the merits of Christ. It is not in our strength and goodness but in His; we do not hope in ourselves and in our virtues, but in Him. We do not hope in our wealth, birth, talents or good works. Saint Thérèse of Lisieux prayed: "When the evening of my life comes, I shall stand before Thee with empty hands, because I do not ask Thee, my God, to take account of my works. All our good works are blemished in Thine eyes. I wish, therefore, to be robed with Thine own justice, and to receive from Thy love the everlasting gift of Thyself" (Act of Oblation to God's Merciful Love). Persons striving to please God do well; without our efforts, we shall not be saved; however, our hope of salvation does not rest upon these efforts, but upon God's mercy.

Hope is not selfish although it concerns the attainment of our end, the salvation of our soul. Charity toward our own soul is not selfishness, it is the fulfillment of the Father's will in our regard; it subordinates our soul to Him and to His will. He has placed His glory in our happiness, in our salvation; and no one but ourself can save our own soul, can give Him our love. This we must do personally, and this He eagerly awaits as if each of us were the only person on the face of the earth.

The value of the theological virtue of hope in preserving the balance of our mental powers is very great, for hope gives strength to the activities of the soul. It makes them joyous and prompt, while freeing the soul from uncertainties, tensions and fears, as well as from proneness to temptation and inconstancy. This stabilizing influence of the theological virtue of hope is expressed by the anchor, the symbol of hope; hope anchors the soul in the Father; it centers our heart in God and frees us from undue attachment to creatures.

It is hope that gives us strength to live in the spirit of the counsel of poverty, just as living in the spirit of the counsel of poverty strengthens our hope. When, on encountering adversities, losses and misfortunes, we turn to the Father, we find our hope and joy mysteriously increased. The soul conformed to the will of the Father never loses creatures without gaining thereby an infinitely greater good, a greater possession of God, a stronger and more confirmed hope. Instead of the misfortunes of life rendering such a soul embittered, depressed, suspicious, fearful and withdrawn, they strengthen it in the possession of infinite happiness. This is the mystery of the Cross, the mystery of fruition through frustration, of conquest through contradiction, of life through death. It is in union with Jesus Crucified that we must endure loneliness, abandonment, suffering. He will teach us how to turn all that is bitter in life into sweetness.

When, in pursuing the spiritual life and conscious of no deliberate habitual attachment, we find that despite all our efforts we are going backward, that our faults are apparently multiplying, that advance is blocked, that our prayers are fruitless, then is the time to hope and to take courage. Such trials are permitted by the Father to strengthen us in faith, in hope and in love. They lead us to abandon all hope in ourselves, to despair of our own goodness and power, and hence they lead us to put all our hope in Him. When we seem to be losing all, to be hanging on to God by only a thread, then is the time to resign ourselves completely into His hands with peace, joy and assurance; for Jesus is closest to the tried, the tempted, the needy, and He will never be nearer than when He seems to have completely abandoned us. He united our dereliction to His own when from the Cross He cried in our name to His heavenly Father: "My God, My God, why have You forsaken Me?" (Mark 15:34 NAB). In our dereliction, then we can be united to Him in His; though we do not feel His presence or this union, it is very real.

"Hope is so pleasing to God that it obtains all that it hopes for," says Saint John of the Cross and Saint Thérèse of Lisieux. Our hope should have the perfection of utter trustfulness and security in the abandonment of ourselves to our heavenly Father, to His loving care.

Utter trustfulness, complete abandonment—for this we should strive with all our energy. This degree of hope we can the more readily achieve the more completely we conform our will to His. While prudence accurately discerns the obstacles and difficulties with which we have to cope, our hearts should remain serene in the assurance that we are the children of a heavenly Father Who is all-powerful.

This was the hope that kept the heart of the Blessed Virgin raised to the Father as she held her course faithfully from her Immaculate Conception to her glorious Assumption. This hope kept her heart in silence and quiet in the grievous trial subsequent to the Incarnation when her pregnancy became apparent to her spouse, Saint Joseph.

Mary embraced the lowliness of her situation and its corresponding duties. She lived sinlessly and took nothing for granted; she gladly practiced mortification and humility, faithfully obeyed all the prescriptions of the Law and persevered in recollected union with the Father. In a word, she strove to practice virtue with all her might and to speedily cut off all the occasions of sin. She accepted all from the Father, and she gave all. She is our model.

The gift of fear perfects the virtue of hope. This fear is not servile fear, which dreads the punishment of God, but filial fear, which dreads to be separated from the Beloved by sin. Hence as love grows so does filial fear.

Hope reposes with certitude upon the divine power and mercy from which it expects all the means necessary to attain its end. Filial fear does not doubt the divine power or mercy but, considering the changeability of the human will, shrinks from the possibility of withdrawing from God by sin. Hence hope and filial fear cling together and perfect each other (S.T. II-II, Q. 19, A. 9, ad 1).

Filial fear leads to submission to the will of the Father and thus opposes the beginning of pride whose origin is in the falling away from God, a lack of submission to Him. Hence the root of humility, the virtue opposed to pride, is the reverence for the Father of filial fear. We should aim at sustaining ourselves in this reverence. Then we shall be submissive to the Father's will; we shall be humble; we shall overcome pride and all the vices that spring from pride; we shall practice all the virtues. This humble reverence is maintained by the practice of the presence of God and perfected by the inspiration of the Holy Spirit. It makes our love pure and true.

The Sacred Heart of Jesus is the most effective school of divine charity.

— Pope Pius XII, Encyclical on the Sacred Heart

24 Charity

The Son of God has given us the most beautiful ideal of life: the twofold love of God and of humans. We are called upon to love, and in this is included all our duties; this is the goal toward which we are to tend, an ideal but more than an ideal. We are called to make it a reality. The spiritual life is that life whereby we advance in love. Our love must be elevated by being attracted to what is most worthy of itself; it must become purified of all its defects.

The First Commandment is: "Thou shalt love the Lord thy God with all thy heart, with all thy strength, with all thy mind and with all thy soul." What does this mean; what does God expect of us? If we are sincere and honest we shall admit that we do not love God with all our heart, strength, mind and soul. Theologians explain that we fulfill this commandment so long as we are tending toward such a love. All

Christians are called to Christian perfection, all have an obligation to tend to perfect love. This call is general and remote; it becomes particular and proximate when the individual realizes he too is called to perfection. Perfection, or sanctity, is simply spiritual maturity. The infant must grow and develop or else he becomes abnormal. Spiritually, too, we must grow or else we are spiritually abnormal: retarded. Both love and grace, by their nature, tend to increase.

God said to Abraham: "Walk in My presence and be blameless" (Genesis 17:1 NAB). Jesus says to us: "You must be perfect just as My heavenly Father is perfect" (Matthew 5:48). In the Sermon on the Mount, He explains to His disciples that they should not only love their friends, as even the heathens do, but that they should also love their enemies. This is perfect love, love like the love of the heavenly Father, and if we are to be His sons, our love must be like to His.

Love is not only a matter of affection but must also be effective. Love is effective when it wills the good of, and does good to, the beloved; this is love of benevolence as opposed to mere love of pleasure and utility. When the love of benevolence is mutual between two persons there is friendship, and this friendship expresses itself in some kind of community of life, a sharing of thoughts, desires and activities. The love of God brings about this condition of friendship between us and Him; friendship with God is a sharing of His happiness and of His love. It consists, on our side, not only of affection for God, but also of willing Him good. Love of God leads us to love Him more than ourselves. It leads us to rejoice in His existence and perfections, to praise, adore and thank Him, to repair sins, and beg that all may know and love Him. The Son of God in knowing the Father glorifies Him, He is a canticle of divine praise in the bosom of the Trinity. This glorification of God we continue on earth, by our faith, hope and love.

Love of God and love of humans meet in this, that the welfare and interest of both are really the same; for God has placed His glory in our happiness, and our happiness consists in knowing, loving and glorifying Him. True fraternal charity has as its primary object the eternal happiness of persons for their sake and for the sake of God, our Beloved. To Him all belong; He desires them to share His happiness to which all other goods are subordinate. True love of God always includes love of the sanctification and salvation of humans.

The mutual love of God and humans is characterized by a community of life. "If any man love Me, he will keep My word and My Father will love him, and We shall come to him and will make Our abode with him" (John 14:23). The Father, the Son and the Holy Spirit dwell in the soul in the state of grace, and the soul in the state of grace feels the attraction, or need, to dwell in the Father through knowing, loving and conversing with Him. Such a soul is not alone but has the company of the three divine Persons.

Love of the Father leads to recollection, a wonderful attitude of soul experienced at times by all who are in the state of grace. Recollection is a gathering of the powers of the soul, a union of them in God by which the soul gives its attention, love and worship to Him. This attitude of soul is weakened by dissipation, the undue pouring forth of the energies of the soul upon creatures. Recollection is strengthened by the avoidance of useless occupations, such as excessive use of radio, television, and newspapers, or the frequenting of movies, shows, etc. Dissipation, on the other hand, is marked by curiosity, excessive activity, the splitting of the soul's energies.

The love of the Father is always joined to fraternal charity and expresses itself in obedience to the Father's will together with a contempt for inordinate self-love and self-indulgence, which it checks. As Saint Augustine said: "Two loves have built two cities, the love of God to the contempt of self has built the city of God, and the love of self to the contempt of God has built Babylon."

Fraternal charity, that love by which we love all persons as our brothers and sisters and desire their eternal and temporal welfare, is based on faith, just as love of the Father is based on faith. It is through faith that we know the lovableness of the Father and can respond thereto by love. So, too, it is by faith that we know the lovableness of humans and can respond with love. Faith shows us all persons as the image of God, with immortal souls, with intelligences ordained to know the truth, and above all the highest Truth, and wills ordained to love the good, above all the highest Good.

Faith shows us these souls in the light of Christ's love for them. Our eyes are opened to the lovableness of people when we look at them through the Precious Blood as Christ saw them during His Passion. Whatever their deficiencies, Christ's Blood has paid the price for their ennoblement. All who are living and who are to live are capable of becoming God-like. The more we believe in and understand Jesus and the Redemption, and the Holy Spirit and His power of sanctification, the more capable we are of loving all despite their sins and sinfulness and despite the distortions of character and personality from which they suffer. Our eyes see the externals of men, reason penetrates somewhat to their interior, but faith alone knows all they can become. By the theological virtue of hope we hope absolutely, directly and effectively for our own salvation and sanctification; this we are obliged to do. Insofar as we unite others to ourselves in the love of charity, we can hope for them what we hope for ourselves (S.T. II-II, Q. 17, A. 3), and this in turn helps us to love them.

All people on earth are either potential or actual members of the Mystical Body of Christ. We cannot, then, exclude anyone from our effective charity without excluding Christ Himself. "I assure you, as often as you did it for one of My least brothers, you did it for Me" (Matthew 25:40 NAB). We should not dare to refuse to love. This applies especially to anyone who has injured us; we must forgive him or her in our hearts. "We are members of one another. Even if you are angry, you must not sin: never let the sun set on your anger" (Ephesians 4:25, 26). "If you bring your gift to the altar and there recall that your brother has anything against you ... go first to be reconciled with your brother, and then come and offer your gift" (Matthew 5:23-24 NAB). God wants the reconciliation of adversaries to precede the worship of Himself, to precede the offering of the Sacrifice of the Mass. We must avert to the contract that we make when we say the Our Father: "Forgive us our trespasses as we forgive those who trespass against us." If we do not forgive them, then neither will the Father forgive us. If we hold anger, a grudge, against another, we restrict the flow of grace into our own hearts.

In a parable God shows us ourselves. The servant who owed his master a thousand talents, staved off his master's punishment, saying: "Be patient with me and I will pay you back in full." The master moved by pity forgave him his debt. Then, as we know, this servant going out found a fellow servant who owed him a hundred pence and taking him by the neck, he throttled him and cast him into prison, despite the appeal: "Just give me time and I will pay you back in full."

When the master learned of this he said: "You worthless wretch! I canceled your entire debt ... Should you not have dealt mercifully with your fellow servant...?" And his lord delivered him to the torturers until he paid all the debt. Our Lord concludes this parable: "My heavenly Father will treat you in exactly the same way unless each of you forgives his brother from his heart" (Matthew 18:35 NAB). The injuries we suffer are trifles compared to the injuries that the Father suffers at our hands; for our sins are the greater because they are offenses against so great a Being, an infinite God. We, who are always in need of mercy, dare not be unforgiving toward a fellow servant who has offended us.

It is hard sometimes to forgive; then we must pray for our adversary. This will help soften our hearts so that finally we can forgive fully and free our soul from all the effects of our anger. Or kind actions toward the ones we dislike will help to overcome antipathy. It is well to realize how difficult it is to change ourselves; when we try strenuously and find that we fail repeatedly, then we should have more tolerance toward others. We should hate no one's evil as much as we hate our own, and the force of our zeal should be directed first of all against our own sins and defects.

All of us by nature have antipathies and sympathies, just as we have our own opinions and are subject to movements of discouragement and self-reliance. But if we are seeking to walk in the footsteps of Christ we will not act in accordance with the movements of nature. We will act contrary to our antipathies, just as by acts of faith and hope we oppose movements of nature against those virtues. To do this, besides praying for and acting kindly toward others, we must learn to think kindly of them, especially of those who annoy and irritate us. We are apt to be very short-sighted and subjective in our judgment of others. The person who irritates us has other aspects than that aspect which jars on our nerves, and we must try to consider these other aspects. We must remember that he has an immortal soul and is capable of becoming a saint through the merits of Jesus Christ.

Fraternal charity urges us to free ourselves from all race and class prejudices. These men and women against whom we are prejudiced because they belong to such a class, because of the color of their skin, because of their family, educational or social backgrounds, these are men and women for whom Christ has laid down His life. Who are we to be their judges, or to love them less than Christ did? Let us realize that it is Christ against Whom our prejudices are directed, the Christ Who complained, "Saul, Saul, why do you persecute Me?"

In cities where we see throngs of people, many of them sheep without a shepherd, let us remember that each has a soul, and that that soul has a story known fully to the Father alone. We should pray for all of them; toward all we should exercise courtesy and kindness.

According to our opportunities and circumstances, we should practice the corporal and spiritual works of mercy. Catholic societies provide means of doing this. Their forms are various (such as the Legion of Mary, the Saint Vincent de Paul Society, Focolare, the Cursillo movement, the Sodality of Our Lady, Opus Dei, Third Orders, the Catholic Charismatic Renewal) permitting the interpenetration of society by persons of varying talents variously organized, transmitting helps of many kinds to their neighbors while sanctifying themselves.

We should freely give alms according to our means. "Anyone who says, 'I love God,' and hates his brother, is a liar," says Saint John (1 John 4:20). If a person is hungry, love does not give him a sermon but feeds him or her. We seek our happiness in vain unless we are truly concerned for the happiness of all others, and manifest this in our deeds.

The gift of wisdom makes us one with the Father and one with His point of view, the point of view of Jesus and Mary (the Seat of Wisdom), in respect to God, humans and all things. Through the gift of wisdom the transcendence of the Father is experienced and charity is perfected. This gift is a principle of contemplation in the purified soul. It leads us to see persons as the Father sees them, to see them through the blood-tinged eyes of Jesus as He lays down His life for them. Thus the gift of wisdom fully-developed makes people not only contemplatives but also peacemakers, lovers of the union of souls; it leads them to share with Jesus the prayer: "That all may be one, as You, Father, are in Me, and I in You ... that they may be one in Us" (John 17:21).

THE MENTAL HYGIENE VALUE of charity may be seen in certain of its qualities and effects, and, more basically, in its healing and balancing of the natural tendencies of human nature.

We may take first these qualities and effects. Charity, which resides in the soul together with sanctifying grace, brings the power to love oneself as one should, to love others as one loves oneself, and to love the Father more than oneself. This power expands the human heart, unfurls its wrinkles, blots out its spots. Its exercise brings in its wake peace and joy and a capacity for service hitherto unknown.

This love, we have seen, is based on faith, on a faith which esteems and appreciates others as the images of the Father and members of Christ, despite their human miseries and failings; on a faith which holds God as most precious for what He is. Hence undue esteem for self and contempt for others are checked, and so too is that unconscious, ill-advised and ill-directed self-hatred which secretly accompanies egocentricity. Thus we become more at peace with ourselves and feel less guilty and inferior. We more readily overcome constricting hatreds, antipathies and begrudging thoughts, and find unsuspected pleasure in our capacity for service. The exercise of this capacity increases our power of achievement, and while love remains the motive of this service, humility is unimpaired.

As the love of the Father increases, so does the strength to give up all that is opposed to this love. Hence the love of the Father introduces order into the soul's desires and resolves the conflict among them. A person in whom this love predominates is quick to withdraw from moral harm; thus the conflicts which contact with moral evil tend to engender are halted at their onset. Besides, the recollection that flows from charity strengthens the unity of operation of all the powers of the soul. And conformity of the human with the divine will leads to ready acceptance of events and circumstances. This means greater adaptability as well as an increased capacity to act wisely in varying circumstances.

A human being is an individual with a personal destiny, but he or she is also a social being who ordinarily only functions normally when working out that personal destiny in a congenial society. Charity unites one to a perfect society by introducing one into union with Christ, the Head, and His members, the Mystical Body, the visible

Church. Thus people enter into communion with the souls of the just in Heaven, on earth and in Purgatory. When one lives by faith one is not deterred by the failure of the many Christians surrounding one to embrace the values of Christ, but rather one associates oneself outwardly and inwardly with those who do. Outwardly, insofar as one can establish friendships and associations with others who are so minded; inwardly, insofar as one is a member of the communion of the saints, and is united with all those in this communion.

We have said that the mental hygiene value of charity is evidenced more basically in the healing and balancing of the natural tendencies of human nature. These are threefold: the tendencies to self-conservation, to race conservation and physical intimacy, and to man's end. This last is the tendency to happiness, and to happiness as found in God. Now all these tendencies have been affected and disturbed by original and personal sins. The restoration of the natural tendency to union with God—which is *natively* the strongest, and in uncorrupted nature would be actually the strongest, and whose restoration and primacy is necessary to the balance of all human tendencies—requires grace and is mediated by faith; by the knowledge of God given us by Revelation. Thus too this tendency is elevated, for this knowledge, as we realize, is not merely a creature's knowledge of its Creator but a child's knowledge of its Father, a friend's knowledge of the Friend, a lover's knowledge of the Beloved.

The theological virtue of hope also plays a part in the restoration of one's tendency to one's end. For hope, as we have seen, cuts off two aberrations which would cripple the soul's union with the Father. It cuts off presumption, and thus makes the soul face and fulfill its responsibilities for achieving its destiny, while hoping in the Father and from the Father all that it needs to do so. And it checks despair and discouragement by the assurance of divine help despite human frailty.

When the natural tendency to love God more than oneself is reestablished in the soul, and by its elevation to the supernatural level immeasurably strengthened, then also all the other tendencies of the soul are brought into balance and harmony, as we have pointed out in treating of the first mental hygiene effects of charity. Then, too, we love ourself as we should, knowing ourself not as primarily a sensing and feeling animal, that is, according to the outer self, but as an intelligent person capable of a rich inner life and expansive love, that is, according to the inner self. Inordinate self-love is based on one's loving oneself according to the outer self, which is one's lesser self; the self-love in charity is based on one's loving oneself according to the inner self, one's higher and true self. This love is only complete when one loves God more than oneself, for God is our end, the source of our being and of all our good.

This true self-love is the basis and measure of our love for others, for we love them *as if* they were one with ourself. True self-love does not hinder us from the self-forgetfulness and self-sacrifice of true fraternal charity, but it does give us the solidarity with ourself which we need for wholesome self-forgetfulness and self-sacrifice. In the same way, the hope which we have of eternal blessedness does not conflict with the pure love of God for His own sake; for this hope, like true self-love, is fundamentally subordinated to the love of God, and seeks salvation and perfection, not primarily for our own sake, but *primarily* to please and glorify God.

To CONTEMPLATE the love of Mary is one of the greatest pleasures of her children. It was her love of the Father and of humankind that brought the Redeemer to us; through this love she was the Redeemer's companion, the Co-redemptrix.

Jesus is not only our Redeemer, but He is also our Judge. He wishes His Mother to be the supreme manifestation of the mercy which prevails in His Sacred Heart. Mary is all mercy; even toward those who are enemies of her Child her heart shines rays of brilliant love, and she desires nothing so much as to bestow great benefits and favors upon them. Her heart knows nothing but love. This love is the ideal and goal of the spiritual life.

The contemplation of this created reflection of the mercy of the Father should lead us to the contemplation of the divine mercy itself. It is difficult for us, earthbound as we are, to realize the sublime heights of the Father's mercy, but nothing so purges the soul of its pettiness and frees its affections, so that in turn they may be bestowed generously and purely upon the Father and humans.

The Father is unbounded; infinity marks all His attributes; the Father is love without limit. To the poor, the needy, the little ones, this love expresses itself in the form of mercy. "Whoever is a little one let him come to me" (Proverbs 9:4). "At her breast will her nurslings be carried and fondled in her lap ... like a son comforted by his mother will I comfort you" (Isaiah 66:12-13). So the Father speaks in the Old Testament.

If we were to imagine all the love of the best fathers and mothers on earth united in one person and immeasurably elevated and strengthened, this would be but a faint image of the Father's love and mercy that is directed toward each of us. The Father considers each of us as if we were His only child, indeed in each of us He sees Jesus, His only-begotten Son, His well-beloved. We should often pray for the grace to understand the Father's love, to believe in His love for us; then we shall be enabled to love Him in return. If we see our fellow men and women with the eyes of Jesus, if we see Jesus our God in them, then we will love them as He desires us to love them, that is, as He loved them. "I give you a new commandment. Love one another, just as I have loved you" (John 13:34). This love Jesus showed us by laying down His life for us; indeed, since we are reconciled to the Father by His Blood, we may say that He laid down His life for us while we were still His enemies.

So this is the way we should treat others. Those who seem to be, or are, our enemies, we should be willing to make our friends even at our own expense.

We should note that the Father loves us not because we are lovable, or because of our intrinsic worth; rather it is because He loves us that by giving us His graces He makes us worthy of His love. It is our need, our nothingness, which call forth His mercy and His graces. Saint Thomas tells us that it was the Father's mercy which, regarding our non-existence, had pity on us and led Him to create us.

We should respond to the wonder of the Father's love by receiving the gifts of grace and glory with which He wishes to enrich us. We should not be content to live on a purely natural, lowly plane, after the Father has given us His only-begotten Son to enrich us with a share of His divine happiness. It is the spiritual life which elevates us to participation in this supernatural happiness and which transforms our activities, even those which are natural, by the supernatural motive of love with which they are performed. Hence we should strive always to act simply to please the Father, in union with the intentions of Jesus and Mary; then our lowliest and most tedious duties will be elevated and become beautiful and an acceptable love-offering to Him. Then we shall be truly conformed to the Father's will, which is that we become another Jesus.

It is well to lay to heart concerning the cardinal virtues which we are about to speak, that they can all be exercised through this simple motive of charity, that is, through the intention to please the Father in union with the intentions of Jesus and Mary. For love of Him, then, we will be prudent, just, religious, penitent, obedient, brave, patient, long-suffering, continent, sober, modest, humble, and meek according to the circumstances in which we are placed: charity leads us to the exercise of all the virtues as they are needed.

Our will is conformed to the Father's will, then, when we are disposed to act and consistently do act in accordance with the intentions that animated Jesus and Mary who are our Models. Progress in the spiritual life is a progress of simplification of the soul so that it acts with an ever simpler and purer intention or motive. The passive purifications of which we shall speak are a divine means of bringing about this simplicity and purity of soul.

25 Hinges of the Soul: The Cardinal Virtues

The spiritual organism that comes to us with sanctifying grace includes not only the infused theological virtues which unite us directly to the Father, but also the infused moral virtues by which we rightly use the means to be united to the Father.

PRUDENCE

The infused virtue of prudence chooses wisely between the things that help and those that hinder us in tending to the Father. It takes counsel where this is needed, judges what is to be done, and determines the will to put into practice the resolution it has reached. Prudence is docile in receiving the truths it needs from others who possess them, penetrating in discovering the means, understanding and reasonable in its deliberations, mindful of past experience, foreseeing in ordering means to end, circumspect in attending to the execution of its plans. No adult possesses this supernatural virtue who does not realize that human happiness consists in union with the Father. Besides true prudence, there is the prudence of the world and of the flesh, which is false prudence; this knows how to take the right means to the wrong end.

All supernatural acts must be reasonable if they are to be virtuous. Supernatural prudence moderates excessive mortification and inordinate zeal for the welfare of others, by bringing the reason to bear on the right measure to be observed in these things. The Father is to be loved without measure, but He desires that our service be characterized by the mean of right reason. He will have a reasonable service, not according to the reasoning of the worldly but according to right reason. This is something that some beginners and proficients must strive to bear in mind, because under the influence of divine grace, of faith and love, they are apt to neglect to deliberate and to measure their service. They feel that they are moved by God, by the highest and most sublime motives, and they are barely aware that God expects them to reflect and observe due proportion in all things. We must be little children in loving and serving the Father, faithful, generous, yet not pushing things too far. There is a time to lay down our lives, when it is true courage to do so, and there is a time when to risk our lives (for example, in reckless driving) is not courage but foolhardiness. There is a time when duty demands that we overcome the softness of our nature just as there is a time when we should take relaxation and rest.

In the beginning and course of spiritual life, it is well to have the counsel of an experienced and holy director who knows the way of the spirit. But such are rare, the saints tell us, and we must use caution and be prepared to pray and seek for a long time for such a guide. "Let your acquaintances be many, but your advisors one in a thousand" (Sirach 6:6). One in ten thousand, says Saint Francis de Sales (*Introduction to the Devout Life*, Chapter IV). Having found a competent director, we should remain faithfully under his guidance. He will direct, comfort and encourage us.

Spiritual masters teach that it is better to have no guide at all than a poor guide. But even if we do not have a guide we can always ask for the solution to pressing problems—especially insofar as they concern sin and the avoidance of sin—from a solid priest in the sacrament of Reconciliation. Christ will help us if we approach Him in the person of His priest with living faith. Light that we do not receive in the sacrament He will then give us otherwise.

Prudence places three special strictures upon beginners: to disclose diabolical temptations and such as are accompanied by the desire to conceal them; not to make a vow without the permission of a prudent confessor; not to offer oneself as a victim of divine justice without such permission. The offering of oneself as a victim of divine *mercy* (as did Saint Thérèse) is another matter—this is the offering of oneself as an object of the outpouring of the Father's love and affection and it includes the resolution of generous fidelity to the Father's will. No special permission is required for this.

The relation of prudence to the other moral virtues manifests the nature of prudence and its mental hygiene value. Temperance restrains the lower passions. The temperate person contains himself and, despite the allurement of pleasure, keeps to the path of right reason and eternal happiness. Fortitude strengthens the reason and will that are wavering through fear; the courageous person remains self-possessed and, despite dangers, keeps to the good of faith and reason. Prudence does not determine these ends of temperance and fortitude, for they are principles existing in the natural reason and in faith; prudence, however, determines how these dictates are to be applied in each individual case. Thus in the matter of food, temperance inclines one to take what is useful and necessary for one's body but prudence determines what this is in each one's case and according to the circumstances. If this prudence is not false, it will judge rightly and not be swayed by inordinate desire. Thus prudence draws its principles from natural reason and faith (such as that we eat *primarily* for nourishment, not for pleasure—but not with the exclusion of pleasure); and prudence then, working through the moral virtues, commands temperate, courageous and just acts (S.T. II-II, Q. 47, A. 6).

We see then that the moral virtues preserve the moral order of right reason. The moral virtues put right reason into our passions and actions. Their dictates are not based upon arbitrary conventions or customs, but upon solid, objective moral principles known to natural reason, contrary to the teaching of those who do not recognize that moral principles are natural to man, necessary to the preservation of his natural goodness, and objectively true.

From those considerations we can readily understand, first, the danger of going for advice concerning our actions and passions to persons who lack the virtue of prudence; and, secondly, the value of the spiritual life for ordering our interior and our conduct. Such moral order is preservative of mental balance.

JUSTICE

The infused virtue of justice regulates our intercourse with persons and with the society of which we are a part. This virtue leads us to have the firm will to do what is right and just in all our dealings with others. It also determines us to be fair in our words concerning them; this requires that we be fair in our judgments. We must be especially cautious concerning those whom we envy or of whom we are jealous or against whom we are irritated. Otherwise we shall fail in justice and charity toward them, as by detraction or slander. Justice leads us to pay our debts, to pay just wages promptly, to return promptly articles that we have borrowed and to keep them safely, to use our talents for and fulfill our obligations toward the Church and society, to distribute offices to those who are best qualified if we are in authority, and so on. Justice in those in authority is a resplendent virtue which directs all they do to the common good without the satisfaction of any personal interest.

One of the common failings against the virtue of justice proceeds from lack of consideration and consists in the negligent omission of what we ought to do. This can be remedied by examining ourselves from time to time concerning our relations with others, asking ourselves, for example: Are we treating others as we would wish to be treated if we were in their place? Are we respecting their rights? Are we injuring or neglecting them? These questions are especially serious and ought to be daily answered by those who hold positions of public responsibility and who may easily be led into grave sin and spiritual

shipwreck by selfishness (e.g. by graft, by respect of persons in distri-
bution of offices or contracts, etc.). Such self-examination might also
embrace the virtue of religion: Are we giving to the Father what is
due Him in the way of service and worship? Are we giving Him
what He has a right to expect from us? Or are we curtailing our duties of religion? Are we heeding the persistent warnings and
reproaches of our conscience?

Fraternal charity requires us to love our neighbor as a brother or
sister in Christ; such love must first of all fulfill the duties of justice
toward him or her; these are discharged rightly if we truly love our
neighbor as we should. So also the love of God leads us to fulfill freely
and gladly the duties of religion toward our Beloved.

RELIGION. Connected with the virtue of justice are the virtues of religion,
obedience, penance and liberality. Religion is that virtue by which we
pay to God what we owe Him in prayer, adoration and worship. The
four acts of prayer (adoration, contrition, thanksgiving and supplication), which are also the four ends of sacrifice, are duties of religion.

Religion is a virtue which, as it develops, sanctifies the whole
person (S.T. II-II, Q. 81, A. 8). Of all the moral virtues its object is
closest to God, being not God Himself, the object of the theological
virtues, but the honor and service of God. It lifts up to God and consecrates to Him all the acts of the other moral virtues and all our
activities and sufferings.

By the service of the Father, we submit our minds and hearts to
Him, and by so doing these are purified, strengthened and elevated.

Devotion may be called the innermost act of religion: it is the
promptitude of the will to serve the Father. It is very helpful to consider the cause and effects of devotion. The cause is the meditation or
contemplation of God, especially of Christ, *for love of, and devotedness
to Him is the way to love and devotion to the Father*. This consideration
of His goodness and loving kindness toward us begets devotion. But
devotion—and this touches upon its signal importance—implies a surrender of the will to the Father. We give up our self-will, the root of all
our sins, and conform our will to the Father by this surrender.

Now what brings about this surrender, so important to the happiness and sanctification of each individual? What is the obstacle to

this surrender? It is the strength of self-will, pride and self-reliance. Hence, to bring about this surrender of our will to the divine will and service, we need to meditate not only on the Father's goodness, shown to us by His Son, but also on our weakness, need and nothingness. Then, perhaps little by little, we shall surrender to Him in loving dependence. We may summarize and say that devotion is begotten by the loving consideration of the truth that God is all and we are nothing.

The effects of devotion are the joy which flows from the consideration of the goodness of the Father, and indirectly, a salutary sorrow at the consideration of our own sins. We may also see as an effect of devotion the consecration of all our activity to the Father, which purifies the mind and heart and strengthens them because we rest in our beginning and end. Devotion leads us to be prompt to obey the inspiration of the Holy Spirit, and indeed, prompt to accomplish all our duties in the spirit of obedience. It leads us to practice patience in all our sufferings.

The realization of the Father's greatness and goodness and our nothingness from which devotion springs is effected in us in a unique way by infused contemplation. It is one of the great advantages of contemplation that it thus purifies the soul and consecrates to the Father all its activities and sufferings, while rendering the will fervent in devotedness even during prolonged dryness.

We see then that the virtue of religion and its interior act, devotion, are poised between charity and humility, while from it flow not only the acts proper to the virtue of religion, as prayer of petition, adoration, worship, but also a universal obedience and patience.

Thanksgiving is an important part of religion. The Heart of Jesus is rightfully very sensitive to ingratitude. He gives His benefits lavishly and receives ingratitude in return. Our Lord manifested His feelings when, after He had miraculously cured the ten lepers, He said: "Were not all ten made whole? Where are the other nine? Was there no one to return and give thanks to God except this foreigner?" (Luke 17:17-18 NAB). We ought to be cut to the quick that we, who are members of His household, not strangers, are so ungrateful.

Ingratitude is a destructive wind that dries and parches the soul, leaving it restless, fretful and discontent. It stops up divine favors, for the Father is loathe to give His graces to the ungrateful, as also He resists the proud. Let us, therefore, frequently think over the benefits we have received from the divine bounty in order to thank Him for them. Effects of the spirit of thanksgiving are fervor, zeal and contentment.

PENANCE. Penance is a virtue which is little understood and esteemed. Our Lord says: "Unless you do penance, you shall likewise perish" (Luke 13:3). Perhaps many of those who heard His preaching perished. He said to certain of His hearers, the Pharisees, "You will surely die in your sins" (John 8:24 NAB). If they did penance on remembering these words, as our Lord wished, this prediction would not have been fulfilled; just as God's prediction made through Jonah against Nineveh did not come to pass because king and people did penance. Such divine predictions are ordinarily conditional threats which will be carried out only in the absence of repentance.

Penance means first of all repentance. When Jesus said: "Do penance" He was saying: "Repent," i.e. have a change of heart (*metanoia*).

Penance is a virtue whose work is to destroy and fight against sin. Hence we can understand its importance. It grieves over past sins which it regrets, intending thus to remove past sin in both its guilt and debt of punishment; it willingly resists the tendencies to sin. It takes up the means whereby sin may be repaired. It leads to that curtailment of idle and curious glances which is modesty of the eyes; to a guard on the tongue (cutting off detraction and a host of other sins of speech); to purification of the motives of the heart and of the intentions of the will; in short, to the mortification and sacrifice necessary if the tendencies to sin are to be overcome.

Materialistic psychiatrists and psychologists who believe that there is no free will but that man is determined in his acts have some evidence for their opinion (although, of course, their conclusion is false), for those who become the servants of sin allow their wills to be subjected to the tendencies of their nature. These are they who never go against their own nature. Penance, on the contrary, is ready to do battle with the tendencies of nature, and the will which embraces penance recovers lost freedom.

Penance is not a gloomy, repressive and destructive virtue. On the contrary, it renews the energies of the soul which it refreshes, strengthens and preserves. It eliminates the barriers between the soul and the Father, and thus prepares the way for a union with the Father which it maintains by its opposition to the tendencies of sin.

Penance, as all virtue, is reasonable: it takes into account not only the greatness of the One offended and the malice of sin, but also the value of the Precious Atoning Blood of Christ, and, particularly, of the *limited* physical, emotional and spiritual resources of the penitent whose satisfactions it unites with the satisfactions of Christ. Penance is realistic: it aims, after detesting sin, at prudently resisting, by well-considered steps, the tendencies to sin.

Penance is cheerful and confident, for it knows it is waging a victorious war: each act of contrition overcomes sin, the penalties due to sin and the tendencies to sin.

Penance is not repressive: it does not hide one's personal sins and guilt from sight to molest the soul from their enforced hiding place in the unconscious. Rather it deliberately reveals them, evaluates them accurately (not emotionally), and takes prudent steps against them, assisted by faith, hope, charity and prudence.

Finally, penance does not sympathize with natural remorse and discouragement: rather it eliminates these as the offspring of pride and selfish disappointment, or elevates them to the supernatural level, where meet detestation of sin and confidence in the Father's merciful love.

Penance is undeservedly unpopular, and its unpopularity takes a heavy toll of unhappiness from the men and women who shun it. On the other hand, those who practice it find that, while it always has its place in the spiritual life, yet this place is not central: it yields place to faith in Christ and love and service of Him. Love of God accomplishes the purpose of penance in an eminent manner and includes the acts of this virtue.

The virtue of penance cooperates with the virtue of religion in offering sacrifice to the God it adores: the Sacrifice of the Mass; the sacrifice of sinful tendencies, of sinful and also legitimate pleasures. To please the Father and advance in His love, it is not necessary to be always doing great and heroic things. The Father is well pleased with little sacrifices: idle glances and words curtailed, humiliations patiently accepted, kind words addressed to those toward whom we feel antipathy or who have injured us, done for love of Him. This is the little way of Saint Thérèse of Lisieux. It avoids singularity, pride, and injury to mind and body; it purifies the wellspring of our thoughts and desires; eventually it leads to true greatness and to truly great deeds.

LIBERALITY. Liberality is that virtue by which a person uses well external goods represented by money, and overcomes undue attachment thereto. The liberal person spends money on himself and others when and as he should, and makes gifts for the benefit of others and the glory of the Father. This virtue is opposed to both the vices of prodigality and avarice.

And what better use can one make of one's money than to give alms with it? What one keeps one will lose, but what one gives will be one's forever. "Alms shall be a great confidence before the Most High God to all them that gave it" (Tobit 4:11). "Alms deliver from all sin and from death, and will not suffer the soul to go into darkness " (Tobit 4:10). God means this. A poor man became entangled in sin and left the Church. He continued in his prayers and gave alms out of his poverty, thinking that God might have mercy on him. And indeed God did, restoring him to the Church and forgiving him his sins. "According to thy ability be merciful. If thou have much, give abundantly; if thou have little, take care even so to bestow willingly a little" (Tobit 4:8). "Come, ye blessed of My Father ... for I was hungry, and you gave Me to eat" (Matthew 25:34-35).

PIETY. The virtue of religion is perfected by the gift of piety, by which we reverence God as our Father with filial affection. Right reason and faith know that the Father is the cause of the being and conservation of all that is. It is the Father's loving thought and will that give existence to everything; without His thought and will all creation would cease to be. He is thinking of us at this moment and willing our existence out of love for us. The Holy Spirit, through the gifts of understanding and wisdom, makes us experience the love of this Father, and through the gift of piety moves us to respond with filial reverence. This filial love of God as Father is yet more excellent than the worship of God as Lord and Creator (S.T. II-II, Q. 121, A. 1, ad 2). Often the soul that is seeking the Father experiences His closeness in and through creation and Redemption. It sees Him opening the petals of the flower which He has painted for its enjoyment with delicate art. It sees His hand lovingly moving the sun and warming us with its heat, as a symbol of the fire of His love with which He wishes to enlighten and inflame our hearts. It reverences the divine Lamb offered up in the Holy Sacrifice of the Mass, respects the Father speaking through His priests, honors all persons as the children of the Father, and lovingly assists the unfortunate. As the gift of piety increases in the soul its conformity to the divine will becomes a repeated "Yes, Father."

FORTITUDE

Fortitude is the infused virtue by which we are enabled to face death bravely. And as the part is included in the whole, so the brave man has courage in lesser dangers and trials; he does not shrink from—but faces—the difficulties that beset him. Therefore, attached to this virtue are two others which are more commonly called upon in daily life: patience and perseverance.

PATIENCE. In all the adversities that befall us in daily life, patience enables us to keep our peace and not give way to sadness. "Patience has a perfect work to do" (James 1:4). It works perfection in us insofar as we are perfected by the sufferings which it leads us to endure for the love of God. We might add that this is the virtue whose work is to maintain peace of mind. Our Lord tells us: "In your patience you shall possess your souls" (Luke 21:19); for impatience is apt to endanger them, betraying them into the underlying faults of sadness, anger, rebellion and hatred.

We may note in passing that the first step in impatience is sadness. But anger, rebellion and, finally, hatred lie in wait, ready to break through in progressive stages. Hence to forestall and conquer these, we need but overcome the sadness, the disturbance of mind, which we experience on being subjected to evil. This should be our firm determination.

Meditation on two great principles helps us to keep patience and to overcome the disturbances of sadness. The first is that nothing happens but that God wills or permits it. The second is that God wills or permits nothing but for our good. "To them that love God, all things work together unto Good" (Romans 8:28). Hence the Father will give the graces to turn to good whatever happens. It is our part to accept it, submitting our will; and this preserves peace by excluding turmoil of soul. Then our minds are clear enough to determine with prudence what we ought to do. If it is an evil that we can and should correct, let us correct it. If it is an evil that we cannot or should not strive to correct (for example, we cannot correct an incurable illness; we *should not* interfere in the domestic affairs of others in most instances) we must resolve to endure for the love of God.

PERSEVERANCE. Perseverance is a virtue that strengthens the soul in undertakings which are of long duration and which therefore need a special kind of courage. Such an undertaking is Christian perfection, for it is the work of a lifetime.

Fortitude strengthens us to face the difficulties of life. It checks fear and the desire to escape these difficulties by abnormal means such as by the indecisive stalling of repression and the childishness of regression. It strengthens the soul in the midst of adverse circumstances. It moderates anxiety and insecurity and permits the soul to face its problems first of all in its own mind, admitting its sins, defects of body and soul and external misfortunes, no matter how humiliating these may be. It checks sadness and depression and those aggressive and hostile tendencies that are so often a consequence of sadness.

Prayer, reflection and sound advice are often needed to determine which adverse circumstances are to be endured and which changed, and how such changes are to be effected. Granted prudent changes, some adversities will still be our lot in life; patience and perseverance are necessary to the soul to maintain evenness of mind amidst these.

It is most important to realize that fortitude and the other moral virtues are sustained by faith and love. The believer can say, "If God is for me, who can be against me?" and, "My back is against the wall, but the wall is God." Thus considerations of faith strengthen us in our love of God and in peace of soul amidst inescapable difficulties. Without such difficulties and adversities, there would be something lacking to our love, merit and glorification of God.

26 More About The Cardinal Virtues: Temperance & Humility

TEMPERANCE

Temperance checks and moderates the inordinate tendencies of the soul toward sensible good. *Sobriety* moderates drink; *abstinence*, food; *chastity* and *continence*, sex; *meekness*, anger. Many must fight a lifelong battle against desires for sensible good, a battle in which the virtue of temperance is needed so that the will may remain constant in its good resolution and so that the sensible appetite may be brought into subjection. Accessories in this battle are mortification and sacrifice; the virtue of penance cooperates with the virtue of temperance.

"Do you know that you are the temple of God and that the Spirit of God dwells in you?" Saint Paul asks of his converts (1 Corinthians 3:16).

"If anyone destroys (or profanes) the temple of God, him will God destroy; for holy is the temple of God, and this temple you are." We must respect a body which has become the sanctuary of the Most High. Again, Saint Paul says: "Or do you not know that your members are the temple of the Holy Spirit, Who is in you, Whom you have from God, and that you are not your own? For you have been bought at a great price. Glorify God and bear Him in your body" (1 Corinthians 6:19-21).

But this is not all. "Do you not know that your bodies are members of Christ? Shall I then take the members of Christ and make them members of a harlot? By no means! Or do you not know that he who cleaves to a harlot, becomes one body with her? 'For the two,' it says, 'shall be in one flesh.' But he who cleaves to the Lord is one spirit with Him. Flee immorality. Every sin that a man commits is outside the body, but the immoral man sins against his own body" (1 Corinthians 6:15-19).

Let us descend at once to particular details. It is well to avoid eating between meals and to forego delicacies of food and drink and to make other little inconspicuous mortifications in these matters. These strengthen the will and root it in the virtues of temperance and penance, while at the same time they break the strength of sensible desire. We should also value and willingly accept the inclemencies of weather and bodily inconveniences with which daily life furnishes us, for without bodily mortification there can be no real mortification at all. "I chastise my body and bring it into subjection," says Saint Paul, "lest perhaps, when I have preached to others, I myself should become a castaway" (1 Corinthians 9:27). Sensible desires are meant to be subject to the will and not the will to sensible desires. Persons who let their sensible desires lead them into sin are like dogs who allow their tails to wag them.

Chastity and *continence* both withhold consent to unlawful sexual pleasure. Chastity does this more effactually by bringing the order of reason into the lower appetite itself, which it subdues. Continence does this essentially, by holding the will firm against the onslaught of rebellious passion.

Concupiscence is like the pleasure-loving child who needs to be checked. Chastity checks and chastises concupiscence. If the child is allowed to have its own way, its self-will increases and it cannot be guided. So it is with concupiscence: indulgence strengthens it and weakens the will; hence conflict becomes more acute. If a man permits his will to be weakened and his lower appetite to be strengthened, he will be more and more harassed by his passions. It is not that chastity is above man's strength, but that it is above man's strength to resist the tendencies of the lower appetite and at the same time to permit certain unlawful gratifications.

Hence it is not prudishness which counsels the avoidance of familiarity or concessions in matters of purity, but right reason and the true good and peace of the individual, as well as the law of God. Concessions to impurity lead not to mental but to moral weakness: the subversion of the will to the power of the lower sense appetite. Such disorder does not follow upon the legitimate use of marriage-rights (indeed American wives need to be reminded of their serious obligation in this matter); in such cases the order of reason is maintained. God has attached pleasure to the act of procreation, by which two commit themselves to each other, but that act and that pleasure are lawful only in the state of marriage which alone safeguards their welfare and that of their offspring. To attempt to obtain this pleasure apart from the married state or while placing a positive barrier to conception, which is one of the ends according to nature of the sex act, is a serious sin. The pleasure attached to the sex act is the appropriate accompaniment of the total, exclusive and permanent gift of one partner to another. And this mutual gift, open to the begetting of children, associated with the formalities that the state and the Church surround it with to protect the family, is marriage.

To conquer habitual solitary sin, all the means of the spiritual life, reorienting energies to the true goal of life, may be necessary; prayer, spiritual reading, the sacraments, fidelity to duty, self-denial. It is a weakness that can coexist with true sorrow after each repeated fall. A prompt return to confession and daily Communion are great helps, especially if they are part of an integral program of the spiritual life. Above all, discouragement and fear should be avoided; these persons need encouragement, and the effort to help them to exert the full power of their will should be a positive, encouraging effort. God's mercy is infinite, and He will never give up in these cases; His patience is inexhaustible. Hence the attitude which should be fostered should be one of confidence of eventual victory. If the frequency of the falls can be diminished to less than once a month, the force of the habit is broken, and victory is in sight. The victory is the Lord's and He should get the glory; self-reliance would spell defeat. All the virtues work together, and without humility, they cannot exist—cannot be motivated by charity. Hence humility, together with trust in the love of Jesus, should especially be fostered, though in humbling himself the battler should not allow himself to be crushed and discouraged. Human beings have an opportunity to give to God more glory in this matter than do the holy angels, who, having no bodies, are not subject to human temptations; the chastity of humans is more glorious than the chastity of angels.

Of course modesty must be exercised; bad books and magazines, etc. avoided; and purity maintained by the prompt and vigorous renunciation of wrong thoughts and desires. Devotion to Our Lady as well as to the Sacred Heart are to be recommended. In some cases, this habit has been overcome by saying the rosary until one falls asleep. One must be ready to continue the first night or two as long as necessary. Those whose problem arises during the day must watch the moods that precede their falls; idleness, gloominess and discouragement should be avoided. Wholesome occupation, good human relationships, and the development of natural capacities are helpful.

In some persons this problem is connected with some psychological weakness, for example neurotic scrupulosity (obsessive neurosis) or other neurotic conditions. What is said above applies also to these cases, even though responsibility may be diminished by the psychological weakness (which is another motive for patience).

Meekness is a virtue which overcomes the tendency to anger, the passion whose object is revenge for an injury suffered. There is a righteous anger whose end and object is an upholding of the order of justice in accordance with reason and faith and which does not exceed due intensity. Sinful anger seeks the personal satisfaction of revenge against the injurer apart from the order of justice or it exceeds due intensity. Considerations which check anger and strengthen meekness have already been proposed under the topic of fraternal charity. It may be added here that when we are moved to anger we should direct our energies to the end of restoring peace of soul even though it may take a long time to accomplish this (just as, when we are moved to rebellion, we should concentrate on submitting our will to the extent of our real obligation to do so). During the intervening time we should strive to direct our attention to the duty of the present moment and away from the thought of the injury which angers us, at least keeping this thought in the periphery of consciousness, if we cannot exclude it altogether. We should also pray for the person who has injured us. Then, gradually, the disturbance that clouds our reason will subside and we shall return to truth and charity.

There are some persons who have an abiding sense of being injured and have a tendency to blame others; they rashly impute fault to those with whom they are angry. When anyone recognizes this to be his or her own case, he must make persistent efforts to overcome this unhealthy, depressing and dangerous fault. This may be done by making it the subject of particular examen (of which we shall soon treat) and by praying often, "Jesus meek and humble of heart, make my heart like unto Thine." Persistent anger leads to hatred, and deliberate grievous hatred of any person excludes from our own soul Christ and His love.

The virtue of temperance also leads to a certain simplicity in our external furnishings and clothing. It moderates our recreations so that while we take what recreation we truly need, we do not extend it unduly through self-indulgence and inordinate love of pleasure. It keeps a restraint upon a lively and vivacious temperament, checking frivolity and dissipation. It curtails unnecessary rest and sleep.

It is very important psychologically and spiritually to rise promptly and to give the first moments of the day to God. On awakening it is well to offer to the Father, in union with the Heart of Jesus and His infinite reparation and through the love of Mary, every thought, word, deed and suffering of the day; and to thank Him for preserving us during the night and giving us this new opportunity to serve Him and to grow in His knowledge and love, so that we may be closer to Him for all eternity because of this day. Then we may continue with our customary morning prayers. Vocal and mental prayer may be made in a kneeling posture. This offers God a sacrifice of the body and helps recollection, although no particular posture is essential for prayer. Sitting favors prolonged prayer.

Temperance moderates curiosity, providing us with that beautiful Christian virtue, modesty of the eyes. It restrains an inordinate striving after knowledge while sustaining a right application of the mind to study; for industry is necessary to obtain acquired knowledge, and the acquisition of certain knowledge is a duty. This "due" knowledge should be sought in preference to other knowledge, and should include an understanding of our religion which is up to the level of our intelligence.

HUMILITY

The virtue of humility is a part of temperance. Humility is not the greatest virtue. It is not greater than faith, which is the foundation of the spiritual life, nor than charity, which is its perfection, nor than obedience, by which the love of God fulfills His will in all things. But humility has a strategic primacy which accounts for the importance assigned to it by Our Lord and by spiritual writers. Humility removes pride and thus all the obstacles rooted in pride to our advancement in the twofold love of God and man. Then we are enabled to practice the virtues, all of which are included in charity, for when we have emptied our soul of the obstacles to grace, grace fills it. God resists the proud and gives His grace to the humble. Therefore we must strive to practice the virtue of humility. We shall succeed more readily if we seek to maintain ourselves in recollection before God in the spirit of reverence and submission as we have explained in treating of the gift of fear (Chapter 23).

God's command to Abraham applies also to us: "Walk before Me and be perfect in My sight." This helps us to overcome our native self-reliance, and, remembering that God is all and man is nothing, to surrender our will in devotedness, as we explained in treating of the virtue of religion.

Humility will be exercised by our obedience and conformity to the Father's will, and our conformity to the Father's will in turn will lead us to the practice of all the virtues. It would be a mistake to seek to make progress by keeping in mind as our plan of action a list of all the virtues which we intend to put into practice. Rather we profit most by keeping in mind Jesus, our Model. We understand the virtues better and they are more quickly engraven upon our hearts, when we understand them in Him. With Jesus and the virtues He practiced before our mind's eye, we need but seek humbly to conform our will to the Father's will as it reveals itself in our duties and sufferings, in the commandments, and in the advice of our director or superiors, etc.; thus we shall practice all the virtues. Saint Francis de Sales recommended the two virtues of charity and humility, explaining that all the others are connected with these and will be acquired with them.

The humility of the Christian is founded on faith. Humility is the truth about ourselves as we are in God's sight. Saint Paul asks, "What have you that you have not received? And if you have received, why do you glory as if you had not received it?" (1 Corinthians 4:7).

All our being, natural and supernatural, comes from the Father. Whatever good we find in ourselves, therefore, we should acknowledge as coming from God; whatever evil we find in ourselves, we should attribute to ourselves, even when it may not be voluntary and hence blameworthy.

What the creature has as its own is only its own native nothingness and, in the case of the rational creature, the moral defects of its sinful acts. For it is only the defect, the crookedness in the sinful act of the will which we can produce exclusively by ourselves, without the Father's cooperation (S.T. I-II, Q. 79, A. 2). Everything else requires divine assistance, even the external act of sin, and this assistance the Father gives because He has established us with free wills, and because of the greater good which He intends to bring out of the sin which He permits. Of course the Father's permissive will does not imply that He gives us "permission" to sin—on the contrary He commands us with all His divine authority *not* to sin, and the good He brings out of sin includes in the sad cases of final impenitence the return of the sinner to the order of divine justice in hell—proof of the divine seriousness regarding sin. Ardently does the Father desire to avert this outcome. He wants rather the sinner's repentance and love.

The truths which are the foundation of Christian humility, then, are the truths we enunciate when we adore God in spirit and in truth, saying: "Thou art all and I am nothing." Then we are in harmony with the holy soul of Christ prostrate before the Father in adoration, which counted itself, of itself, as nothing, and, because of our sins, sin.

"Christ … Him, Who knew no sin, He was made sin for us" (2 Corinthians 5:20-21). Humility leads us into the interior of Mary's Most Pure Heart; she esteemed her lowliness to be the cause of the good pleasure which the Father took in her. "He hath regarded the humility of His handmaid" (Luke 1:48).

And if we know that of ourselves we are nothingness and sin, we are strengthened in the midst of scorn, contempt, indifference, misunderstanding, for we can say in the humility of Jesus and Mary, "I am only receiving my due." As sinners, humiliations are due us; through accepting them we make reparation to the Father for our sins (and those of others); we give Him what is due to Him; we unite ourselves to the humility of Jesus and Mary, whom we are imitating. Jesus as our Redeemer made our sins His own and accepted the humiliations He received in His life and Passion as His "due"; He was atoning for our sins. If, then, we atone for our sins (and those of others) in our turn, we shall become truly humble: humiliations are the way to humility. We may think that we can obtain self-knowledge an easier way than this, but true self-knowledge will only be gained by souls who accept humiliations.

This teaching is necessary at all times, and for a special reason in the early stages of the spiritual life. As they begin to appreciate the gifts of the Father and to make a return of love to Him Who loves them, newcomers to the spiritual life may consider that they are excelling those whom they fancy (perhaps truly) are not following the spiritual life. A secret pride is easily generated; pride remains in all of us throughout life and must be fought right to life's end. This disorder in beginners may make life miserable for those with whom they are associated in marriage, family or business.

We shall speak soon of how the Father helps to expose and cure this disorder; now we will be content with pointing out that the beginner should grasp the truths upon which humility is founded and recognize that progress depends upon the acceptance of humiliations. The spiritual good growing in oneself one must refer to the Father as its Author; one ought to compare what is divine in others (the good in them) to what is one's own (the evil in oneself) and thus to honor the Father in humans, while retaining one's own lowly place before the Father. Otherwise one will hold others in contempt as lacking in spirituality and so place oneself in danger. We must also beware of speaking indiscreetly to others of spiritual matters, thus exposing ourselves to an increase of secret vanity and pride and to making the esteem of others a partial motive for our spiritual practices, to our own detriment. Vain discussion of the higher states of prayer and of controversial opinions should also be avoided.

Humility leads us to cut off systematically the excessive efforts which we make to convince ourselves and others of our own intrinsic worth. It leads us to a measure of silence, for there is a time to speak and a time to be silent, and undue speech, as the humble person realizes, is not without sin.

Saint James tells us that the tongue is a member no one can tame. "It inflames the wheel of our nativity, being set on fire by hell" (James 3:6). The wheel of our nativity is the wheel of the seven capital sins which engender many other sins. We shall fall into these sins to which we are prone when we begin to speak too much: lies, boasting, murmuring, criticism, complaining, detraction, and so forth. Our envy, jealousy, anger, sensuality, sloth, pride and vanity will express themselves. Furthermore, Our Lord said that we shall be judged for every useless word that we speak. But rightly ordered words used in charity and recreation are not useless.

Silence is also important because speech can so readily empty the heart of devotion. Silence is the seal of love which keeps us close to the divine Master and preserves in our souls the graces we have received.

Humility also overcomes envy and jealousy, leading us to rejoice charitably in the good of our neighbor as if it were our own, for we are one in Christ. Humility inclines us to see the virtues of our neighbors rather than their defects; by it we are inclined to esteem and respect them rather than to criticize and detract from them. Humility takes from us the desire to elevate ourselves by belittling others.

Neither does the truly humble person belittle himself unduly. First, in his or her own mind, he (or she) is disposed to acknowledge all the value he has, for if he does not he cannot be grateful to its Author, as he ought. She does not exaggerate but neither does she minimize, although this would be more in keeping with humility than exaggeration.

Were one to belittle oneself in words by denying that one has some good that one knows oneself to have, or by affirming of oneself some evil or defect which one knows oneself not to have, one would lie. But, without violating truth, one can conceal the greater things in oneself, while revealing or affirming the lesser things, and this is in accordance with humility (S.T. II-II, Q. 109, A. 4; Q. 113, A. 1).

HUMILITY AND SELF-CONFIDENCE: THE VIRTUE OF MAGNAMINITY. It may seem to some that humility paralyzes the soul; sometimes it is pressed to the point where it does; then it is no longer humility. Some persons, often of real value, are naturally diffident of themselves; they may also be indecisive, fearful of taking the initiative, and easily discouraged or saddened. The truths on which humility is founded seem to such persons to confirm their doubts about themselves, and hence to leave them in the rut of their native tendencies. Such persons need to recall that just as there is an ordered self-love which is part of charity, so there is an ordered self-confidence which arises from humility, from truthful acknowledgment of the good one finds in oneself, and this self-confidence Saint Thomas assigns to *magnanimity* (S.T. II-II, Q. 129, A. 6, esp. ad 1). This acknowledgment helps diffident persons to stand firm in their own mind and in their activity when faced with difficulties and opposition, and not to give in to the tendency of their nature to doubt themselves, or to withdraw. They need to be self-assured, to take into account their assets, to have that confidence in themselves and in their opinions which correspond to the truth. In being self-assured they will do themselves violence, overcome their native diffidence; they will practice humility and simplicity; and they will glorify God as the Author of the good they acknowledge in themselves, and in Him they will rest.

Diffident persons tend naturally to efface themselves. As Pope Pius XII pointed out in an address to the Fifth International Congress on Psychotherapy and Clinical Psychology, on April 13, 1953, they need to realize that virtue is compatible with and sometimes requires not only self-esteem but also an orderly self-defense; all self-assertion is not egotism. This Pope said: "There exists in fact a defense, an esteem, a love and a service of one's personal self which is not only justified but demanded by psychology and morality."

True humility is joined to fortitude and magnanimity by which the soul while acknowledging that of itself it is nothing, says, "In Him Who strengthens me I can do all things." Pusillanimity, which makes the soul shrink from doing the things of which it is capable, is not a consequence of true humility. By true humility, as we have said, the soul acknowledges the gifts and talents which it has been given; recognizes that the Father has elevated it to a supernatural order, having made it His son or daughter (and reflects often on this high estate); appreciates the assistance of the Father's grace, and is not abashed in what it undertakes for His honor and glory and in fulfillment of His holy will. The humble soul unfolds and develops its supernatural and natural potentialities for love of the Father as a part of His service.

True humility, then, does not lead to a sense of inferiority, but heals the sense of inferiority which is basically a sense of inadequacy and of incapacity. Our pride, our desire to exalt ourselves, make us uncomfortable at the realization of our limitations. True humility, on the other hand, takes us as we are. It does not assert that we are unable to become or accomplish anything. It knows that the more miserable material we are, the more glory will be due the Father for making something wonderful of us; it knows no material is so wretched that His power could fail to make a masterpiece of it if only it is placed and kept in His hands.

Humility accepts the limited functioning of our capacities when these are hindered in any way, and awaits patiently the time when they will be exercised fully. Humility is content with the knowledge that we are what we are in the Father's sight, and is grateful to Him for all the good things it finds in itself, including capacities to be realized. It is willing to accept and work with the material the Father has given it. If it uses this well, it knows that it is on a par, in a certain sense, with those who, having greater capacities, are doing greater things. The humble soul has as its goal the fulfillment of the Father's will for it.

Humility is not by its nature associated with depression. Depression is a sadness at the evil which the soul finds present in it. Hidden pride complains, "How could *I* be such an inferior being?" But humility joins itself to confidence in the Father. The humble soul knows that by the two arms of humility and confidence it can embrace the Father and hold Him, even when it seems to be precipitated into hell itself. Humility and confidence are terrible to the devil, and are strong in frustrating his attacks; they generate perseverance in all manner of temptations and trials. Humility abases the soul before the Father while allowing the soul to bask in the sunshine of His love, in which it believes. It has confidence that through the Father's assistance it will be able to fulfill fully His will. Thus the soul that is truly humble does not lose itself in endless introspection, but turns confidently to the Father and, mindful also of all His benefits, which it frequently recalls, it gives Him thanks while hoping for even greater assistance. The development of Christian humility, therefore, relieves the soul of the sense of inferiority and inadequacy.

Confidence in the Father and fortitude increase as undue self-reliance and self-confidence decrease. As we have explained in treating of devotion and self-surrender, undue self-confidence hinders the soul from giving itself completely to God and from realizing in Him the strength and power of grace. Therefore the awareness of one's powerlessness, frailty, failure, is a springboard to the Father, if one accepts it, and accepts also the power of Christ's grace and resolves to cooperate with His will, which is our sanctification.

All the virtues are contained in an eminent manner in love, which is the form of them all but does not excuse from the exercise of any. Love bases itself on faith, strengthens itself by hope, purifies itself by humility and patience in sufferings, exercises itself in obedience and justice. The practice of the presence of the Father keeps the soul under the influence of the Holy Spirit so that all its actions may proceed from love. This presence is strengthened by daily-renewed periods of prayer.

27 Progress in the Virtues & Gifts; The Particular Examen

The virtues and the gifts are a supernatural organism given us together with sanctifying grace. For purposes of discussion, the virtues can be treated separately; in operation several work together much as the parts of a motor work together in propelling a car. Thus all supernatural acts proceed from belief in God, and from love of God; to be virtuous they must also be reasonable and humble. Acts which fulfill what is due to God or others proceed from justice and its annexed virtues; acts which are made despite inordinate desires or fears or which withstand them, proceed from the virtues of temperance or fortitude.

The gifts of the Holy Spirit are present in all souls in the state of grace. As the soul advances in the practice of virtue, in detachment and in purity, the Holy Spirit works more frequently through His gifts.

The virtues work by the human mode of reasoning leading to willing, whereas the Holy Spirit, through the gifts, works by a divine mode, directly enlightening the mind and moving the will. It is much like rowing a sailboat; from time to time a wind arises and catches the sails and propels the boat, then the oarsmen are carried along with no effort of their own. The Holy Spirit breathes where He wills, enlightening the mind with wisdom, understanding, knowledge and counsel, strengthening the will with fortitude, moving the soul with the reverence of piety and filial fear. The gifts are like the sails, spread out by detachment, mortification and docility, to catch the wind of the Spirit when it blows.

The understanding of the spiritual life is fostered not only by a knowledge of the supernatural organism with which we are endowed by the redeeming grace of Christ, but also by insight into its development. We are elevated to a supernatural state of sanctifying grace which casts out original sin from the essence of the soul and takes its place, making us pleasing to the Father, partakers of His divine nature, His children. The infused virtues and the gifts of the Holy Spirit begin the healing of the wounds of original sin, which progresses as we act in accordance with them, as we imitate Jesus, or as Saint Paul puts it, as we walk in the Spirit. Faith heals our ignorance of the divine things we need to know. Charity heals the malice of our wills, leading us to love God as our last end, and to love Him more than ourselves, something that wounded nature cannot do without the help of grace (S.T. I-II, Q. 109, A. 3). Fortitude, with its attendant virtues of patience and perseverance, heals the wound of weakness; temperance checks concupiscence, anger and pride, and keeps the lower appetite under the domain of right reason.

Thus our faculties are strengthened. The remnants of sin remain in us so that, embracing the struggle, we may merit and advance in the virtues and in the healing of our soul. We must lay it well to heart; this struggle is necessary; unless it is undertaken, there can be no perseverance in the state of grace nor progress in the spiritual life.

The gifts of the Holy Spirit complete the supernatural endowment, making us amenable to the breath of the Spirit Who sees our needs as we do not, and moves us to acts pleasing the Father, giving us the special help we need to persevere and grow in divine grace.

This supernatural endowment remains unused to a great extent by many Christians. It remains like a buried talent undeveloped in the soul which continues to follow its natural tendencies dominated by its predominant fault, which is elicited by certain patterns of circumstances, and which mobilizes the energies of the soul and commands its powers. The activity of such a soul remains the same even though it receives additional grace through the continued reception of the sacraments. It is not living in accordance with this grace nor with the virtues which it has received, and it will continue to stagnate until it undergoes a spiritual awakening, until it determines sincerely to deny itself, to put off the old man and to put on the new.

On the other hand, the soul that embraces the spiritual life in earnest begins to live in accordance with its supernatural endowment of virtues and gifts. Charity begins to dominate the activities of the soul. In prayer, charity believes, hopes, loves and worships God; in social relations, charity is kind and gives each one his due. With regard to self, charity is humble, sober, continent; in the face of danger, it is brave; in annoyance, patient; under injuries, meek. Thus charity exercises all the virtues in accordance with the circumstances in which the soul is placed. As progress continues, the soul learns to know its predominant fault and the pattern of circumstances which elicit it, and fights against it, so that it can maintain itself and its conduct more unbrokenly under the influence of reason and faith. "Complexes"—emotional attitudes which resist reason—resemble the predominant fault in their action, are often connected with it, and are overcome in the same manner.

The quickest and most efficacious way of growing in all the virtues and in adapting oneself rightly, i.e. virtuously, to all circumstances of life is through the earnest cultivation of the spiritual life. Through the soul's application to God in prayer, spiritual reading, self-denial, mortification, good works and conformity to the Father's will, the growth of charity is greatly accelerated and with charity all the virtues grow.

As the Father leads the soul into dryness, He purges it of many of its faults and evil tendencies through the passive purifications of which we will soon treat briefly. These purifications complete the action of prayer, mortification and the practice of virtue in removing the hidden obstacles to the growth of charity.

With the growth of the virtues (connected with each other and the gifts as they are), grow the gifts, and the mode of action of the soul changes. The Holy Spirit's own immediate action in the soul's life becomes more pronounced as the soul is moved more and more through the gifts. Perhaps the principal purpose of the passive purification is to facilitate this change. This development of the action of the Holy Spirit depends upon the soul's fidelity: patient, trusting perseverance in the trial of the passive purification, docility to His inspiration, fidelity to its spiritual exercises and to the practice of mortification and self-denial so that it may fulfill all its duties out of love of Jesus.

To be truly docile to the Holy Spirit, it is necessary that the soul check its tendency to act through its own natural spirit and temperament, and that it become and remain detached from all things: that is, free from inordinate voluntary attachment. If the Father makes the soul aware of a habitual inordinate attachment, the soul must show itself willing to make whatever sacrifice the Father may demand and so rid itself of that attachment. But sometimes it is not the Father but the devil who asks for some imprudent or great sacrifice with the intention of discouraging the soul.[1] Here reflection and advice may be needed to discern what is the Father's will and what is not; imprudent commitments ought to be avoided. The sacrifice of something legitimate or good which the soul does not seem to have the strength to undertake, may not be a sacrifice asked by the Father at all, or not at this time. Sometimes the Holy Spirit wishes only to elicit readiness to make the sacrifice without requiring the actual sacrifice itself, as in the case of Abraham who was ready at God's bidding to sacrifice Isaac.

The soul has been exercised in the practice of the infused virtues before the change in its mode of acting occurs. And then it is not accomplished all at once, but over a prolonged period of time. When the Holy Spirit does not act through the gifts, the person acts through the infused virtues. In the case of the action of the Holy Spirit, the person experiences sudden, peaceful and unpremeditated enlightenment,

---

[1] Cf. Dom Eugene Boylan, O.C.S.O., *The Spiritual Life of the Priest* (Westminster, Md: Newman, 1947), p. 20.

solution of doubts and difficulties, strength in the will, reverence for divine things, the desire to remain still in the Father's presence in prayer, etc. In the case of the person's action through the infused virtues, he or she arouses himself or herself to acts through the human manner of placing considerations or reasonings based on faith and right reason, which motivate the will to the act proposed by the intelligence.

The period of the proficient is a period intermediate between that of the beginner and the perfect. It is in fact the period of transition from the mode of prayer and action principally through the infused virtues, which characterizes the beginner, to the mode of prayer and action chiefly through the gifts of the Holy Spirit, which characterizes the perfect. Still it should be noted that sometimes beginners, in the stage of sensible consolation when they are being led by grace to embrace the spiritual life, are moved passively through the gifts by the Holy Spirit Who takes them under His wings, or to speak in another metaphor, Who takes them in His arms and carries them. Furthermore, the Father acts through the gifts from time to time in the case of all who are in the state of grace. Finally, *He* is the sovereign Master and varies His action as He pleases, although ordinarily following a certain order in the conferring of the graces of the spiritual life.

Growth in the spiritual life is possible to all, including the layman living in the world. The supernatural organism is given to all Christians by the sacrament of Baptism. Its development is a progress in charity to whose perfection all are obliged to tend by the First Commandment. Without spiritual exercises and a program of the spiritual life everyone encounters difficulty in promoting the welfare of his soul and in growing in the spiritual life, whether he is a layman, cleric or religious. We are approaching a summary of the elements that such a program should contain.

Here we have spoken of progress in the spiritual life. Now we wish to say, as we shall say again, that this progress is not necessarily felt or understood as such. Indeed as the soul makes progress it becomes more aware of its deficiencies; it loses the sensible devotion it experienced; it no longer derives sensible fruit from meditation as it formerly did when companionship with Jesus in prayer was so evident. It seems to itself much less devoted to the things of God for which it may now feel a repugnance, although it is conscious of a more or less constant painful desire for God and effort to please Him. In short, it believes sincerely that it is going backwards; perhaps it is even tempted to think it is abandoned by the Father, a temptation that occurs to those who are making true progress. The Father does not allow the soul whose well-being He is promoting to feel unduly satisfied with itself. But all that is required to make true progress is perseverance in the effort and in the practices whereby one is striving rightly to give oneself to God despite the temptations, the dryness, and the apparent coldness of the soul toward Him. The constant desire to please God, together with real effort to do so, is always in fact pleasing to Him. It is true love and a certain possession of Him in which the soul can and should rejoice. For when God is desired, He is loved; in being loved, He is possessed; and in being possessed, He may be enjoyed by the soul with rejoicing.

Before concluding this chapter, we wish to speak briefly on the virtues of those who are not in the state of grace. We shall then better value the spiritual life.

All have certain happy natural inclinations of temperament which they are apt to mistake for virtues. In addition, in those who are not in the state of grace, there may be certain acquired virtues, such as industriousness, honesty, temperance. However, in them the intention which refers acts of these virtues to God is absent because of the absence of charity and so these virtues are imperfect; the full assemblage of the virtues is also absent. These souls cannot rise above a certain basic egotism, cannot love God more than themselves. But in the act of their acquired virtues, their motive is elevated to the level of right reason. In such souls one often notes a certain naturalness in their mode of action, sometimes a more or less unmitigated selfishness that may resemble candor and sincerity and which may therefore have a certain attractiveness. This is also noted in souls in a state of grace for a time, but who do not embrace the struggle with the tendencies required for perseverance in the state of grace.

In connection with this topic of natural virtue, we may remark that the object of psychotherapy which seeks to relieve the symptoms of the less serious mental disturbances, is to lead the sufferer to replace his faulty mechanism of response by one that is in accord with right reason; in brief, its object is natural virtue as a remedy for the defective symptom-laden mode of response—which is a very real and important accomplishment.

The psychotherapist with a full understanding of natural virtue is aware that among them is included the virtue of religion: the acknowledgment of the pre-eminence of God and the honor which man as a reasonable being owes Him. The psychotherapists who understand also the order of grace, realize that they are freeing their patients from obstacles to grace by removing defective and unreasonable attitudes and modes of response, and that the more freely grace acts in their patients the more their mental health is benefited. In the chapter "Religion and Psychiatry" of Vandervelde and Odenwald's *Psychiatry and Catholicism*[1] a pertinent account is given of the discoveries of the European existential analysts who have found repressed religious tendencies in the unconscious of irreligious patients. These analysts recognize the therapeutic importance of helping their patients to integrate these repressed tendencies into their conscious lives, which thereby gain purposefulness and balance.

THE PARTICULAR EXAMEN

The particular examen, unlike the general examination of conscience, has for its object one particular fault which we wish to correct or a particular virtue which we wish to practice. It is made ordinarily before the noonday meal. A good subject is the weakest point of the soul, the predominant fault against which we are fighting, or the particular virtue opposed thereto which we realize is most necessary at the time. This subject may be retained for a varying length of time as, for example, a month or longer. Praying for the help of grace, we spend one or two minutes noting in God's presence the frequency of this fault since our last examen; we reflect on the means we should take, propose to act as we should in the circumstances we foresee; begging God's help, we make resolutions and thank Him for the improvement that we notice. All these acts need not be elicited in each examen. A review of the capital sins and of the virtues may

[1] New York: McGraw-Hill, 1957, 2nd ed., p. 179.

reveal to us what root defect is responsible for our falls or what particular virtue we are most lacking, and so may provide the subject for our particular examen. Or the subject may be some practice, such as that of the presence of God, of making aspirations, of doing and suffering all for love of Jesus, or of uniting all one's acts and sufferings with His infinite reparation.

28 True Devotion; The Faculties; Temptation; Retreats

DEVOTION is a promptitude of the will to do the things that are pleasing to the Father; it resides essentially in the will. Sensible devotion, on the contrary, is a *sensible pleasure* in the things of God. This sensible pleasure makes the soul eager to perform its spiritual and religious exercises and duties; it is often given by the Father to beginners in the spiritual life. Under its influence they devote themselves so whole-heartedly to God that they begin to think that they are on the verge of sanctity and that they are already practicing great virtue.

The soul that receives sensible devotion should make strong acts of the will; thus it forms good habits that remain when the Father takes away sensible devotion, as is His wont. This He does when it has accomplished its purpose of helping the soul to devote itself to His service (even in the lay state). He withdraws it so that the soul may realize its true condition, for it is far from sanctity. Then the soul feels desolate and dry and finds a repugnance to doing the things to please the Father that previously gave it so much pleasure. At this point, those who are guided primarily by self-seeking, or who are too readily discouraged, or who lack proper advice and encouragement, drop out of the spiritual life and abandon their spiritual practices. Others continue to seek God; they should realize that the prayer, spiritual reading and practice of virtue which is now more painful to them is more pleasing to the Father. Now they come face to face with the strength of their sinful tendencies; this begets in them self-knowledge. This state of dryness is also called aridity by spiritual writers; it may be the night of the senses, which is common in those emerging from the stage of the beginner as we shall see in Chapter 32.

True devotion is in the will and can exist without sensible devotion. When the soul experiences the loss of sensible devotion which is not the punishment of deliberate infidelities to its spiritual exercises or to the practice of virtue, it should not believe that it is abandoned by the Father or that it is going backwards; for this is rather a sign of progress. When this state is the result of infidelity there is a loss of interest and application to spiritual exercises; then it is necessary to renew prayer and spiritual reading, to repent infidelities to grace and to accept the new difficulties in the service of the Father in the spirit of reparation.

THE SPIRITUAL AND SENSIBLE FACULTIES

An account of the faculties of the soul will explain further the difference between sensible and essential devotion, as well as other aspects of the spiritual life. The intelligence and the will are the master faculties; they are purely spiritual in nature and are rooted in the immortal and spiritual soul. Our conduct and external movements are normally under the absolute control of the will; while the sensible faculties—the imagination, sensitive memory and sensible affections—are only partially under the control of the will.

These sensible faculties are the more perfect the more docile they are to intelligence and will; but they often rebel against the will as a consequence of original sin and the wounds resulting therefrom. Nonetheless, the will retains its absolute control over external conduct.

We must expect, then, from time to time, rebellion on the part of the lower faculties. Thus the passions, such as anger or sadness, may oppose the will which is striving to retain a contented peace of soul; and the imagination may present thoughts in accordance with the passions and contrary to the will and its commands. The will has some direct power over these lower faculties, as we have said, and even when they resist the will, it retains its control over external conduct. The person can and should fulfill his duties, not allowing his passions to unduly influence his deliberations or actions.

Sin is only committed when the will consents to sin; the rebelling lower faculties increase the merit of the will which resist them. This interior conflict and opposition, when the issue is clearcut and a moral principle is involved, serves greatly to strengthen virtue in the faithful will: the disorder consequent upon sin, which provokes this conflict, becomes a remedy for sin.

The importance of the sensible faculties should not be overemphasized. Such overemphasis tends to occur because the sensible faculties by their own nature are *sensible* and produce vivid and pronounced impressions, while the spiritual faculties of intellect and will are spiritual and their acts may be barely perceived. Nevertheless the spiritual faculties are the ones which by the very constitution of human nature are in control. The will can apply the intellect to judge according to truth and real goodness; it can always redetermine itself, pursuing real goodness as opposed to the apparent goodness to which the imagination and passions incline us. Thus in prayer and spiritual reading the will and intellect are directed anew to truth and goodness and this renewal can be repeated indefinitely till the end of life. On the other hand the senses, seeking to gratify themselves with pleasure and to avoid pain, are changeable: now they seek this pleasure which has made an impression upon them; then, forgetting this pleasure, they seek another. In the time of sensible devotion the senses are amazed to discover how much pleasure they can find in the things of God, and it is their cooperation with the intellect and will that then gives the soul the impression of wholehearted devotion to God. But the Father knows that the senses are fickle and that the will is still weak and needs to be tried, strengthened and purified by the withdrawal of sensible devotion.

Because of the vivid impressionability of the senses as compared to the spiritual faculties, the soul is prone to underestimate the strength of its will when it finds the lower faculties in conflict with the higher, as happens when sensible devotion is withdrawn. But it is the spiritual faculties which have the upper hand. They will remain in control against the onslaught of temptation, if we direct them to our true good, while relying on the Father's grace.

This doctrine concerning the sensible and spiritual faculties is important not only for understanding true devotion but also in combatting temptations of the flesh, scrupulosity and other neurotic tendencies, all of which have their roots in the sensible faculties but gain strength through confusion of mind and weakness of will. The vivacity of these sensible faculties and the pleasure they take in sensible things (regardless of whether they are morally good or evil) make the soul think at times that it has given consent of the will and has sinned. The soul has an experience of its will, true, but this experience is not so sensible nor so vivacious; it knows that it has not wanted to sin, so that there could not have been full consent.

The passions sometimes exercise an influence upon the conduct by way of the imagination. The imagination presents pretexts and arguments in accordance with and moved by the passions. Because of the secret leanings of the soul, there is a tendency for it to judge in accordance with these pretexts. Drawn by the passions and not sufficiently supported by clear convictions, the soul is apt to accept these pretexts and not avert to the advantages of following the right solution—the one in accordance with the Father's will and its true welfare. This failure may occur more readily if the conscience is burdened with overstrict notions. Then the soul intuitively fears to advert to its conscience at the moment when it is drawn by its passions to what its imagination or intelligence suggests as good (which may be a real or an apparent good). In the anxious, insecure soul with a neurotic predisposition, it is just at this moment that it may permit a neurotic mechanism—repression—to intervene.

Our spiritual powers are strengthened when we enlighten our intelligence with truth and determine our will in the love of the good, personified in Jesus and Mary. Repression and disorder are hindered when we take right counsel and quietly examine important and emotionally-charged matters that await our decision, frankly desirous of finding the Father's will and what is truly best; and when we foster a detachment of soul which fearlessly will acknowledge the truth. This will be accomplished and confusion of mind resolved by spiritual reading and prayer, discussion with well-informed advisors, or by a retreat. We must clear our minds of false views, enlighten them with truth, renew the determination of will to pursue the good and to suppress promptly and perseveringly the pretexts and arguments of the imagination, so weighty when they coincide with our secret desires. But we must also give a fair hearing *at the proper time* (when we are at relative peace and are self-possessed) to these secret desires, which sometimes represent right reason and the Father's will, but tend to be banished by an overstrict conscience which fails to acknowledge the good they represent. This overstrict "conscience" is sometimes *unconscious* and *not* the true conscience, as will be explained in Chapter 30.

TEMPTATION

Temptations are sometimes brought about through our own fault. This happens when a person does not use discretion in avoiding the occasions of sin and thereby invites temptation. Such conflicts should be avoided by circumspection and by generosity in sacrifice and mortification. Sincere and earnest resolution makes short shrift of the temptations and conflicts brought on by halfheartedness. Sometimes circumstances of life detrimental to the spiritual life may be modified. Thus certain friendships, reading, pastimes, place of residence or work may be of crucial importance. Open discussion with a good spiritual director or with Our Lord in prayer may lead to a wise decision.

However, there are temptations throughout the spiritual life that occur without any fault on the part of the soul. It is important to realize that temptations refused are meritorious, and that no matter how long they continue, they are not sins. Temptations and trials are part of the Father's plan for the sanctification of the soul. They make the soul more humble, more aware of its own weakness, more dependent on the Father and His grace, and more circumspect in its actions.

They also point to the weak spots in the soul and to the object of the soul's inclinations and attachments. Hence the soul can learn from its temptations and trials its weak points, and can strengthen these by the practice of the opposite virtues; it can identify its inordinate attachments and detach itself.

Temptations also come to indolent souls who do not strive to practice virtue. Temptations are then like the dogs which the shepherd sends after his lagging sheep to urge them onwards, as Father Faber puts it in his book *Growth in Holiness*.[1] To be delivered from these, it may be sufficient to undertake the practice of the spiritual life in earnest.

While resisting temptations humbly, confidently and perseveringly for love of the Father, we should accept them as permitted by the Father. The Father allows these trials and temptations to befall us because He has accepted original sin and its consequences. But He ordains these consequences to our advance in the spiritual life, and to the various advantages thereto which we have mentioned. In this sense, He sends these trials and temptations. Temptations and trials are a participation in the sufferings of Christ, Who also allowed Himself to be tempted for love of us.

RETREATS

A retreat is a short interval during which we withdraw from the world and our customary occupations, and under favorable circumstances devote ourselves to spiritual exercises. Retreat-houses are available for this purpose. In such surroundings and circumstances, it is easier for us to look into our heart, see where we are going, consider our life— its past and future—with new seriousness and balance. Thus we take stock of ourself, clarify our objectives, settle our problems, renew our energies, and eliminate attachments that may be sapping our strength, occasioning conflict, conscious or unconscious, and undermining our mental health.

When the soul is withdrawn from its usual external affairs and round of habitual thoughts and desires, it more readily receives the

[1] Baltimore: Murphy, 1854.

inspirations of the Holy Spirit. Obstacles in our path are then resolved in the light coming from above; decisions and resolutions of far-reaching importance for our spiritual welfare (and sometimes for our mental health) are often reached. Conferences, prayer, spiritual reading and reflection bear greater fruit when we are making a retreat.

However, although a retreat may help to safeguard mental health at the same time as it promotes the interests of the Father in our soul, it is not the place for a person to betake himself, or to be sent, because of impending mental disease. The exercises and withdrawal are suited for a normal person, but may have an untoward effect on the mentally disturbed.

Ordinarily, at least two or three days are necessary for a retreat; when this time is not available, a "day of recollection" may be made instead.

In "formal retreats" group conferences are given. In most retreat-houses, a retreat-master and confessors are available with whom we may discuss problems that are of special concern to us. It often happens that the grace to solve our problem comes to us as a consequence of our exposing it in this way, an act of humility and faith that is very pleasing to Our Lord.

It is well to make an annual or semi-annual retreat, if our circumstances allow. Retreats may be made to coincide with special liturgical seasons, permitting a fuller participation in the liturgy. "Family Retreats" permit husbands and wives to make their retreats together.

A retreat gives a new impetus to the spiritual life, and can be a potent factor in safeguarding and forwarding the life of grace. In virtue of the qualities of one's temperament and spiritual life or the nature of one's problems, one tends to have a particular period during which one can persevere fruitfully in one's spiritual endeavors without making a retreat. But if, before one reaches the end of this interval one makes another good retreat, one will maintain one's spiritual momentum. Those who have special problems may find that by making their next retreat within this interval they avoid a relapse into their particular difficulty. Such additional retreats may sometimes be made profitably at retreat-houses that provide "informal retreats," where retreatants have the help of a prudent retreat-master and of a schedule of spiritual exercises but where they also have ample time for private reflection, prayer and spiritual reading adapted to their individual needs.

29 The Last Things

Love is the strongest motive and the best. The teaching of Saint Thérèse of Lisieux (recommended to us in the brief of canonization of this saint by Pius XI, who affirmed that her mission was to teach her little way to the people of our time) makes it clear that love is a suitable motive even for beginners.

Love makes the soul expand and strengthens its energies, and gives the Father what He so earnestly desires to receive from us. Therefore we have emphasized the Father's love of us and the love we should have for Him in return. Our endeavor should be to make love grow in our soul and to make it predominate.

Nevertheless, charity can avail itself of the assistance of a wholesome fear—even servile fear. Saint Gemma Galgani, a great saint, very intimate with Jesus and Mary, declared: "I will dread the punishments of my sovereign Lord." She was determined to dread them, and she realized that by doing so she was strengthened against sin.

The person who is wholly without fear is apt to be abnormal. Intelligence shows us that there are dangers to be avoided. *Perfect* love casts out fear—servile fear—but not all fear, not reverential, filial fear, which is the fear of offending God and being separated from Him. Excessive fear is moderated by reflection on the goodness, love and power of God; such reflection engenders confidence and tranquility in the soul. In this matter the measure of prudence is needed. Considerations which produce immoderate fear should be curtailed if the immoderate fear cannot otherwise be checked and no great evil would result from this restraint. They should be used when they are helpful and necessary to strengthen our love so that we can fulfill our duty and avoid sin. Servile fear is often a necessary means to draw a soul from mortal sin to repentance, whereby it regains charity.

DEATH

When we look ahead into the future, the one thing of which we can be most certain is that we shall die. It is important for us to prepare for death now, and this we do when we embrace the spiritual life, that is, the life for which we were created and which has the Father as its goal, and when we pray: "O my Jesus, for love of You and in atonement for my sins, I accept the death which You have chosen for me, together with all its circumstances." This act of acceptance of the divine will in regard to the conditions of our departure from this world is very pleasing to the Father and very meritorious for the soul, which it helps to establish in serenity and peace.

Scripture says that the man who remembers his last end will not sin (Ecclesiasticus 7:40). The thought of our last end helps us to detach ourselves from creatures and to put our life in order.

Since the grace of final perseverance is a free gift from the Father, it cannot be merited. We should pray for the grace of a happy death. Continence also is a grace which requires prayer. We can combine the petition for these two graces in a beautiful evening prayer, thrice repeated, consisting of a Hail Mary followed by the ejaculation, "O, Mary, by thy Immaculate Conception purify my body and sanctify my soul."

JUDGMENT

Immediately after death the soul undergoes its particular judgment. The thought of this solemn interview with Christ, our Judge, should help us to overcome one of our greatest enemies, human respect. At that time the soul will be alone before Christ and He will judge it upon its merits. No one will be there to help it. It will not take into account what others were doing but only what it did. That others were tepid or sinful, that it was surrounded by a multitude of scoffers, will be no excuse then. If we frequently anticipate the particular judgment, we shall free ourself from the influence of the thought of others which holds us back from accomplishing our duty.

The remembrance of the particular judgment will help us to overcome our rash judgments of others, if we are also mindful of the words of Christ: "Judge not and you shall not be judged."

PURGATORY

All those who die in a state of grace are saved, but only the undefiled can enter Heaven. The Father's mercy has prepared a means whereby the defiled who have been saved can be purified. These are they who did not use the means the Father had prepared for them during life to satisfy for their sins, either because they died with the guilt of unrepented venial sin upon their souls, or because, repenting sin, they died with the temporal punishment of mortal or venial sin unpaid. "The night comes," Our Lord says, "when no one can work" (John 9:4). He tells us that there is for the debtor "a prison" from which "you will not be released until you have paid the last penny" (Matthew 5:26 NAB).

The souls in Purgatory are saved, and in them reigns deep peace and submission to the holy will of God. They are tormented by a twofold pain, the greater of which is the pain of Heaven deferred, the lesser the pain caused by the fire which binds and fetters their souls, according to tradition.

The soul separated from the body is separated from creatures and from creature satisfactions. Then the infinite longing of the soul for God makes itself manifest in all its urgency. There are no trifles with which the soul can distract itself; there is nothing but that infinite longing which, when its satisfaction in deferred, is terrible. Moreover, the soul is afflicted by knowing that it is through its own fault that it does not now see the Father Whose love had desired it to be otherwise.

The pains of Purgatory are purifying but they are not meritorious. They do not prepare the soul for a higher place in Heaven; its place is determined by the degree of charity that it had at death.

The remembrance of and meditation on Purgatory should beget charity toward the souls who can do nothing for themselves but whom a prayer, a little word from us, can free or help. It should also lead us to resolve to endure our Purgatory in this life, to make the sacrifice which the love of the Father asks us to make, which the practice of virtue in conformity to the Father's will requires. We should accept the humiliations and sufferings of this life in reparation for our sins, so that our souls, purified and strengthened, and deepened in divine love, may fly at the moment of death from earth to Heaven. If we act wisely, then, we shall have but one lifetime and not two— for we shall exclude a lifetime in Purgatory. In addition our suffering here will be meritorious and will "earn for us an eternal weight of glory" (2 Corinthians 4:17).

Hell

When we act, we should consider the end, the goal, to which our action is leading us. The end, the goal, of mortal sin is hell. The soul that remains in a state of mortal sin, unless it prays much, will fall into many further mortal sins, and in this condition may be surprised by death.

If we look through the Gospels for the references that Christ made to hell, we shall be surprised to find how frequently Our Lord spoke to us on this subject. It is divine love which teaches us the wages of sin. The Father knows that through the knowledge and the fear of hell many, who would otherwise not be saved, will be His friends forever in Heaven. We should realize, then, that it is divine love and mercy which desire us to reflect on hell so that we may not suffer there, and so that we will do our utmost to prevent others from such an end.

The Church declares that certain persons are saints, that they are in Heaven, but it does not declare the names of persons in hell. It does teach, however, that whosoever dies in a state of mortal sin has for his portion eternal punishment. In regard to particular persons we cannot pass any judgment. It is possible (and what is possible we can believe God's mercy accomplishes in some cases) to commit a mortal sin of suicide, to die refusing a priest's absolution, and yet to repent before the moment of death by an act of perfect contrition and thus to be saved. The Curé of Ars was divinely enlightened to know that a certain man who had committed suicide by throwing himself into the River Rhone was saved by making an act of contrition before his death.[1]

It is also possible to enter into a fatal coma in a state of mortal sin, and in this state to receive a divine favor such as a vision, together with the grace of perfect contrition. Father Hermann Cohen received a letter informing him that his mother had been saved in this way. The receipt of this letter—written by a woman to whom God revealed this fact—had been foretold to Father Hermann by the Curé of Ars six years before it was written.[2] Our Lord's words, "Judge not and you shall not be judged" apply here.

It is not unjust that eternal punishment be meted out to those who have committed sin. One mortal sin really deserves hell, though it is possible that no one who has committed only one mortal sin has been allowed to die without recovering the state of grace (or without committing further mortal sins), as certain theologians teach. One mortal sin is an act with sufficient knowledge and full consent by which the soul kills the supernatural life that the Father had freely and lovingly bestowed upon it. It is an act by which the soul drives the three divine Persons out of the living temple in which They had taken up their abode. If it dies in this state, it knows that the Father has not rejected it but that it has rejected God, and that for all eternity.

The Father does not annihilate such a soul, to which He gave existence, but He restores the order which it had overturned by subjecting it to Himself in a state of punishment.

The greatest pain of hell is the pain of loss, for even the condemned soul that has abandoned all hope tends by its very nature toward God as toward its last end. Its desire for its happiness is like a catapult whose missile is blocked each time it takes off, because the force of nature is checked by the will fixed in sin. The "pain of sense,"

---

[1] R.-M. Garrigou-Lagrange, *Life Everlasting*, St. Louis: Herder, 1952, p. 47.
[2] Hermann Cohen, *Life*, New York: Kenedy, 1925, p. 104.

before the general judgment and resurrection, is the pain that the soul experiences fettered and imprisoned by a material creature: fire. After the resurrection, the body which has sinned rejoins the soul to share in its punishment by enduring a fire whose flames are never quenched.

Even in hell the Father's mercy makes itself felt, for the punishment is mitigated by His clemency so that the condemned do not suffer as much as they deserve; their punishment is infinite in duration but finite in intensity.

Sometimes it is very difficult for us to realize that the sin that fascinates and allures us is as hateful as it really is. It is in Christ's wounds that we should learn the malice of sin. But when this fails to check the force of temptation, let us meditate upon hell. Then we shall learn what it is to our advantage to know. The wise anticipate the hour of temptation.

HEAVEN

We were created for Heaven, redeemed that we might attain Heaven. Jesus died, rose and ascended that He might open the way for us to enter Heaven. It is for Heaven, then, that we are destined, and the more we realize and think on this, the better our perspective on life will be.

Many object to viewing life as a pilgrimage, a road to another world. They want to do full justice to the pleasures of this world or they fear to be diverted from contributing their full quota of energy and talent to the building up of the earth. They wish their personalities to mature in all the respects which will fit them for their present life, and they do not want to chance an underdevelopment of their capacities for this life, such as might ensue if they set their sights on, and directed their energies to, the life to come.

This may evidence a want of appreciation of the grandeur, extent and certitude of the next world, an overevaluation of this world, or a lack of understanding of the consequences of "set your hearts on His kingdom," namely, "and these other things will be given you as well" (Luke 12:31). Among these "other things" are, in appropriate cases, the wisdom and energy to build up this present world in accordance with the Father's will.

If Heaven exists and can be attained, and then lasts forever, it is most improvident and unwise to neglect to give it the consideration that is its due. Nor does the orientation of all our powers, talents and energies to this goal diminish, squander or inhibit, in the long run, the development of these capacities or of our personality. Rather it gives them an unfailing, ever-present, and invincible incentive, such as nothing else can provide. Heaven and Heaven alone is worth all our energy at any moment—and this will remain the case for every instant of our life.

Finally, if we are Heaven-bound in our thinking, desires and activity, this will not prevent us from giving our full attention to the temporal aspects of our personal, or of social, welfare. Rather we will see these illuminated by God's wisdom and supported by His will.

It is foolish to imagine that because we go in for the longest range planning that we render ourselves incapable of shorter range planning. There is no reason why, for love of God and of His universal reign over all mankind, we cannot plan not only for our lifetime, but for the generations to come, insofar as it falls to our lot so to do. Earth, and the establishment on earth of a renewed and splendid society, is the more worthwhile, the more we appreciate our final destiny, which only our efforts expended in time can make into an everlasting reality. To this, intellectual, scientific, moral and spiritual progress contribute, nor can it be achieved without continually enhancing the beauty of moral and supernatural virtue. God is Himself wisdom and knowledge; science, progress, personal and social development are not stunted by a true and full allegiance to Him. If they are stunted, then there is something defective in the allegiance, something withheld which should be given Him.

Heaven is God participated, His happiness made ours, the enjoyment of the society of the saints, the fulfillment of our personal aspirations and capacities in a measure and manner inconceivable. And since the thought, remembrance of, and the desire for Heaven is so basic to the entire spiritual life, it has been discussed at the beginning of this book. For, as we said there, only insofar as we keep in remembrance the joys of Heaven will we understand the Father's plan for us, and His permission of the many evils in which we tend to become enmeshed, but which can become instead the means to accelerate our travel to the Father and to enrich our service of Him.

Part Six:

Mental
Balance
& the Degrees
of the Life
of Happiness

30 Psychological Advice

In Chapter 28, an account of the faculties of the soul was given. In this chapter, psychological advice will be offered, and, in the next, the role of grace in preserving psychological equilibrium will be discussed.

The integral program of the spiritual life has a mental hygiene value which is sufficient for the mental hygiene needs of many. For others, who are mentally ill, psychiatric treatment is indicated; and as we said in the first chapter of this book, the spiritual life is not a substitute for psychiatric treatment, *just as psychotherapy is not a substitute for the spiritual life*.

Between these two groups is a third, composed of persons who need help additional to that contained in a spiritual program, and yet who do not require psychiatric treatment. For them psychological advice which can be easily integrated with a spiritual program is enough.

Many persons are disturbed at certain times by anxiety, fears, harassing desires and thoughts, moodiness, irascibility, etc. These emotional states may be complicated by psychosomatic symptoms: inability to concentrate or sleep, dizziness, symptoms referable to gastrointestinal tract, heart, etc. Such persons may be unable to give their attention to their duties and obligations (which they leave partially or entirely unfulfilled); they may be disturbed in judgment, as well as in peace and contentment. Under this strain they may be subject to moral trials and temptations to which they may succumb.

A thorough physical examination by a competent doctor may reveal an organic disease underlying their distress: the emotions have a physical foundation which may be undermined by physical disease. (The medical world is now giving its attention both to the influence of the emotions on the body—to psychophysiologic or psychosomatic disease—and to the influence of bodily disease on the emotional balance. We need to understand all the implications of the union of body and soul.)

A psychiatric examination may reveal some serious mental disorder underlying these symptoms, and may lead to helpful or curative therapy. With any existing organic disease receiving due attention, and in the absence of a mental disease requiring psychiatric treatment, psychological advice may prove helpful. Sometimes, as has been said, a moral and spiritual problem is connected with psychic distress. This problem may range from the evasion of God and of one's true purpose and place in life to a concrete moral problem. In the case of fairly normal personalities, psychological advice often greatly strengthens their grip on themselves, and helps them to profit by a spiritual program, while the spiritual life and spiritual guidance renews their grasp on their purpose and place in life, and procures for them the light and strength to solve moral problems. The spirit of detachment from self-will relaxes the strain induced by the fixation of desires upon what cannot be reasonably and properly attained.

Spiritual guidance will include the correction of errors existing in the conscience, which may be too rigid and severe, or too broad.

There is a vast difference between the conscience and the "unconscious conscience," which exists in one of the inner senses: the estimative sense.

The imagination forms an image, for example, of a rose; the sensitive memory places a date on this image: "I saw that rose yesterday;" the estimative sense attaches a value judgment: "it was very beautiful." The estimative sense is the equivalent in the human of instinct in the animal. By their instincts, animals, without prior experience, know what is harmful or useful to them: for example, the lamb knows that the wolf is an enemy. The instincts are determined by nature. The estimative sense, however, because the lower part of man is destined to union with the higher rational part, is not determined by nature, but receives its initial determination in infancy and early childhood. Hence, the importance of the values inculcated in the child before the age of reason is reached, values which are communicated through authentic love, including much physical caressing—especially during the first three years.

This estimative sense cannot reason, but it can form a sort of *estimate* or judgment concerning concrete things. It lacks the flexibility of reason which can take circumstances into account in forming a judgment. The estimative sense, the seat of the "unconscious conscience," simulates our conscience and is the source of many injunctions, commands and censorious judgments concerning ourselves and others. We must learn to distinguish the true conscience from this unconscious likeness, and learn to ignore the unconscious conscience. Sound spiritual direction which corrects errors of conscience leads us to a greater reasonableness of conscience, and to a greater discernment of the dictates of our true conscience which is located in our reason.

To appreciate the nature and value of psychological advice, it is important to understand it in the light of the mutual influence of the powers of the soul. We are especially concerned with the relation of the rational powers (intellect or reason and will) to the sensitive powers (sense appetite and inner senses, especially the imagination and estimative sense).

First, the intellect and will may directly exercise an influence over the lower powers by intimating directives to them, for example, to restrain them; but this should be done gently, and without violence, and not beyond the point where they readily respond—we should never do violence to our *mind*. Since the imagination and lower appetite are not under the absolute control at the will and do not always respond to a direct act of the will, those who are suffering from a disorder of these faculties are undergoing a real affliction deserving of sympathetic and extended help, rather than the cursory: "snap out of it"; "it's all your imagination"; "forget it." This may help those in whom the disorder is very superficial; otherwise it does not suffice.

Secondly, the intellect and will influence the imagination and passions by suggestion and persuasion: by the thoughts and desires which the intelligence and will produce. These tend to reform the estimative sense according to reason as well as to influence the imagination and passions. Thus fear is overcome by thoughts of confidence, anger by calming thoughts as well as by the diversion of the mind from grievances and by attention to one's present duties. Mental prayer and spiritual reading and the discussion of one's troubles with a competent adviser have manifold benefits which include their influence over the estimative sense, imagination and passions by suggestion and persuasion. Misinformation and ignorance may be corrected, obligations clarified, difficulties which have previously hindered prudent decisions resolved, and this may greatly increase the control of the higher over the lower powers.

At this point we may take a moment to reaffirm the importance of doctrine and a philosophy of life on one's emotions, temperament, character and conduct. The doctrine a person holds (consciously or unconsciously) may be a *result* of his temperament and life, but it also *shapes* his temperament and life. Once the errors have been aired, exposed, resolved, a person's view of life and control of himself may be greatly improved. So a person with a tendency to anxiety who becomes a Christian realist, as, for example, on the basis of the doctrine presented in this book, may thereby modify his anxious tendencies. This important fact is fully recognized in, and is the basis of, Dr. Viktor Frankl's logotherapy.

There is no doctrine of life so conducive to the re-establishment and perfection of psychological equilibrium as that delivered by Christ to the Church He founded, and this truth will be examined in the next chapter. Those who pursue an integral spiritual program will progressively discover new aspects of Christian doctrine, which will replace their practical errors, with great benefit to their spiritual and psychological health and outlook. This mental growth serves as a basis for the unfolding of new energies in the will. We remind the reader of what was said on the mental health value of mental prayer. This deepening appreciation of spiritual doctrine, reforming erroneous views, occurs especially through spiritual reading and mental prayer in conjunction with the integral spiritual program.

The estimative sense, imagination and passions may *suggest* certain opinions and attitudes; thus in fear, a pessimistic outlook is apt to be engendered. To counteract this, the intelligence and will can utilize *countersuggestion* and *counterargument* (which is something more than autosuggestion). Countersuggestion and counterargument, as the work of the intelligence and will, should be based upon the truth and the good as the *intelligence* sees them; among the faculties, the intelligence is the final judge of truth (even in the act of faith it is the intelligence which tells us that there is a sound motive for believing).

This presupposes that we recognize the real issue raised by our emotions and imagination for what it is, that we analyze and resolve it. Then we may utilize counterargument and countersuggestion to enlist the support of our lower powers and overcome the opposition which they are waging against the intelligence and will. In countersuggestion the will embraces the truth which the intellect presents, and may utilize the imagination to represent this truth to itself in a more concrete and moving form. Thus the power of the will to engender affections (passions) in accordance with reason is utilized; it counteracts the power of the imagination moved by the passions and the *appearances* of truth and good. These appearances do have a certain grip on us by virtue of a repetitious trend of thought (apprehensive, angry, or gloomy thoughts, for example), and because we are disposed by our passions to give credit to them. Hence to overcome them, we need to repeat and develop the truth, as we do in prayer and spiritual reading, at the same time closing our ears to the discussion raised by our lower powers and which has been already analyzed and judged. That is, we refuse to dwell on the thoughts and emotions raised by the recalcitrant lower powers. The repeated thought of loved ones also is useful in stimulating some persons to follow a right course of action.

Thirdly, the influence of the intelligence and will over the imagination and passions is exerted through the will's command of the external members and external conduct. Thus we may perform an external action contrary to our feelings, and this will help to change them. So when we are unreasonably annoyed with someone, we may act kindly toward him—and feel better toward him as a result. This is not hypocrisy, as is sometimes *felt* to be the case: one is acting in accordance with the attitude of one's will and judgment, and contrary to the attitude of the imagination and feelings. So, too, sadness may be lessened by lifting the corners of the lips upward, trivial as this means may seem; tenseness and anxiety, by relaxing the different parts of the body including facial muscles, by directing the attention to each part successively; also by assuming a bold and calm posture. Pride may be diminished by kissing the ground; distraction by a recollected, kneeling posture; dejection by an upright, confident posture.

Fourthly, the power of imaginative and emotional trends of thought and the strain of preoccupation may also be broken by placing ourselves in contact with our surroundings by our senses; by seeing God's beautiful nature, a picture, a color, hearing good music, etc. When the senses operate it is easier to suspend the workings of our imagination and emotions ("conscious sensations"); a few minutes of this is refreshing, and allows us subsequently to reassert the act of the intellect and will in accordance with our duties and against the trend of emotion. Such means as these are treated more fully in *Achieving Peace of Heart* by Father Narciso Irala, S.J.[1]

However, the possibility of a repressed conflict is present in cases of emotional disorder; then complete openness with a competent adviser may lead eventually to insight and resolution: this occurs

[1] This book has been helpful to many. It is not necessary to make use of all the methods suggested, but to use what is applicable to oneself, and to grasp the principle behind the methods (as these principles are exposed above); one then can practice the principle in one's daily life. This book should be read slowly and studied. A list of helpful points may be made, so that these may be reviewed daily and so put into practice. What is said in this book about "brain waves" (and we could add, the improvement of eyesight) has been rightly criticized and could well be eliminated in future editions.

often in psychotherapy or in conferences with a sympathetic, under-standing and enlightened person if the conflict is not too deeply repressed. In the case of deeply unconscious conflicts, which seriously jeopardize mental health, psychotherapy with a trained therapist with spiritual values, may be helpful. This kind of case may be suspected, for example, in the engaged person who is thrown into a depression by the prospect of marriage—in the absence of any rational or con-scious explanation. We need more trained psychotherapists with a balanced spiritual philosophy of life for the treatment of such cases.

PROPER MENTAL and working habits should be encouraged. Preoccupy-ing trends of thoughts must be set aside. Interruptions in thought are necessary: the mind should not be always thinking; it needs rest, and so does the tongue; a proper spirit of interior and exterior silence is mentally healthful. Thus in the performance of simple routine tasks, trains of thought that produce themselves spontaneously should often be set aside, especially if they arise from pressure or are accompanied by tension. To escape such disturbing, preoccupying trains of thought, we may give full attention to our task, to performing it without ten-sion or haste, deliberately, with consciousness of the sensations in the members we are using,[2] from which we should eliminate tenseness.

[2] Psychiatrists have observed that the neurotic and those with neurotic tendencies lack the experience of a proper relatedness to their own body and are not duly con-scious of normal bodily sensation: the normal tone of their muscles, the swing of their limbs in walking, the stability of their body in standing or sitting, etc. Instead they give undue attention to disordered sensations and preoccupations. By concen-trating their attention on these disordered sensations, they are magnified, and also function as disordered, forming a vicious circle. A radiologist demonstrated how he could get the spastic pyloric valve (between the stomach and small intestine) of per-sons undergoing a barium gastrointestinal series to open by diverting their attention from themselves: asking them about the weather, the way they had taken to come to the hospital, etc. It would be better for many to become a little more conscious of their normal bodily sensations—at times—deliberately sensing their members and movements, and simultaneously breaking the thread of overemphasized trend of thought. How a paralytic (e.g., polio victim) must envy the sense of the tread of the foot, the swing of the leg, the power of self-locomotion, which the self-centered (and others) take so much for granted. So, too, with the use of hearing, sight, smell, etc. For instance, when unpleasant sounds (snoring) and other sensations are accepted, the disturbing effect they produce is at once diminished.

We should avoid that splintering of attention which occurs when we are rushed or under pressure, and which causes us to give our attention to the next thing to be done while we are still engaged in the present act. This is detrimental to mental health, and causes diminished control over the lower powers. The habit of recollection, and of doing what we are doing when we are doing it, is most conducive to the integration of our powers, and offsets this harmful tendency, so common in our contemporary life. To repeat, we should act deliberately, at a steady (not hurried) pace, doing one thing at a time, doing with full attention what we are doing.

Some of these reflections will strike many as petty commonplaces. Yet appropriate attention to small things by those suffering from minor emotional disturbances—even attention to bodily relaxation, body consciousness, singleness of attention and lack of haste—can have healthy consequences. When the psychological condition causing distress is based on a slight disorder, such minor advice (especially when combined with a spiritual program) may suffice to correct it. Then the soul, freed from its psychological pinioning, can raise itself to God or apply itself to its responsibilities. And this is the important point: such advice as this should not become a source of self-entangling introspection, of involvement with self. On the contrary, it should be used as needed to free the person *from* himself, so that he can direct his energies to his work, to loving and serving others, to enjoying the simple pleasures of his life—and to loving God.

The beauty and harmony of a well-integrated person's activity rest, in part at least, in its spontaneity. Dwelling on our psychological powers and their interrelations may become detrimental to this spontaneity and to simplicity. It is much better to be engrossed with God and His will, and to have our conversation in Heaven, as Saint Paul counsels; or, simply to take Our Lord and Our Lady as our models, and think of them and of doing what is pleasing to them; or to give our full attention to the proper discharge of our responsibilities. So long as everything works out smoothly, this is by all means the way to follow. And when psychological advice frees us to do this, it is surely in order.

We might make a comparison with the operation of an automobile. Without a thorough study of its mechanism, we can step on the starter, then on the gas, grasp the steering wheel, shift gears, and drive. Still, it is well for a chauffeur to recognize and be able to cope with a choked carburetor, a plugged gas-line, burned-out brakes. For this he needs to know something more than how to start, accelerate and steer. So we, who are more permanently connected with our faculties than the chauffeur with his car, can profitably study their operation, and have in mind psychological advice to be used (but not overused), when we find ourself in need of it.

WE ENTER NOW into a last phase of this psychological advice. This regards the decisiveness of the act of the will. Quite different psychological schools have recently affirmed the crucial importance of the will, and have coincided in their hints on decisiveness: the new European psychiatric schools (represented especially by Dr. Frankl) and Father Irala.[3] We shall utilize the hints of these writers in the framework of the psychology of Saint Thomas, as has been our method throughout. His psychology corresponds to the facts without distortion, and serves as the best framework into which to integrate a more detailed understanding.

Dr. Frankl tells of the remark of a paranoid schizophrenic patient who, when asked about the strength of her will, replied: "When I want it to be weak, it is weak, and when I want it to be strong, it is strong." No matter how "weak" the will is, no matter what vices it has subjected itself to, so long as the person remains sane, his will retains a certain mastery which nothing can wrest from it. The will can say "yes" or "no," it controls external conduct absolutely despite emotion (yet we must use our will to avoid the occasion of sin, lest under stress of its proximity, we "change our mind": the will may reverse its decision). It can exert an influence over imagination and emotions, as we have explained; it can apply the attention of the mind to what it chooses. Here, too, a certain precaution is needed: one ought to avoid dwelling upon thoughts and images that will arouse the emotions and lead to an imprudent change of will. It is wise to choose the occupa-

[3] Thus, psychosynthesis founded by Dr. Assoglioli. Dr. Silvano Arieti also has written works with this emphasis, e.g. *The Will to Be Human*, Quadrangle Books, 1972. Also assertiveness training, cognitive therapy, and affirmation therapy manifest the importance of the will.

tions, companions and circumstances of life which will conduce to the thoughts and desires we wish to have. Such a choice may have great importance: while one might become a devil in one set of circumstances, one might, through changing them to another set, become a saint. Even in the world one may build up a set of circumstances which will be an orbit in which the star of one's life rotates without ever ceasing to be enlightened and to shine.

The will by the very constitution of human nature has a mastery which cannot be taken from it, but which it may surrender. It works together with the intellect, applying the intellect to its object and act, subjecting itself freely to the results of the search of the intellect for what is best for it to will.

In previous chapters, we have explained how prayer and the virtues, especially true love and self-denial, exercise and strengthen the will. We wish now to touch on the means of overcoming indecisiveness and inconstancy. A decision means the choice of one alternative and the rejection of another. It should be preceded by sufficient deliberation (and prayer and counsel where needed), and followed by constancy, being put into execution at the proper time, either immediately or later as one has appropriately decided to do. Contrary arguments, the realization of the advantages of the alternative which one has duly excluded, should be promptly suppressed. If the decision is to be executed later, in the interval it should not be reconsidered; to offset the contrary arguments that crop up in the mind, one should rather dwell on the preponderant good effects to be secured which have motivated the decision. One must have the courage to make the sacrifice: one cannot have both of two contradictory alternatives; one must go if we are to have either. It is better to sacrifice one than both, as does the indecisive will.

Having made our decision prudently, we should consider the alternative impossible: that is, impossible for us in view of the decision. If the matter is a question of avoiding sin, if it involves moral obligation, then we should judge all the more firmly that only one way exists— the right way. This way alone leads to true happiness.

31

The Role of Grace in Mental Balance

We have discussed the psychological powers with which we are endowed, the disorder to which they are subject, and appropriate advice for curbing such disorder. But it is especially *grace* that engrafts into these faculties the virtues by which order is established and maintained, and through which they attain unity and the power of accomplishing their functions. In the discussion of the spiritual exercises (such as prayer), and of the virtues (theological and moral), we have pointed out their respective mental hygiene value.

The doctrine of grace, as it is delivered to us by the Church, shows us not only the way to salvation and perfection but also, at least indirectly, the way to mental health. According to Catholic doctrine, grace is a gift of *being*—an assemblage of virtues together with their principle, sanctifying grace—which operates through actual graces. This gift is totally opposed to mortal sin, since by it the creature adheres above all to the Creator, whereas by mortal sin he adheres above all to his fellow creatures and to himself rather than to the Creator. Consequently they cannot coexist in the same subject: "Wisdom will not enter into a malicious soul, nor dwell in a body subject to sins" (Wisdom 1:4).

According to the doctrine of Saint Thomas (S.T. I-II, Q. 89, A. 6), when a child comes to the age of reason, it turns either toward God as its last end, or toward the creature (or to put it another way, toward God or toward itself). If toward God, then it receives the gift of sanctifying grace. So also perfect contrition expels mortal sin and obtains the restoration of sanctifying grace.

Catholic doctrine holds that the human is lifted and elevated to a supernatural level, to become a partaker of the divine nature (2 Peter 1:4), endowed with supernatural powers and energies. This elevation of nature and healing of one's native wounds, after the age of reason, occur only on the condition of a repudiation of sin and a turning toward God—on the condition of perfect contrition for past sins, together with a firm purpose of amendment. The sacrament of Baptism forgives all past sins and any expiation due to them. The sacrament of Reconciliation forgives sins committed after Baptism.

Sins are not merely "covered over" by God's favor. It is not true that serious sins continue to remain in the justified soul, which God no longer imputes, because the soul has faith in Christ; or that through this faith, without any other adjustment of its interior or its conduct to what is right, a human being is saved. Nor is it true that once having experienced this faith, one is then assured of being among the predestined, one is saved.

On the contrary, the human sense of justice, intrinsic to one's reason, requires repentance and amendment of life and reparation for wrongs done. Nor does this view harmonize with the nature and wisdom of the Father. The Father's love must have a worthy object—even if, by a divine act of recreation, this object is *made* worthy. Moreover, the love of friendship requires a certain equality: one may love an animal, but it is not his friend. One must be elevated to a new state, a supernatural state, to be worthy of the Father's friendship; one must become His son or daughter. Sonship requires identity of nature; adopted sonship or daughterhood, a participation of nature. This is accomplished only when the Father makes us partakers of His nature by the gift of sanctifying grace, by which we become a new creature (2 Corinthians 5:17; Galatians 6:15). We are not worthy of the Father's friendship, but the Father makes us worthy and that, not by an "imputation," but by a new creation: "Unless a man is born through water and the Spirit, he cannot enter the kingdom of God" (John 3:5).

The greatest human happiness, then, does not require initially any wonderful natural endowment, heroic struggle or practice of virtue; it is a *gift*; the person is given grace and thereby enters into a mutual love with God. Whatever one's physical, mental, social lot may be, one's happiness is assured by this mutual love. And it lies within the power of one's will (sufficient grace being always forthcoming from the Father) to retain this mutual love by one's fidelity: here prayer for grace, struggle and the practice of virtue are required.

There is a desire in the human person for truth, for absolute truth, which is not satisfied by anything less. This desire is fulfilled in the truths of faith, whose certitude is absolute since the Father Himself vouches for them. And these truths bear on the most important matters: personal immortality, eternal reward, divine everlasting love, divine perpetual helpfulness and beneficence, the means of pleasing the Father.

Moreover these sublime truths are embodied in the events of the life of Christ, which can be pictured by the mind. They are truths which express the simplest and most fundamental relations and so are intelligible to all: man's sonship and woman's daughterhood, God's fatherhood, reward and punishment.

Yet the power to believe, like the power to love, is *given* to us, and without this gift, we cannot believe or love. So long as we do what is in our power, we will obtain this gift. By the power to love I here mean the power to love benevolently, beneficently—to love what is most worthy of love, unselfishly and sacrificially—to love God, and humans for God. This is love indeed, and true maturity.

While the acts of the theological virtues make a person conscious of God Who is their object, *humility* makes one conscious of the truth about oneself and of one's relationship to God and to others. Humility overcomes the natural repugnance to recognize painful truths about oneself and sets one at peace with oneself.

Penance enables one to preserve and extend this peace within oneself, and to pay one's debts to God and others.

Fortitude strengthens one to face dangers and difficulties calmly, *patience* to preserve one's peace in the midst of disturbances. Patience quiets anxiety by firmly putting the objects of one's solicitude in their proper place.[1]

Fortitude and patience cooperate with the theological virtue of *hope* which anchors one in the Father and in His will, and thus strengthens one to fulfill it. Hope routs discouragement and despair as well as presumption. It assures one not only of attaining one's goal, but of receiving from the Father all the means one needs to do so; but it leaves one the "initiative" to take all the means necessary for attaining this end. This virtue is marvelously strengthened by the Resurrection of Christ, which lights up the world to which we are journeying, and points out clearly the life which we will lead and the happiness of immortality. Something comparable to the Resurrection is effected in the spiritual person in this life as the powers and energies of grace expand and render him or her buoyant and triumphant over difficulties previously insurmountable.

The assurance of the communication of grace is contained in the sacraments, which conform both to the Father's wisdom, mercy and goodness and the needs of human nature. They unite two opposites: the sensible (being signs) and grace which is invisible and superior to the entire natural order; through these signs, grace is communicated. It is given *ex opere operato* (through the work performed by the minister). Certain minimal conditions are required of the recipient of the sacraments, otherwise there is an obstacle to the reception of the grace of the sacraments. And the better the dispositions of the recipient, the more grace the recipient will receive through the sacraments. But the dispositions of the minister do not place an obstacle to the flow of grace through them, so long as he validly dispenses them—be he holy or not holy.

Another safeguard to human nature conferred by the Father's plan

---

[1] Archbishop Ullathorne, *Christian Patience.*

is the *living* testimony to the truths of faith and morals, both in themselves and in their application, and this may take the form of spiritual guidance. As humans we have an interior and exterior life, and they are or should be coordinated. What we believe and experience interiorly should suffer the check or correspondence with what we sense and experience exteriorly. We rational beings have this check in natural matters, that is the basis of empiricism and natural science and the foundation of true philosophy. We need it even more in supernatural affairs. The Father fulfills this need through His Church. One's interior experiences and mandates, one's inspirations, can be checked against the teaching and advice of guides instructed in divine matters (and those properly instructed must be sought) who speak in unmistakable language, correct one's misinterpretations, and are watchful of the particulars of situations and problems, while respecting, not interfering with, proper human liberty.

Grace enlarges the vision, opens new vistas, integrates experience and knowledge of the natural and supernatural orders. Besides this intellectual integration, it procures a spiritual, moral and psychological integration. It reforms one's ideal and conscience, rendering it more sublime, sound and practical. It harmonizes one's desires and affections; provides powerful, clear and reasonable motivation; strengthens one's will; renders one's conduct consistent and constant; eliminates deficiencies; makes one capable of facing, acknowledging and fulfilling one's responsibilities.

The psychological advice given in the preceding chapter attains new significance in the spiritual life, which tends to incorporate it. The strength of the will is increased by the spiritual life and the practice of the virtues. After all, it is the spiritual life, the pursuit of Christian perfection, which is the true *education* of the mind and its values, of the will and its habits.

In this education, grace plays a healing and elevating role. The will is strengthened by little sacrifices and by the performance with full attention and care of little actions such as make up the routine of the day. The spiritual life proposes motives for giving this full attention and care to our actions, for suspending preoccupying and worrisome thoughts, for ridding our actions of their load of half-conscious repetitious defects. It teaches us to leave the past to the mercy of the Father and the future to His Providence; it teaches us to accept and give our full attention to the realities of the present. The present alone is ours and in it are focussed our responsibilities. By using the present rightly, we purchase an increase of happiness and eternal life. The spiritual life teaches us to accept the pleasures and pains attendant upon the right use of the present and to sacrifice on the altar of duty and charity those dissipating attractions and selfish desires which would disintegrate us and deflect us from our true purpose, aim and goal. It teaches us to accept the love of others, and to give love to others. The little pleasures enjoyed *on the way* are strengthening; pleasure made the *target* of our desires, weakens us and turns us off our path.

As we have explained, the lower powers are often at variance with the higher powers, which place us in contact with reality. The senses place us in contact with one kind of reality, it is true: the reality of the appearances of things, to which the nature of things is joined. But it is reason which penetrates to this nature, separates the accidental from the essential, foresees consequences and weighs effects. Now grace dwells in the higher powers of reason and will; it strengthens them, helping us to produce clear, true thoughts and judgments, and firm acts of the will. Grace makes the higher powers predominate, so that one's life, acts and sufferings may be reasonable and human. As the virtues grow and the soul is purified, this action extends to an ordering also of the lowers powers.

Hence it is that a fully developed neurosis, which involves unreasonable defects in the attitude of the will, is not compatible with sanctity, which implies the full development of the virtues and rectitude and reasonableness of the will.[2] Various reflections throughout this book bear on this point: the attitude of the reason and will to

[2] See Jordan Aumann, O.P., S.T.D., in *Faith, Reason and Modern Psychiatry* (a symposium by eminent psychiatrists and theologians, edited by Francis Braceland, M.D. N.Y.: P.J. Kenedy & Sons, 1955). See also Vandervelde and Odenwald, *Psychiatry and Catholicism*, op. cit., p. 298, footnote 6 (second ed., p. 356, note 6). Also note what Albert Pie, O.P., writes in *Vocation* (trans. by Walter Mitchell, Westminster, Md.: Newman Press), p. 108: "The expectation that grace and virtue will have a good influence on the unconscious life and that in some cases, where there is neurosis, this influence will have a genuinely therapeutic effect, is thus justified. Of course, it is not easy to foresee to what extent grace will have this curative effect. That depends on the severity of the neurosis. It also depends on the quality and intensity of the grace given and the depth to which it sends its roots."

neurotic tendencies and disturbances modifies these to the point of excluding neurosis (partially or totally), or its intensification or repercussions; humility, self-examination, self-knowledge bring to mind the painful and humiliating experiences which pride and repression would exclude from consciousness; and charity centers the soul in others and the Other, rather than in the self, makes us acknowledge and fulfill our responsibilities in action, suffering and conscious union with Christ. Grace actuates the reason and will, orders the emotions and actions, stimulates a due, appropriate self-consciousness and self-respect, a consciousness and respect of others and a due relatedness to them.

However, while sanctity and neurosis (in its full form) seem incompatible, sanctity and psychosis may concur in the same person, if that person has sanctity at the time a psychosis occurs. (Such, it seems, was the case of Monsieur Martin, Saint Thérèse's father.) Even in psychosis, grace may modify its form, or hinder its development, or hasten recovery. Yet here, even more than in neurosis, proper psychiatric observation and treatment are essential. Professional men and women of high religious and moral convictions and professional competence can offer great assistance to the mentally sick or emotionally disordered without subjecting their patients to risk of injury to their faith, morality and, consequently, to their psychological welfare. Sometimes they assist their patients to a spiritual reorientation and a more rapid and thorough recovery or improvement by their own example and conviction, to which their patients are often very susceptible (even those who have been and remain impervious to their own clergy). For in some cases, the religious conviction of the psychiatrist or psychologist carries more weight than that of the clergy, and psychotherapy can remove emotional obstacles to the action of grace. Then the patient is in a position to cooperate better with a spiritual adviser. Other persons give their full confidence to their clergy and are distrustful of their psychiatrist or psychologist, unless he is competent in the understanding of their religious and moral values and knows how to respect and safeguard them.

Just as the neurotic disorder may lead the patient to resist or misuse psychotherapy (and that is something the skilled psychotherapist is ready to deal with in the therapeutic process), so the neurotic disorder may lead to the misuse of the means of grace and of religion. Here the understanding of neurosis by the spiritual director will be of help.

The salutary influence of the spiritual life does not imply that the religious or clerical state of life is the solution for neurosis. These states of life, on the contrary, require normal personalities, capable of bearing the additional responsibilities proper to them. The neurotic has enough of a cross in his neurosis, and neurotic tendencies, without adding the penances and sufferings of religious and clerical life.

Paranoid personalities may also profit by spiritual development, promoted prudently, with an emphasis on genuine humility and obedience, yet they are not suited for clerical and religious life, especially not for the contemplative religious life.

32 Two in One Spirit: Degrees of the Spiritual Life

The living water to which Our Lord refers is the abundance of His grace which flows ceaselessly in the soul perfectly united to Him. It is well to speak of this union of love and the graces that are connected with it because this encourages the soul in its pursuit of God. On the other hand it is necessary to caution beginners fired with the zeal of immature haste that perfection is not the work of a day, but that it requires years. It is also necessary to lay to heart the danger of presuming that we are further advanced in the spiritual life than we actually are, since this would cause the soul to lose much ground and greatly hinder its progress. Saint Teresa of Avila tells us that it is better to think that we are not yet worthy of being admitted to a higher degree than to strive to push our way into it (Epilogue, *The Interior Castle*). We are striving to push when we imagine ourselves to be more advanced than we actually are; and thereby we lose the divine favor, for as Saint Teresa says in this connection: "Our Lord dearly loves humility."[1]

The true doctrine concerning the goal and stages of the spiritual life deals with deep and hidden mysteries and is difficult to understand without experience. This is because the realities referred to cannot be grasped in the abstract, any more than a man born blind can grasp the descriptions of what others see.

A clear brief explanation of the stages and degrees of the spiritual life is not readily obtainable. Here we follow especially the teaching of Saint John of the Cross, a master of the spiritual life raised up by God to guide us in the hidden things of the way to God. He was possessed of an eminent degree of reason, faith and theological knowledge, and was especially enlightened by the Holy Spirit through the gifts of wisdom, understanding, knowledge and counsel, operating in a soul of consummate sanctity and natural genius. The Church in declaring Saint John of the Cross a Doctor testified to the excellence and orthodoxy of his teaching and to its utility for the faithful. (Even so, his works are not recommended to those not already well-instructed in the spiritual life and somewhat advanced in its practice.)[2]

---

[1] Ordinarily it is best to read no further in books on prayer than the degree to which we have attained. Thus we receive the advice suitable to our present needs. When, in reading descriptions of successive degrees of perfection, we experience excitement in anticipation of finding our present state, we must beware of that inordinate love of our own excellence which would blind us to the truth and lead us to think we are more advanced than we are. Urgent prayer and a delay in pursuing our reading may be needed.

[2] While Saint John was enabled to generalize the laws of the spiritual life (God's manner of acting in sanctifying souls), Saint Teresa of Avila gave a concrete expression of these laws as she knew them through personal experience (and the experience of her daughters). Her teaching completes Saint John's. In Saint Francis de Sales and Saint Thérèse of Lisieux we have two later saints and teachers of special enlightenment, and we may understand Saint John better through understanding them. More will be said on this subject. The teaching of John and Thérèse, who follows him closely and with great simplicity, has more weight because of its conformity with the doctrine of Saint Thomas Aquinas, and with a long tradition, reaching back to the Scriptures and the desert fathers.

Jacques Maritain has well said: "Happy they who choose for their masters, after Christ Himself, Saint Thomas Aquinas, that they may thus obtain supreme communicable knowledge, and Saint John of the Cross, that they may be guided towards supreme incommunicable knowledge!" From his Introduction to *Saint John of the Cross* by Father Bruno, O.C.D. (N.Y.: Sheed & Ward, 1932).

Before going on to speak of transforming union, a few remarks about this and the following chapter may be helpful. In a short compass, the entire development of the soul is covered, and with such detail as may be helpful to many in different stages of growth or following different paths. For that reason, all will not be pertinent to everyone. In particular, details given in the footnotes may be very useful to some and of little use at the time of reading to others. For spiritual directors and priests, the entire chapter will be of benefit.

With regard to transforming union, it is well to note that this degree of spiritual maturity does not deliver the person from his or her fallen human nature, which continues to be a burden and a source of temptation, frustration and trial. One in this state may be more acutely aware of it than ever, and even to an extent which tempts one to discouragement.

It is well to look at this whole process of sanctification from the point of view of the Father. He deals with His children with the utmost gentleness, tact and consideration. He knows well that people extend themselves mightily to achieve success in various endeavors: sports, business, love, professions. He knows that those who extend themselves in seeking Him and His kingdom are the wisest. And He does not hesitate to allow them to proceed with the courage and generosity of deep and humble love, of which He Himself is the source.

Those who enter Heaven without such exertions of love and generosity are assured of complete happiness—but on a lower level. Those who wish to attain the highest Heaven, will have the Father's help in doing so. Each person in Heaven is full to the brim with happiness, but those who have striven for and attained a higher degree, will for all eternity have a greater degree of happiness and intimacy with the

---

This chapter will be found to be substantially in agreement with Father Garrigou-Lagrange's *Three Ages of the Interior Life*, which is used by laymen, seminarians and priests as a textbook of mystical and ascetical theology. Compare also Chapter 12, Grades of Prayer, of *Spiritual Theology* by Jordan Aumann, O.P. (Our Sunday Visitor, Inc., Huntington, Indiana, 1980). Increasing unanimity is to be found among the various Catholic schools of spirituality on matters which have been controverted from the beginning of this century. Thus Father De Guibert's teaching is closer to Father Garrigou-Lagrange's than was that of Father Poulain; and Father Marie-Eugene's than was that of Father Gabriel of Saint Mary Magdalen, to speak only of spiritual theologians of the Society of Jesus and of the Order of Discalced Carmelites.

three persons of the Trinity and with all of the society of Heaven. The more one opens one's heart to the purifications of love, and allows Love Himself to enter more deeply into one's heart, the higher will be that person's place in Heaven. For the larger will such a person's heart be and the greater his or her love.

A Cistercian abbess on the occasion of a feast day greeting, asked me: "Where are you on the ladder (of holiness)?" I replied in my thank you note: "I am standing at the bottom of the ladder. Here I expect to remain for the rest of my life. One cannot fall when one is at the bottom. But I shall continue to try to reach the first rung, and, being on the ground does not prevent me from aspiring to the heights."

TRANSFORMING UNION

The goal to which the Father leads the soul that desires to belong entirely to Him is, above all, of course, Heaven, where the soul is completely transformed into God, sees Him face to face, and loves Him with a perfect, constant, actual and unblemished love. The soul and the Father are truly then one spirit in one knowledge and love.

All souls who are saved attain this state in Heaven; some, however, only after the purification of Purgatory. But God desires that we be purified on earth where our purification is meritorious and leads us to a higher degree of glory for all eternity.

There are many degrees of the transforming union—not only in the increasing perfection of the soul in this state but also in the comparison of different souls in this same state, for some are placed by God on a higher path than others.

The transforming union is a union of love. It is characterized by a greater charity which results from the greater purity of the soul. We shall soon see how this purity is attained. In this state, says Father Alexander Rozwadowski, S.J., echoing Saint John of the Cross: "God and the soul give to each other total possession of each other by the union of love, consummated in the measure possible on earth ... two natures are in one single spirit, the love of God."[3] Saint John of the

---

[3] R.-M. Garrigou-Lagrange, O.P., *The Three Ages of the Interior Life*, Vol. II, p. 558, compare also Chap. XL.

Cross says: "The state of this divine union consists in the soul's total transformation, according to the will, in the will of God, so that there may be naught in the soul that is contrary to the will of God, but that, in all and through all, its movement may be that of the will of God alone."[4] And Saint Paul says: "Whoever is joined to the Lord becomes one spirit with Him" (1 Corinthians 6:17 NAB).

The soul in this state retains a relatively constant effortless consciousness of God, possible only because this consciousness is not the result of its own application but is infused. Because God acts on the intellect and the will in a most general way (to enlighten it and inspire love), it seems to the person as if this action were taking place in the substance of the soul itself instead of in its faculties. The soul dwells interiorly in this infused imageless awareness of God which subsists without the activity of its senses and imagination, without strain or illusion. Here the attacks of the devil cannot reach it, and it views the ripples and commotions in its senses and lower appetites as from a high fortress in which it is secure. Hence it enjoys habitual peace and tranquility. The Father directs and strengthens it in its actions through the gifts of the Holy Spirit; He watches over it with a special providence keeping it from sin and in the fulfillment of His will, not however, without the continual exercise of the person's free will.

Just as marriage establishes a stable and secure union between the partners, so this state in which both God and the soul have given themselves completely to each other constitutes a stable and secure union, one of expanding love and divinely inspired and supported service. Since God communicates Himself to the soul in a special manner as its own possession, the soul, appreciating this gift, returns it to God, offering Him Himself and itself in Him. So too the priest and people offer God to God, and themselves in this offering, in the Holy Sacrifice of the Mass.

Since the soul now dwells in truth, it is peacefully aware of its evil inclinations; and this is one of the advantages of this state. The soul is thereby constantly reminded of what it is in and of itself and hence

---

[4] *Ascent of Mount Carmel*, Bk. I, Chap. XI, in *The Complete Works of Saint John of the Cross*, translated and edited by E. Allison Peers. Westminster, Md.: Newman Press, 1953. Other quotations from this author are also from this edition.

glorifies the Father by humble acknowledgment of its own nothing-ness and sinfulness, which it resists, while striving to abide in the charity and peace of the Spirit of Jesus. It is supported by the long-held conviction that the worst of people (and hence itself) is safe in relying entirely and for everything upon the infinite goodness of the Father and the merits of His Son. It abides in the presence of the Father, covered with the mantle of Jesus, like Jacob who approached his father Isaac in safety and was acceptable because he was clad by his mother Rebecca with a special covering so that he might simulate the eldest son.

STATE OF BEGINNER

When one first starts out on the spiritual journey one may experience sensible consolations by which the Father teaches one that all one has been seeking up to now in the world He can give directly. These sensi-ble consolations, therefore, tend to wean one away from the pleasures of the world. One occupies oneself in time of prayer with such medi-tation as we have outlined at the beginning of this book. As one progresses, one's considerations lead more quickly to affections and to acts of the will, until these predominate (affective prayer).[5]

In the Charismatic Renewal, persons are often introduced into these sensible consolations and affections by the "Baptism of the Spirit," which is a new awareness of the Spirit and a new facility of prayer and attraction to spiritual things. This grace is a stirring up of the grace of Baptism and Confirmation in those who have received these sacraments.

This period of sensible consolations is a "honeymoon" period,

---

[5] One's affections become simpler and one tends to remain longer in a single affection or act of the will (the prayer of simplicity). It may well be that souls cannot maintain this prayer of simplicity without the assistance of infused graces of prayer, as seems to be evident from the descriptions of Bossuet and others down to the present day. In that case the prayer of simplicity (or acquired contemplation or prayer of simple regard) is a form of prayer identical with that which the soul experiences when passing from the purgative way to the way of proficients, through the night of the senses. The "prayer of simplicity" is not mentioned by Saint John of the Cross, who speaks simply of the transition from meditation to the obscure infused contem-plative prayer of the night of the senses.

which is very beautiful. In it persons feel that they are on the verge of sanctity, one more push and they will be in Heaven!

Eventually this period is succeeded by a period of aridity when the bottom seems to have fallen out. Then one feels that one more push and one will be in hell! Actually this aridity is a sign of progress, and marks the transition to the state of the proficient as we will soon explain.

However it is at this transition when aridity occurs that persons are apt to give up prayer, just when they are really making progress. More progress is made in aridity. The person is more aware of his or her native tendencies and is closer to an awareness of her or his faults, which is a boon, so long as one realizes that the mercy of God is attracted by our faults and not repelled by them.

The Father loves to exercise His mercy towards His children, and our faults acknowledged with the desire to improve, gives Him the opportunity to do so. This knowledge of our faults also makes us compassionate towards the faults of others, for we realize that the Father will have mercy on us only to the extent that we are merciful towards others. But before this transition to the proficient occurs, the person reaches the Third Mansions described by Saint Teresa of Jesus.

Those who have established the habit of mental prayer and persevered in it despite difficulties and obstacles, experience an increasing domination of faith and charity over their acts and conduct, which become well-regulated. This is no small triumph of grace, as is attested by Saint Teresa in the Third Mansions of *The Interior Castle*. She considers that such persons have reached this degree, while making use of meditation during the time of prayer. She encourages them with the teaching that they have now so won the divine favor that they will be able to attain even to the innermost mansions, if they will but allow the Father to act within them and not put obstacles in the way by preserving too human a set of values. They must rather honor the divine transcendence and prize the riches of the Father sufficiently to be willing to relinquish their grasp on those of this earth, and especially they must be willing to sacrifice their own judgment, their private views and their own wills, inclinations and tastes.

In the Third Mansions there is experienced a great desire to belong completely to God, together with the resolution to do so, and to live recollectedly in the presence of God throughout the day (but strain on the mind should be avoided, and one should freely give attention to one's duties). This determination of complete self-renunciation is the forerunner of further progress: of the night of the senses and of the subjection of the powers of the soul to the operations of the gifts of the Holy Spirit.

Often the Father deals in a special manner with those whom He does not intend to lead into the night of the spirit, because of their inability to undergo its sufferings or for some reason known only to Himself. The Father purifies these persons from time to time with the purification of the senses while encouraging and helping them to persevere in the spiritual life and to practice virtue. These persons retain the practice of meditation and affective prayer except when they are periodically undergoing this purification; then they find themselves unable to meditate and should remain at peace in the silent desire for God, or in the restful general loving knowledge of Him which they experience. Thus, for them, times of consolation alternate with periods of aridity (Saint John of the Cross, *The Dark Night of the Soul*, Bk. I, Chap. IX, XIV).

TRANSITION TO STATE OF THE PROFICIENT

At the time of transition to the state of the proficient spiritual persons experience a considerable change in prayer. They find that they are no longer able to derive pleasure and fruit from their meditations. They seem to be drawn to a simple, loving gaze upon God, resembling that of a peasant who explained his prayer to the Curé of Ars in the words: "I look at Him and He looks at me." Or we may say, the soul in prayer feels drawn to persist in its ample desire for God. Now these persons no longer experience sensible consolations or sensible devotion (sometimes this is lacking from the very beginning). They may be troubled and dismayed, believing that they are going backward. Now, too, they often experience violent temptations against faith, purity and patience. They are becoming more aware of their native tendencies (whatever these may be), of their weakness and sinfulness, of their native helplessness. If in the past they have experienced neurotic, depressive or other mental tendencies, they are now apt to experience them again, although with this difference, that now these tendencies do not exercise as much effect on conduct or on the will, which is stronger and resists them more effectively.

These persons may reproach themselves for their lack of devotedness to God, yet they are more faithful to Him than ever. Indeed, they cannot find pleasure in creatures and they are more or less constantly oppressed by a painful desire for God, painful because they feel so distant from Him. These are the signs given by Saint John of the Cross (*Ascent of Mount Carmel*, Bk. II, Chap. XIII; *Dark Night*, Bk. I, Chap. IX), which denote the transition from discursive prayer to a prayer of simple, loving attention to God without discursive (particular and successive) acts of the mind and will.[6]

The state in which such persons find themselves constitutes a trial which should be accepted from the hands of the Father with a readiness to endure it as long as the Father wills. They should pray for perseverance, continue their spiritual practices, trust in God and realize that all is well. They should follow their desire to remain still and quiet while at prayer, waiting upon God with a loving attention so long as they are unable profitably to do otherwise—from this prayer they will

---

[6] These three signs, in the order they are given in the *Dark Night*, are: 1) The soul finds no pleasure or consolation in the things of God, nor in creatures. This excludes aridity consequent upon recently committed sins or multiplied imperfections, for in such cases the soul seeks and takes consolation in creatures. We might add that these signs also distinguish the aridity of the night of the senses from the aridity of the Second Mansions of Saint Teresa, through which the meditating soul passes to attain the Third Mansion, where its habit of meditation (and of regulating its life by the fruit of meditation) becomes established. 2) The memory is habitually centered on God, with painful concern, because the soul thinks it is going backwards. This excludes tepidity, in which the spirit has lost its solicitude to serve God. In the night, there may be associated sadness (manifesting a melancholy temperament or depressive tendencies), which arise because now the lower appetite is deprived of all pleasure by the arid night of the senses; but this does not prevent (but rather increases) the purifying effect of this night. But if, instead of the night of the senses, the aridity represents simply a depression in disguise, the will lacks the promptitude and constancy in serving God which are characteristic of the soul in the night of the senses. This is especially manifested in its failure to maintain acts (not feelings) of hope. 3) The soul no longer profits by meditation or use of discursive acts and of the imagination, as previously; for those going on to the higher degrees, this inability increases rather than passes off, as it does if its cause is a temporary indisposition, as fatigue, illness, etc. Yet at first even in those who are advancing in this way, this inability may be temporarily suspended from time to time; then the soul should resume its meditations.

derive strength to deny themselves and to practice virtue. This trial is common among those who generously give themselves to God and has as its purpose to purify the sensibility of beginners of attachment to the consolations of God and of hidden self-love, pride and vanity. Saint John of the Cross says frequently throughout his works that the dark night of the senses is a trial marking the passage of the soul from the stage of the beginner to that of the proficient.[7]

At times such persons may find themselves able to profit by meditation and affective prayer; then they should do so, especially uniting themselves to Our Lord in His Passion, or talking simply to Jesus and Mary. They turn from these occupations to the simple and loving attention to God when they feel drawn thereto, and are unable to reflect, or if they find reflection distasteful. Before terminating their prayer, they may make acts of self-renunciation and detachment. These people may rightly and profitably hold to the thought that in this dryness they are within the Sacred Hearts of Jesus and Mary and they may persevere in a prayer which consists simply in the mute desire for God.

There is no stage of the spiritual life in which one can neglect safely the companionship of the sacred humanity of Jesus (or that of Mary), or the remembrance of His sufferings, which is a source of strength in this as in all trials. This remembrance may be made outside the time of prayer by reflections on the redeeming sufferings of Christ; it is well also to reflect upon the vanity and emptiness of the world, and thus to foster and maintain detachment of heart which is essential to this state, and which is also a direct result of the simple prayer itself.

---

[7] It is to be noted that some authorities, including Tanquerey, author of the very helpful book, *The Spiritual Life*, place the night of the senses at the transition of the proficient to the perfect. Father Garrigou-Lagrange rightly considers this a mistake (*The Three Ages of the Interior Life*, Vol. I, p. 486), which is contrary to the clear and often repeated teaching of Saint John of the Cross. It is a mistake which may be very costly, for the soul that is undergoing this trial knows well that it is not far advanced; indeed, it fears it is going backward, and fails to receive the encouragement that it needs from those who follow such an opinion. It needs encouragement so that it may persevere with courage in its prayer and keep free from attachments, anxiety and activity while maintaining a simple and loving attention to God, at the time of prayer. A good little book which will help persons in this and subsequent trials is *Common Mystic Prayer* by Father Gabriel Diefenbach, O.F.M. Cap. (Paterson, N.J.: Saint Anthony's Guild Press, 1947).

Or this remembrance may be made by a simple gaze on Christ in one of His mysteries, e.g. in His infancy or Passion.

The night of the senses is a passive purification, and passive purification is effected in the soul through a mysterious action of God. These persons are strengthened in virtue, self-denial and the spirit of sacrifice, and their sensibility is supernaturalized and subjected to the spirit.

This action of God is really the beginning of infused contemplation, but the person is not conscious of the divine light, which manifests itself, however, in the signs given previously (see footnote 6 to this chapter).

Saint John of the Cross summarizes in these words what we have said of the night of the senses:

> These souls whom God is beginning to lead through these solitary places of the wilderness are like to the children of Israel, to whom in the wilderness God began to give food from Heaven, containing within itself all sweetness, and, as is there said, it turned to the savor which each one of them desired. But withal the children of Israel felt the lack of pleasures and delights of the flesh and the onions which they had eaten aforetime in Egypt, the more so because their palate was accustomed to these and took delight in them, rather than in the delicate sweetness of the angelic manna; and they wept and sighed for the fleshpots even in the midst of the food of Heaven. To such depths does the vileness of our desires descend that it makes us long for our own wretched food [that is for the sensible consolations which formerly accompanied the work of the mind in meditation] and so be nauseated by the indescribable blessings of Heaven [which Saint John will characterize in the next sentence].
>
> But, as I say, when these aridities proceed from the way of the purgation of sensual [i.e. sensible] desire, although at first the spirit feels no sweetness, for the reasons that we have just given, it feels that it is deriving strength and energy to act from the substance which this inward food gives, the food which is the beginning of a contemplation that is dark and arid to the senses; which contemplation is secret and hidden from the very person that experiences it; and ordinarily, together with the aridity and emptiness which it causes in the senses, it gives the soul an inclination and desire to be alone and in quietness, without being able to think of any particular

thing or having the desire to do so.... If those souls to whom this comes to pass knew how to be quiet at this time, and troubled not about performing any kind of action, whether inward or outward, neither had any anxiety about doing anything, then they would delicately experience this inward refreshment in that ease and freedom from care [in the time of prayer. This is to be understood in the following paragraph also. For persons in this state are free to devote their energies to their duties and work.]

For in such a way does God bring the soul into this state, and by so different a path does He lead it that, if it desires to work with its faculties, it hinders the work which God is doing in it rather than aids it; whereas aforetime it was quite the contrary. The reason is that, in this state of contemplation, which the soul enters when it forsakes meditation for the state of the proficient, it is God Who is now working in the soul; He binds its interior faculties and allows it not to cling to the understanding, nor to have delight in the will, nor to reason with the memory. For anything that the soul can do of its own accord at this time serves only, as we have said, to hinder inward peace and the work which God is accomplishing in the spirit by means of that aridity of sense. And this peace, being spiritual and delicate, performs a work which is quiet and delicate, solitary, productive of peace and satisfaction, and far removed from all those earlier pleasures, which were very palpable and sensual [sensible]. This is the peace which, says David, God speaks in the soul to the end that He may make it spiritual (Psalm 84:9 (85:8)) (*Dark Night*, Bk. I, Chap. IX).

PROGRESS WITHOUT PASSIVE PRAYER

Many do not undergo the night of the senses. In prayer they continue to occupy themselves in meditation, affective prayer, and acts (a-c-t-s) such as we have described. They practice the virtues, especially charity, and perform certain devotions and good works, including almsgiving and other works of mercy. They are to be encouraged to continue in their way of life, which is meritorious and pleasing to the Father, and in this path they will increase in charity and in the other virtues.

They do not undergo the night of the senses, perhaps because the circumstances of their life involve them in activity that is too prolonged and unbroken to permit them to become strong enough interiorly to be surrendered entirely to the divine action; perhaps because their psychological substratum contains weaknesses which would not permit them to withstand the severity of the passive purifications (although we have seen persons with various types of mental weakness undergoing passive purification); or perhaps because they do not mortify and deny themselves to the extent necessary for such advance: they do not surrender themselves entirely to God. Yet these souls are precious children of the Father, and the particular love He bears them is manifest in the grace of persevering fidelity He gives them, or the grace to keep returning to Him and to the practices of the interior life. Such souls, persevering with Christ through various trials, rendering Him many services, attain deepening insight into the things of God and are enriched by abundant merits. Perhaps some of them undergo the nights unknown to themselves, or at the end of their life, as in a last illness, etc.[8]

THE PROFICIENT

After persons have passed through the night of the senses (which may last years), they experience a more penetrating faith through which they are drawn into closer intimacy with Jesus in the silent absorption of love; at times, they are quietly held in prayer pressed against the bosom of the Father. The soul "now very readily finds in its spirit the most secure and loving contemplation and spiritual sweetness without the labor of meditation, although as yet the purgation of the soul is not complete ... it is never without certain occasional necessities, aridities, darkness and perils" (Saint John of the Cross, *Dark Night*, Bk. II, Chap. I). These aridities in fact increase toward the end of this stage and are a forerunner of the night of the spirit. (Some persons whom God is not leading to the transforming union He nevertheless purifies from time to time with an aridity such as that experienced in

---

[8] Some spiritual authorities hold that there is a "non-contemplative" way to perfection, and that souls following this way reach the states of the proficient and the perfect without passing through the passive purifications or attaining to transforming union. For these authors, there are two ways to perfection, one by the help of infused graces of prayer, which they deem "extra-ordinary," and the "ordinary" way followed by those who continue to meditate without receiving special graces of prayer.

the night of the spirit without subjecting them to this night in its entirety and full severity—compare the intermittent night of the senses.)

Persons undergoing aridity, such as the "nights," must renew their appreciation of the wonderful gift of prayer they have been given, for as time goes on and the prayer remains always much the same, it may appear monotonous and restricting. The works of Saint John of the Cross and of Saint Teresa of Avila will help to do so. While their prayer may seem to them at times to be idleness and emptiness, in reality it engages the will in intense activity (though unfelt), and with great fruitfulness. But they must be on guard against surrendering to a sensual sweetness, which the devil may produce, or to vagueness and real inactivity (a vague daydreaming), in which the will is not engaged. Here the conscience must be the guide (this problem is treated in Dom Belorgey's *Practice of Mental Prayer*, p. 73). At such times God is waiting for the soul to resume the activity of the will in prayer by acts, or to strengthen its will in the firm desire for Him alone, in true detachment and humble search.

The prayer of the proficient is the prayer of quiet, engaging the will alone (Fourth Mansions) or the prayer of union (Fifth Mansions) when the divine action engages all the faculties, suspending the lower powers. In the former prayer, the soul is conscious of opening its eyes to God, of directing its gaze to Him; in the latter, God's action so takes hold of the soul that even this effort is unnecessary (these two degrees are described by Saint John of the Cross).

How long does the state of the proficient last? "A long time, even years," says Saint John (*Dark Night*, Bk. II Chap. I). But in what concerns the time element, there is much variation in all the stages of the spiritual life.

Concerning this period, the interval between the nights, we learn further interesting and helpful details from Saint Teresa, especially in her *Interior Castle*, Fourth and Fifth Mansions.[9] (Saint Francis de Sales

---

[9] The First Mansions describes the state of the person without an interior life. The Second Mansions describes the person taking up the spiritual life and trying to enter into himself. The Third Mansions follows the person as he or she succeeds in establishing an interior life through habitual mental prayer. She has organized her entire life according to the dictates of faith and right reason. Then may come the experience of passive recollection (*Interior Castle*, Fourth Mansions—a digression; *Second*

follows Saint Teresa and elaborates on her descriptions in his own unique way.)

In the prayer of quiet which occurs in the Fourth Mansions, the will alone is engaged by the action of God, and the soul is drawn to a silent repose in Him. The senses and imagination may be hushed or they may be active and distracting. This prayer may be prolonged sometimes by occasional acts of love; it may occur in the midst of activity or at the time of prayer. This prayer begins in the night of the senses (compare Saint John of the Cross's descriptions of the night of the senses). However when the night of the senses is traversed and the interval between the two nights is reached, this contemplative prayer becomes sweeter in a refined way: this sweetness is not so much sensible as spiritual.

The Fifth Mansions are reached when the soul experiences a new form of prayer in which the senses are completely suspended and the soul is, as it were, completely lost in God, for about fifteen minutes. During this prayer and afterward, the soul is impressed with the certitude (a brightness of faith) that though it saw nothing, it was in God and was fully united with Him. (In this prayer the soul experiences no particular thoughts or sentiments: nothing but God Himself, in blind, yet bright, faith.) The certitude that in this prayer the soul is in God is the special characteristic of this prayer, which is known also by its effects, and which is called by Teresa the prayer of union, by other authors the prayer of simple union—because as yet the transforming union has not taken place. This prayer changes the soul exceedingly, endowing it with new energies which surprise it; with ardent longings for God, desires for humiliations and sufferings which it had not experienced before or in such a degree, great zeal for good works, fresh courage of a degree unimaginable to it previously. Henceforth, until it reaches the transforming union it is restless, seeking ever the union with God which it had experienced in this prayer, and thinking that it is never doing enough for Him, and so not entirely at peace with itself. Now, and in the impending night of the spirit, it needs to learn

Relation to Father Alvarez; compare also Lamballe's _Mystical Contemplation_, p. 141). This passive recollection precedes the prayer of quiet.

that its involuntary faults which irk it so much are not displeasing to the Father (as Saint Thérèse of Lisieux learned in the retreat the year following her profession). After the soul has experienced this prayer of union for the first time, as much as a year may (but need not) elapse before it experiences it again, according to Saint Teresa of Avila.

Saint Teresa brings out the significance of this prayer in a comparison with a custom of her time. When the marriage of a young man and woman was arranged, and while the contract of the engagement was being drawn up, they were given an opportunity to see one another on a short visit in order to become acquainted and to see if they desired this match. It is to this "visit" that Saint Teresa likens the prayer of simple union. The engagement contract is being drawn up between God and the soul and the soul is admitted to an intimacy with God—a visit with Him, which declares what its future state is to be if it goes ahead with the engagement and the marriage. It needs this experience to prepare it for the great trials ahead which it must surmount to reach the transforming union.

It seems then that when persons reach the Fifth Mansions they are destined by God to the transforming union (Seventh Mansions), on the condition that they remain faithful to Him, especially during the intervening trial of the dark night of the spirit which awaits them in the Sixth Mansions.

Saint Teresa warns these people that they are not yet strong enough to be able to enter freely into occasions of sin without danger to themselves. Also she calls attention to the zeal of the devil against them. He desires to hinder and stop their progress and to lead them away, into sin (which is still possible), because he recognizes the great things that God intends to do in and through them, and to what extent their perfection will threaten his kingdom. It is only after they have reached the spiritual marriage or transforming union, that he can no longer threaten them with such hope of success. Indeed, then, Saint Teresa says, he is afraid to attack them because he knows that his attacks only lead them to greater merit (especially when he sees them in actual union with their divine Bridegroom). But he does, especially when they are under some stress.

The change that the prayer of simple union works in the soul is brought home to us by Saint Teresa's metaphor of the silkworm, which from its cocoon has now hatched a little white butterfly. This soul is more active than ever in its good works and has an energy of self-sacrifice and self-denial that it never knew before.

33 Degrees Concluded & Illustrated by Saint Thérèse

The transition from the state of the proficient to that of the perfect is characterized by a second passive purification, the night of the spirit. Persons undergoing this trial experience their own poverty and imperfection intensely—and as if they were separated from the Father. They have a sense of the infinite majesty of the Father, and experience a painful desire for Him. While these experiences are the effect of an obscure infused contemplation and increasing love of the Father, these persons are not aware of the cause of their suffering, they do not directly experience the contemplative light, but rather feel as though they have been abandoned by the Father to whom they realize they cannot as yet completely unite themselves. Their spirit is being purified from those inordinate affections for self and creatures which it contracted from their sensible nature (Saint John of the Cross, *Dark Night*, Bk. II, Chap. VII, 5). By faith they adhere to the Father in darkness and emptiness of soul; by hope they expect their salvation through the merits of Jesus Christ crucified alone, without admixture of self-reliance, for they have an overwhelming experience of their own wretchedness; by love they desire greatly to please the Father, while they are afflicted by the conviction that they are serving Him poorly, and thus their motivation, provided by the theological virtues, is purified. This night, like its predecessor, and the intervening peaceful period, ordinarily lasts for years (*Dark Night*, Bk. II, Chap. VII, 4, p. 390: "If it [the night of the spirit] is to be really effectual, it will last for some years, however severe it be").

Thus so far as it is possible in this life, the intention of such people becomes entirely simple and sincere, having God alone as its object without that admixture of selfish interest and self-deceit so difficult wholly to preclude. This is possible because the very depths of the will and senses are purged by the divine action. As a result of this purgation, sense and spirit enter into a harmonious union and the gifts of the Holy Spirit can reach their full development in the soul. The soul comes to dwell in proximity to the tendencies of its lower nature, which are thus enlightened so that it can readily recognize them. The awareness of the lower tendencies keeps the soul in mind of its own natural baseness and continued need of the Father's support.

During both nights there may be associated sufferings inflicted by persons, the loss of friends and temporal goods, bodily illness or infirmity, etc. Thus such persons are greatly exercised in fortitude and prepared for those graces which render their virtues truly heroic. This development is assisted by the mystical death which they undergo in the night of the spirit.

As in the night of the senses, such persons must generously accept the trial of the night of the spirit as long as the Father wills it to last, a period which is known to Him alone; they must remain content with their present state and live in dependence upon the Father's will, repeatedly asking for perseverance in faith, trust and love, while remaining in the assurance that all is well. Also, as in the night of the senses, these persons derive profit from the remembrance of the

Passion of Christ and of the humiliations which Jesus endured for love of them, and from the thought that in this painful darkness they abide in the interior of the Hearts of Jesus and Mary.

Saint John of the Cross says:

> The purgative process of the dark night of the spirit allows of intervals of relief, wherein, by the dispensation of God, this dark contemplation ceases to assail the soul in the form and manner of purgation ... the soul feels and experiences great sweetness of peace and loving friendship with God.... This is to the soul a sign of the health which is being wrought within it by the purgation and a foretaste of the abundance for which it hopes ... until the spiritual purification is complete and perfected, the sweet communication is very rarely so abundant as to conceal from the soul the root which remains hidden, in such a way that the soul can cease to feel that there is something that it lacks within itself or that it has still to do. Thus it cannot completely enjoy that relief ... when the soul is most secure and least alert, it is dragged down and immersed again in another and a worse degree of affliction ... and the soul once more comes to believe that all its blessings are over forever (*Dark Night*, Bk. II, Chap. VII, 4, 6).

The night of the spirit is rare, but if more persons were willing to give up all for the love of Jesus perseveringly, it would become less rare. As *The Imitation of Christ* says, the reason there are so few contemplatives is that so few are willing fully to renounce and mortify themselves.

THE PERFECT

Upon emerging from the passive purification of the spirit—just when trials are blackest and hope seems vain—the soul receives wonderful graces and joy from the Father, graces of knowledge of God, and of virtues which will complete its sanctification. Now the soul is prompted to give itself to God more completely and purely than ever, and God gives Himself to it. This commitment is called by spiritual writers the spiritual betrothal, or engagement, and after such persons have persevered in abandonment to the divine will throughout the ensuing period, and have been further enlightened and enriched by divine gifts which strengthen them greatly in virtue, making their virtues heroic, the spiritual marriage takes place. Then God and this person give themselves to each other in total possession, to enter into a stable and secure union of love.

The spiritual marriage is a contract entered into by two persons whose wills are competent to do so; the human will is competent, because through grace it has been sufficiently purified and rendered heroically generous and compliant to the divine will. The person may have no overwhelming experience of the divine ratification of this contract, no special revelation; but he or she may experience this acceptance by the certitude of hope inspired by the Holy Spirit or by some other communication made to it by the Spirit through the gifts. Saint Bernard says of this contract that when the human will gives itself, then the divine will has done so too. In other words, the complete and irrevocable gift of the fully purified will is an action proceeding first of all from God and signifies His ratification of the contract.[1]

Sense and spirit having now been refined, these people "taste" God and experience Him in a very intimate manner. He delicately and gently inspires them with divine love which bears the glorious impression of eternal life. (Saint John's work, *The Living Flame*, treats of the experiences of the transforming union, especially in its more advanced degrees.) They sing His praise while being consumed again and again by the flame of His love, and thank Him for having purified them in the crucible of His love (as does Saint Thérèse in her prayer "Oblation to Merciful Love"). They recognize that the pure and sublime delight of one divine embrace has repaid them for all the years

[1] It sometimes happens that the soul disregards the intimation that it has reached the state of transforming union, because it cannot bring itself wholly to believe, or to believe perseveringly, that this is the case. This happens sometimes because of misunderstanding: it thinks that transforming union is an extraordinary state, identifies it with extraordinary phenomena often described in connection with it. It also happens because the soul considers its remaining imperfections and deficiencies as incompatible with transforming union, etc. But this state is only relative perfection, and descriptions of it are apt to be misleading. Saint Teresa, in the Seventh Mansions, tries to forestall erroneous conceptions; while not neglecting to signalize the exalted character of this state, she points out its limits: that the soul is still capable of imperfections and faults of frailty, that the grace of the transforming union with all its *habitual* effects may be interrupted for as much as a day, when the soul tastes again its native indigence, etc. This should be kept in mind in what follows.

of suffering they have undergone during their passage through the passive purifications and the trials of the way, and traces of these sorrows are swept clear of their spirit, which, however, strives to retain the memory of them that it may be more grateful; meanwhile their love for the cross has not abated—nor are they left without crosses.

Such persons have now reached perfection and spiritual maturity; their virtues are now perfect and heroic (Saint John of the Cross, *Spiritual Canticle*, XXIV, 3, 4), through the gratuitous gift of the Father. This final stage of the spiritual life corresponds to full adulthood in the physical maturation of the human body. Such persons, now purified in sense and spirit, are completely subject to the Father and conformed to His holy will, and moved habitually by the Holy Spirit through His gifts. Through the gifts of wisdom and understanding in particular (which makes their faith penetrating and sweet), they experience the almost continual quasi-experimental presence of the Father; through the gift of counsel they are directed in their difficulties; through the gift of fortitude their love is strengthened by the strength of the Father, making them generous in detachment and readiness to suffer; through the gift of piety they are made filially reverent in the divine service, as well as in all their relations with persons and things whom they see as belonging to their Father and whom they revere for this reason. Finally the gift of fear keeps them before the Father in humility and checks their tendencies to sin. They are also protected by a special providence of the Father from external occasions of sin, but not from trials and suffering, including that which comes from their own fallen nature, a fallen nature they still have!

It is a striking principle in the doctrine of Saint John of the Cross that the virtues are made perfect and heroic only by the special graces of the divine bridegroom, after the "bride" has been long tried and purified and has perseveringly renounced and mortified herself. This shows the gratuitousness of perfection, as well as the preparatory graces required, and also how high a state it is.

Transforming union is a transformation of the soul in which its operations henceforth proceed more from God than from the human person. That this may be, such persons must be fully receptive of the divine influence. So long as they follow their own human way of thinking and acting, marked also by their own defective habits in exercising their faculties, they cannot be fully receptive of the divine influence or fully activated by the divine Spirit. They are rather acting through the infused virtues (in their mode of operation) than through the highest potentialities conferred upon them by their supernatural equipment. Saint Teresa has pointed out in the Third Mansions that on the threshold of passive prayer too human a manner of reckoning halts the soul from advancing further (compare also Father Marie-Eugene, *I Want to See God*, II, Chap. X).

When persons have passed through the purifications, they have separated themselves from themselves to the point of a mystical death; they have subjected themselves to the divine action with the persevering fortitude of complete self-renunciation and have accepted a complete and annihilating dependence on the Father's grace. They have tasted their own misery so long and fully that they know their utter worthlessness and poverty, and depend no longer upon themselves. No longer does their sensibility preclude their attentiveness to the Father in pure faith, nor does self-reliance exist to turn the will from the operation of God. Consciousness is now not of self but of God who is experienced as an operating principle within the soul, by the effects of His action. Thus Saint Thérèse of Lisieux felt that it was Jesus who was loving souls ardently in and through her, and so also she recounts many evidences of God habitually acting in and through her.

Transformation means, then, that one is actuated by the Holy Spirit, acting through the gifts habitually; instead of through one's own reason and virtues. The new form, which one has by participation in the divine nature (by Baptism), has become one's principle of operation. This principle is divine, and hence one's operations are divine. But they proceed instrumentally from one's human nature, and so remain characterized by one's own personality and thereby stamped as human, and often as imperfect. When one is not under the operation of the grace of transforming union, one acts through the infused virtues.

It is more perfect for one to be dependent upon and moved by a divine principle than to move oneself by the human principle of one's own reason and will: no higher mode of union with God is open to the human than that of this transforming union. That union is more perfect in which the divine will predominates and directs the human will.

Hence the importance in the spiritual life of external and internal silence, of the guard of the thoughts and desires, of mortification and self-denial—as well as of the practice of the virtues and good works. Thus one keeps one's lower nature in subjection to one's reason and will, and one's reason and will in subjection to the motion of the Holy Spirit. Thus too we can understand the spiritual wisdom underlying discipline in the cloister, such as silence, solitude, abnegation and obedience.

Transforming union makes people contemplatives whether they are in the contemplative or active life.[2] The lives of the saints convince us of the contemplative character of sanctity. The saints esteemed their intercourse with God for its own sake, and then too they realized that it was the source of the fruitfulness of their activity. This is verified in a beautiful way in the lives of those Jesuit saints of the first period of the Society, who attained such an astonishing degree of perfection: Saint Ignatius, Saint Peter Canisius, Saint Francis Xavier, Saint Jean de Brebeuf, Saint Isaac Jogues, etc., and it is explicitly taught by

---

[2] Jacques Maritain, and other writers after him, distinguish two forms of perfection, active and contemplative, one in which the contemplative gifts of the Holy Spirit—the other in which the active gifts—are predominantly developed.

Although the virtues and gifts are connected and develop together, in different individuals different virtues and gifts will be outstanding. This point has been well presented by Benedict XIV in his *Treatise on Heroic Virtue*, following Saint Jerome, Saint Thomas and other authors. Grace acts to develop the virtues commanded by one's state of life, and those which are in accordance with one's natural aptitudes, tendencies and opportunities. The distinction of M. Maritain has this much in its favor. We might add that if in the perfect, some virtues will be more readily elicited than others (although in the readiness of the mind, as Saint Thomas puts it, they are present in the same degree), then much more so is this the case with the imperfect. Some persons by expecting too much of themselves (in ready practice of all the virtues) induce tension.

But we must also observe that wisdom is both speculative and practical, contemplative and active, and contemplation is practical, being essentially a supreme love of God. We cannot in theory or practice push M. Maritain's distinction too far. Actually the great active saints were great contemplatives, and the great contemplative saints were highly gifted in their activities (as soon as they were called upon to act), even if they were restricted by their mode of life as in the case of the cloistered Saint Thérèse of Lisieux, who showed herself, however, when made acting novice-mistress, to be very accomplished in this office. In summary, the activity of the perfect is regulated by their contemplative wisdom; contemplation directs action as Saint Gregory and Saint Thomas say.

the greatest Jesuit masters of the spiritual life such as Father Louis Lallemant (author of *Spiritual Doctrine*).

The great contemplatives whose mode of life permitted a very restricted apostolic overflow, as Saint Thérèse of Lisieux, were no less apostolic. Indeed the purely contemplative life has a necessarily apostolic stamp in its spirituality. The expression of this apostolic fervor is manifested in the perfection (perfection, not iron-clad rigidity) with which the rule is kept, in the charity and joy abounding in contemplative communities, in fraternal charity; it rises to the Father as an ardent plea for the temporal welfare, the salvation and sanctification of humankind. But it also finds expression in the highest external apostolate: the apostolate of contemplatives to contemplatives, guiding, directing, forming, teaching them. One of the advantages of the contemplative life when sincerely and faithfully lived is the availability of good spiritual directors, formed to the heart, virtues and wisdom of Christ by the contemplative life.

Transforming union, then, makes persons not only contemplatives but also apostles. This is the source of that wonderful activity which has illuminated the life of the Church. It is impossible for love to grow perfect in good works without a corresponding impulse arising from this love toward its object which is Jesus Whose Kingdom, as He says, is within the soul; just as it is impossible for love to grow perfect in contemplation without an impulse toward the welfare of Jesus living (or wanting to live) in souls. Love is a unitive force seeking union with its beloved; that union occurs within the soul. Love applies the intelligence and will to bury deep into the beloved by knowledge and love, and to seize upon *Him* with a heart aflame, and this occurs preeminently in contemplation. Thus true lovers seek Him continually, interiorly in their own hearts, and exteriorly in the fulfillment of His will in all things, especially in the temporal and spiritual welfare of others for His sake.

The love of charity is a love of friendship which makes Jesus and His disciple images of one another. It does not confer upon the disciple the beatific vision which Jesus always had during His human and apostolic life; but it does give the disciple an equivalent of this vision, which is the infused contemplation of the transformed soul in whom, through the operations of the gifts of the Holy Spirit, the companionship of God, the consciousness of His presence, is more or less continual. Thence proceeds great joy because the aim of love, real union, is accomplished. The beloved is truly present and united to the lover, Jesus is with and in the soul, the soul is with and in Jesus, and their wills are one.

A BEAUTIFUL EXAMPLE of the way of perfection which we have traced is furnished by Saint Thérèse of Lisieux. We do not mean to be categorical in what follows, but merely to offer a provisional opinion. At the same time we shall only touch lightly upon facts which are well known.

Saint Thérèse divides her twenty-four years of life into three periods: the first before her mother's death; the second from this event, at the age of four, until the Christmas just preceding her fourteenth birthday. She underwent the night of senses during this period, at least during the last two years of it, which was characterized by "a martyrdom of soul"—a siege of scruples. For this, she had been prepared by the graces of her first Communion and her Confirmation at the age of eleven, when she affirms, she received the gift of fortitude in suffering, so soon to be needed because of the impending two years' trial.

The third period of her life, "the most beautiful and the most filled with graces from heaven," began with the cessation of the night of the senses and in particular with the Christmas grace, which was probably the prayer of simple union, when "I felt charity enter into my soul, and the need to forget myself and to please others; since then I've been happy!"

To understand what happened in this Christmas grace, we have to recall that between the age of four and a half and the time of this grace, Thérèse was in some respects a neurotic and immature child. She cried easily, was excessively sensitive and shy, did not make her own bed or fulfill the ordinary personal or household tasks of her age. We must not exaggerate this picture as she was practicing virtue throughout this period.

It was at the age of four and a half that Thérèse's mother had died. This was not the first maternal deprivation that Thérèse suffered. She was sensitized by a previous one, which made the death of her mother the more traumatic. Madame Martin had lost three children before Thérèse was born. At the age of two weeks, Thérèse became critically ill, and manifested the same symptoms of digestive disorder which had characterized the illnesses of the two brothers and sister who had died before her birth. The doctor said that unless Thérèse was given a nursing mother she would likewise die. Madame Martin wished the nursing mother, Rose, whom she was able to obtain for Thérèse, to live in the home with her. Since Rose had children of her own this proved impossible. So Thérèse visited her home only once a week, and knew Rose as her mother. She cried if separated from Rose. When fifteen months of age, she was taken from Rose's home to her own. Thus sensitized by a separation from her mother surrogate, the only mother she really knew until fifteen months of age, the loss of her real mother was a traumatic shock, from which she did not recover until the Christmas grace on the eve of her fourteenth birthday.

No doubt her mother's death was the most serious shock which Thérèse's developing personality underwent. However this was not the end of her maternal deprivations. She took Pauline as her "little Mother" after her mother's death, but then Pauline entered the Carmel when Thérèse was nine years old. This precipitated a serious illness of six months duration. Meanwhile Thérèse took her other elder sister Marie as her little Mother. When Thérèse was thirteen Marie entered the Carmel, three years after Pauline had done so.

Saint Thérèse experienced a transformation in this Christmas grace on the threshold of her fourteenth birthday. What she had been unable to accomplish since her mother's death—the conquest of her extreme sensitivity and shyness—was achieved in an instant, as she tells us. Then she "discovered once again the strength of soul which she had lost at the age of four and a half." Now new fires of zeal burn in her: for virtue, for suffering, for souls, and she wins through prayer her first soul, the notorious criminal Pranzini. These are the effects of the prayer of union.

But this is not all. "God did for me what Ezekiel reports in his prophecies: 'Behold your time was the time of lovers: and I spread my garment over you. And I swore to you, and I entered into a covenant with you, saith the Lord God, and you became Mine. And I washed you with water and anointed you with oil. I clothed you with fine garments, and put a chain about your neck. You did eat fine flour and honey and oil, and were made exceedingly beautiful, and were advanced to be a queen" (Ezekiel, 16:8, 9, 13).

Thérèse goes on: "Yes, Jesus did all this for me. I could take each word and prove it was realized in me..."[3] (These words were written about two years before her death.)

This "Christmas grace," then, seems to have been the first instance in Thérèse's life of the prayer of union: that "visit" between the two contractants of the marriage-to-be. They already manifest to each other their entire willingness to enter into the covenant, which shall be sealed in the spiritual betrothal and spiritual marriage after the night of the spirit has been completed. Then Thérèse would be able to say of this passage of Ezekiel, that she could apply it word for word to herself and "prove it was realized in me..."

There is something analogous in the interior life of novices who, in receiving the habit, already in their hearts give themselves to God in the religious state for life as far as they can (without actually obliging themselves permanently by vow even interiorly, which they should not do without a special permission until they make final vows). Again at the simple temporary profession, one may will to be Christ's forever in religion in so far as one is accepted. Thus, in the "visit" of the prayer of union, before the spiritual betrothal or marriage, the person has an intimation of the Lord's intentions and of what is being offered, and responds with the willingness to make the proffered covenant.

Between the time of the Christmas grace and her entrance into Carmel fifteen months later, Thérèse experienced the radiant period between the two nights. At this time her soul expanded under the influence of tranquil, sweet, passive prayer.

Upon her entrance into Carmel spiritual aridity, the dark night of the spirit, set in, and increased for a period of years.

Finally Thérèse reached the summit of the mountain of love, as she herself declares, and as she adds, all her desires were fulfilled. She

[3] *Story of a Soul, The Autobiography of Saint Thérèse of Lisieux*, a new translation from the original manuscripts by John Clarke, O.C.D., ICS Publications, Institute of Carmelite Studies, Washington, D.C. 1975. Quotations from the autobiography are taken from this translation.

was living in the peace and quiet of the transforming union, aware that Jesus was habitually living within her and acting through her, when she was subjected to an additional trial, a further "night," this time reparatory—not for her sanctification but for the souls of those whom she wished to save and who were living in the darkness of unbelief. This "thick darkness," this "tunnel," this trial against the faith, which robbed the thought of Heaven of its light and joy, came on her during the Easter season, about a year and a half before her death. So too, Saint Paul of the Cross, after reaching the transforming union before the age of thirty-one, endured a reparatory "night" for forty-five years, through which he gained the graces which the religious of the Order he founded would need.[4]

Saint Thérèse tells us that during her seventeenth and eighteenth years (that is in the year during which she made her profession and in the succeeding year while she was undergoing the night of the spirit), her "only food" was the works of Saint John of the Cross. Pius XI in his sermon at her canonization affirms that "in the writings of Saint John of the Cross, she found her mystical theology." Saint John deals with the essence of the path to God, detouring all the accidental extraordinary graces, and so he was in a special manner equipped to be the teacher of Saint Thérèse. She was the shining exemplar of his teaching, reflected with all the more purity because of her ordinary mode of life. She has become the best teacher of the doctrine of Saint John for our day and for all, because of the simplicity of her writing and the absence of technicalities. Everything is ordinary, except the extraordinary love and willingness to surrender entirely to God in complete confidence in Him, and these dispositions she transmits to the legion of little souls who follow her.

She is raised up by God, as Pope Pius XI tells us, as a model for all Christians, to lead them to that perfection which she so signally attained. To encourage all, Thérèse writes: "If all weak and imperfect souls such as mine, felt as I do, none would despair of reaching the summit of the mountain of love, since Jesus looks only for gratitude and self-surrender."

---

[4] R.-M. Garrigou-Lagrange, O.P., *Three Ages of the Interior Life*, Vol. II, p. 507.

By our prayer to her and our study and imitation of the writings of this little Saint, what was fulfilled in her, will be fulfilled in us: "I ask Jesus to draw me into the flames of His love, to unite me so closely to Him that He live and act in me. I feel that the more the fire of love burns my heart, the more I shall say: 'Draw me,' the more also the souls who will approach me ... *will run swiftly in the odor of the ointments of their Beloved...*"

In the way of the spiritually mature, charity continues to grow and more quickly as persons approach the end of their life and the consummation of their union with Jesus in Heaven. They know that of themselves they are nothing, that all their welfare is the gratuitous gift and work of grace, for which they thank God. They realize full well that in the merits of Jesus, Mary and Joseph, not in their own, they have the foundation for all that they hope and confidently expect, and so they guard against the pride and presumption that can even now enter surreptitiously in, to spoil their love and works. They know that perfection here below is great imperfection compared to the perfection of the saints in Heaven, and that the perfection of Jesus and Mary on earth is in a different order completely from the perfection of the saints, and that many others are called to a higher degree of perfection than are they.

In the passage soon to be quoted, Saint Paul expresses the sentiments of the spiritually mature, as is clear from the words which follow this quotation: "We who are called 'perfect' must all think in this way." But the quotation is applicable to all, even to the greatest sinners, who turn to the Father with sincerity and seek Him wholeheartedly:

> I believe nothing can happen that will outweigh the supreme advantage of knowing Christ Jesus my Lord. For Him I have accepted the loss of everything, and I look on everything as so much rubbish if only I can have Christ and be given a place in Him.... All I want is to know Christ and the power of His Resurrection and to share His sufferings by reproducing the pattern of His death.... Not that I have become perfect yet: I have not yet won, but I am still running, trying to capture the prize for which Christ Jesus captured me. I can assure you my brothers I am far from thinking that I have already won. All I can say is that I forget the past and strain ahead for what is still to come; I am racing for the finish, for the prize to which God calls us upward to receive in Christ Jesus (Philippians 3:8-15).

34 Spiritual Direction

This chapter is intended for those who are unable to obtain spiritual direction, for those giving or receiving spiritual direction, for those who might become spiritual directors (including seminarians). It will show how this book may be turned into a handbook of spiritual direction. As a handbook for spiritual direction it contains the instructional reading which those undergoing spiritual direction need, the formation needed for those becoming spiritual directors, the appropriate advice for different stages and ways of the spiritual life, and advice for those with special problems.

WHAT IS SPIRITUAL DIRECTION?

What do we understand by "spiritual direction"? It is a means by which one person helps another in his or her response to the call of God's love. The one being directed exposes his or her needs, strivings, conflicts, manner of coping. The director listens compassionately, seeks to understand, and to discern by God's grace what the Holy Spirit is doing or wishes to do in this person, and gives appropriate help.

In common with counseling, there is listening, discovering and identifying the emotions which are present, and the factors which need to be understood and evaluated, allowing conflicts to enter awareness and to be resolved, and this as much as possible through the self-discovery of the person directed.

Specific to direction is the agreement on the goal of the two parties: union with Christ. There is agreement that conflicts, desires, and behavior be evaluated in terms of Christ's Revelation, the teaching of the Church, the will of the Father.

Both must be alert to the dispositions of the other, and whether this goal is really motivating the transactions which take place in this relationship. If not, this is not spiritual direction.

WHAT THE DIRECTOR NEEDS

The first thing that is required of a director is that he or she be truly seeking God and be experienced in the use of the necessary means. The director then will have some self-knowledge and purity of motivation and detachment in the relationship with those directed.

WHAT THE BEGINNER NEEDS

The first thing that a beginner needs is instruction on the goal of the spiritual life and on the basic means of pursuing this goal, such as is provided in this book. The beginner needs to learn how to make mental prayer, do spiritual reading, avoid the occasions of sin, practice self-denial, frequent the sacraments fruitfully, particularly the Eucharist and Penance, be faithful to the duties of his or her state of life, and in general to put his or her life in order in accordance with the Gospel, overcoming bad habits and practicing charity in sincerity and truth.

NEEDS OF THOSE WHO PERSEVERE IN SEEKING GOD

The director should know the signs of the transition which marks the passage from the stage of a beginner: the transition from discursive meditation to a more simple form of prayer, as is explained in the chapters on the degrees of the spiritual life (and exemplified in the life of Saint Thérèse). He will then understand what is taking place at this juncture, and be able to give the needed support and encouragement.

Throughout the spiritual life encouragement is needed in the face of dryness, distractions and temptations. Deliberate sin needs to be frankly faced and overcome, involvements hindering or jeopardizing the spiritual life recognized, and hindrances to spiritual growth eliminated.

Vocational decisions including marriage and the ministry require discernment and perhaps special consultation. Counseling may be required in the case of marriage difficulties. Psychiatric disorders need referral.

Some of the points made in this succinct statement deserve elaboration.

THE RELATIONSHIP OF THE DIRECTOR AND THE ONE DIRECTED

In the process of spiritual direction, it is important that the aim, union with Christ, be kept in view, and the transactions and relationship judged with respect to this aim. On the part of the director, spiritual direction is not an opportunity to exercise control over another person, to dominate someone, to impose one's personal views and preferences or even one's own way to God. It is not an opportunity for the spiritual director to air his or her pet opinions, or to discuss topics of special interest to him or her, or to obtain information from the one directed about which one is curious. In her autobiography, Saint Thérèse explains how careful she was in these matters when acting as novice-mistress.

The spiritual director should not go beyond his or her light in giving advice. The one directed usually has the best knowledge of the circumstances and situation in which he or she is involved. Discussion, reflection and prayer should help the one directed to perceive the best course to take, the one most in accord with the will of the

Father. Often this is discovered by the person directed only after a sufficient period of time. In finding the will of God, discernment is needed and this topic is treated below.

Direction should lead the person directed to an increasing dependence on the Father "from Whom all light proceeds" (James), on Jesus, on the Holy Spirit "Who will lead you into all truth" (John), rather than to a dependence on the director.

The director should not interfere with the directee's fulfillment of the duties of his or her state of life. For married persons, the marriage bond is a source of graces and the director is not a substitute for the light which comes from a spouse. The director should not interfere with the directee's obtaining light and direction, if a religious, from his or her Superiors and Rule. He should also not hinder the person directed from obtaining counsel from others than himself, although "shopping for opinions" is an abuse of direction.

On the part of the one directed, a spiritual director is not someone to lean on, a substitute for a missing or failing marriage partner, someone from whom one looks to gain backing for one's own unexamined desires, projects, experiences. In other words, the spiritual director is neither someone on whom to be dependent, nor someone to dominate and use to further one's own purposes.

The one directed must be very honest and sincere, and reveal to the director whatever is pertinent to the matter being discussed. Neither fear of the director's adverse judgment, nor expectation that the director can give advice without knowing the relevant facts should deter openness and freedom of communication.

The director's advice and opinions are not as important as the Lord's and this is what both should seek. If the director fails habitually in this regard it is time to change one's director, something which should not be done lightly, nor postponed when necessary.

THE BEGINNER

The beginner needs instruction on how to do spiritual reading. Spiritual reading done properly is a source through which Christ Himself gives spiritual direction. Helpful instruction on spiritual reading is given in the chapter on that subject.

The beginner also needs to be taught how to pray. It is important to pray as one can and not as one cannot (Dom Chapman). Prayer is personal and intimate conversation with Christ. An entire chapter is devoted to this subject.

The beginner needs to appreciate the graces that flow from the sacraments of the Eucharist and Reconciliation and to frequent them. Instruction on these sacraments is contained in chapters of this book. One must understand that the Eucharist is Jesus Christ, Who loves *me* and Who is waiting for me to participate with Him in His sacrifice and to receive Him in communion. By prolonging my thanksgiving, I give Him my love and accept the blessings which He wishes to confer on me, perhaps in a way which at the time is imperceptible. By participating daily in the Mass I grow in love of Him, and by visiting Him in the Blessed Sacrament I both testify to this love and receive the fruits of His love. Thus I am strengthened and enlightened to deal with the problems which are never lacking.

The spiritual life is unreal if fidelity to the duties of one's state of life, or genuine love for those with whom one comes in contact is lacking. Authentic spiritual life requires the denial of gratifications which interfere with the activity of love, in which true peace, joy and fruition is found.

The person embarking on the spiritual life needs to be informed about the elements of the spiritual life, and needs to be encouraged to become wholehearted in the love of Jesus and of persons, making a total gift of self to the Father.

What is Required of the Spiritual Director

The first requirement for the spiritual director is to embrace the spiritual life seriously himself or herself, using appropriate means. The second requirement is to persevere in it. Spiritual reading forms the reader in Christ and imparts the light and the zeal needed to help others. In turn this activity will increase the director's enlightenment and zeal. But he should beware of doing spiritual reading in order to obtain lights for others to put into practice instead of doing it for the guidance he himself needs. Once assimilated and put into practice, these lights will then be available for others, without impoverishing the director.

DIRECTION FOR THOSE PERSEVERING IN THE SPIRITUAL LIFE

But what of the direction of those who are no longer beginners? Chapters of this book give not only instructions for beginners, but also describe and explain the growth and progress of the spiritual life.

It is very important that the director understands the transition between beginner and the advanced, and identifies it when it takes place. This transition comes early in a generous person—perhaps one or two to four years after conversion or dedication to Christ and the spiritual life. False ideas can be disastrous. They may lead to insistence that the person directed continue in discursive meditation when he or she is unable to meditate and needs to pursue a more simplified form of prayer. Such directors have a point in not wanting people to advance too quickly—a foundation for simplified prayer is laid by discursive meditation and the practice of virtue. But when this is accomplished the person needs encouragement at the transition point because he or she feels that the bottom has dropped out, that they are going backwards, that they cannot pray. In reality if the signs of the transition are present, then they are making progress and will find support and sustenance in a simpler form of prayer.

If such a person subsequently finds an attraction to discursive prayer or is able to practice it, he or she may take it up again. Here again Dom Chapman's rule pertains: Pray as you can and not as you can't.

I have given in one chapter the degrees of prayer, marking the development of the spiritual life. This may be helpful to some in obtaining the advice they need for the stage they are in, or for the director who can identify this stage. If this identification is not readily apparent to the person directed or the director, this is not important. That is, one need not try to fit one's inner life into a schema—one takes it as it is and pursues it as best one can. The director can be satisfied with this both for himself and his or her clients.

EXTRAORDINARY PHENOMENA

It is important not to make much of extraordinary phenomena. To show a special interest in these may encourage someone whose experiences are not authentic to develop and elaborate them. Moreover such an attitude is apt to cause the recipient to overvalue these experiences, and to become open to them, and thereby to invite the intervention of Satan, who can also duplicate such experiences. The recipient of authentic experiences will be content if they are not the object of special interest or curiosity.

Those presenting special experiences should be listened to attentively, treated courteously, and judgment should be reserved. It is important to judge the mental and emotional balance, the character of the person, his or her humility, obedience, charity, fidelity to the duties of state of life, etc. The Church is rightly cautious in such cases, and so should the director be.

The principle governing the director in such cases should be based on the preeminence of virtue over extraordinary experiences.

Supernatural virtues, particularly the theological virtues of faith, hope and charity, are a participation in the divine life and nature, by which the Christian is a son or daughter of the Father. This is infinitely higher in value than visions, locutions, the working of healings or miracles, prophecy, etc. These are all *gratiae gratis datae*, i.e. gratuitous graces given for the building up of the body of Christ, and therefore valuable, but they are not sanctifying graces, graces which give the recipient increasing participation in the divine life, such as are the virtues and gifts of the Holy Spirit (wisdom, understanding, knowledge, counsel, fortitude, piety, and fear of the Lord).

In the wake of the charismatic movement there are many imitations of the extraordinary graces, many who seek them, many who thereby are led astray. Such people are apt to be self-centered and lacking in humility, obedience and sincerity.

WHO NEEDS DIRECTION

The priests' and directors' time is limited. Parish priests, through spiritual direction of those whom God is calling, can raise up a number of lay ministers who can help in the varied needs of the parish, diocese and Church. But it is not only those destined for high holiness, for special ministries in the Church, lay or clerical, who can profit by direction. There are many weak persons, persons who have difficulty sustaining spiritual growth, people who relapse into mortal sin, who can be helped by direction.

Homosexuals, neurotics, persons with depression or alcoholic or chemical addiction can also profit by direction, as can those who have been visited by some catastrophe, tragedy or misfortune, such as the loss of a spouse, child or parent, divorce or separation, illness and so on.

People with special problems need to have a reason which makes life worth living, something to believe and hope in, something which enriches their life. They need to learn how to bring a rich full life out of one which has been gradually or suddenly impoverished. They need to know how to deal with failure and how to make failure the foundation of a new and better life.

Above all, such people need encouragement, they need hope, they need support, and this not through sweeping the hard realities of their situation under the rug, but by turning to a power great enough to come to their rescue, and willing to do so, if they will accept it—the power of an Almighty God, Who does not help us by invading the sphere of our free will and operating in it independently of us, nor by miraculously changing reality, though He can do this, but by His grace and the means of the spiritual life through which we practice virtue and become better people. Thus we become partakers of an unending peace and joy—unending because we are called to immortality.

People with problems, if these problems are of their own making, which is not always the case, need to know how to face themselves, how to acknowledge their mistakes and faults of character, how to recognize the extent to which they themselves are the cause of their failure or suffering or misfortune, and how to become better and wiser people. They need to see through the pretenses by which they have alienated themselves from God without realizing it, by which they have created a philosophy or views of life which excuses their self-seeking or seeking of gratifications contrary to the love of the Father, His commandments, the teachings of His Church, while consorting with those engaged in a similar (and often mutual) self-deception.

Jesus Christ proposes Himself as this new rich fuller life and offers it to all who will accept it. Those with special problems need special grace and this is a call from Him to a special closeness to Him in which they will find these graces and be able to walk straight and humbly with and before Him in sincerity and truth. So homosexuality, alcoholism and chemical addictions, depression, neurosis and neurotic personality disorder, separation and divorce are a call to come closer to the Savior to make a more complete and entire gift of oneself to Him and to receive from Him the special graces needed to persevere in an increasing ever-richer intimacy with Him, such as the teaching of this book, based as it is on His revelation and the teaching of the Church, proposes. These people need to be oriented to their supernatural goal. They need to seek God with sincerity. Such motivation as the spiritual life provides can bring purpose, order, peace and some degree of stability into their lives.

The director can avoid wasting his time with those who do not sincerely wish to be converted, to turn to God, to make progress, to overcome their disorderly mode of life, while indicating to them that when they do decide to turn to God, His help will, hopefully, be available to them.

35 A Complete Program of the Spiritual Life

To those who ask what they must do to attain eternal life, God replies: One thing is necessary, keep My commandments. Let us dwell on this, let us keep it in mind and not lose sight of it; everything else is secondary.

Yet we must bear in mind that we cannot keep God's commandments perseveringly without grace, and grace is obtained through prayer. We must therefore always pray for the grace we need to keep God's commandments. Hence Saint Benedict says, in the Prologue to his Holy Rule: "First of all, when commencing any good work, let us beseech Him with most fervent and persevering prayer to perfect it, so that we may never have the misfortune to grieve Him by our evil deeds, after He has vouchsafed to reckon us among the number of His children."

Now if we are to pray perseveringly, we need to dwell upon the truths of God; and this spiritual reading, and sermons, the equivalent of spiritual reading, help us to do.

The first and greatest of the commandments is to love God with our whole mind, heart, strength and soul. By this commandment we are obliged to seek perfection. The principal means of fulfilling this obligation is the ardent and sincere desire for perfection, which arises from spiritual reading, expresses itself in prayer and good actions and needs to be frequently renewed.

Since God is our Beginning and End, we seek perfection not for our sake, but to honor and glorify Him: our spiritual life is a service, a worship of Him. But He has so made us that His glory and our happiness are identified; He takes His glory in our happiness, and our happiness can only be attained in Him and in seeking sincerely His glory.

In this book, we have pointed out, in conformity with the documents of Vatican II, that while we and we alone can give to the Father our love, and that we alone can pursue personally our sanctification, which according to Scripture is His will for us, nevertheless, He saved us not as individuals alone but also as a people. We are responsible not only for ourselves but also for our family and for society. But if we are to fulfill our mission to bring the happiness of Christ to all people, which is laid upon each of us, we must advance in an ever purer and more complete love and gift of ourselves. The importance of accomplishing this, and how to do so, is the theme of this book.

Since some of the distinctively Catholic spiritual ways and practices have been lost in the general confusion and disorder which followed Vatican II, some of the recommendations of this book, and particularly of this chapter, will seem archaic. That simply shows how topical they are, how badly needed, so that Catholics may recover their blurred and lost identity. The appealing needs of social justice, of world peace, and of current movements, can only be fostered by people who themselves are personally converted, turned to the Father and at home in His will, and able to maintain and advance their union with the Father in the Son and through the Holy Spirit.

The truly Catholic soul acknowledges that Jesus is God and regards His Father lovingly as its Father. It receives all that happens in life as coming from the Father's loving hands, and does all in conformity with His will in imitation of Jesus and in union with Mary. This attitude of soul, nourished by prayer, spiritual reading and the reception of the sacraments, leads to the practice of all virtues, to the faithful performance of the duties of one's state of life and to patience in trials and sufferings. It is secured by the spirit of self-denial, the avoidance of occasions of sin, and generosity in sacrificing legitimate pleasures which touch upon personal weaknesses, especially when these weaknesses are serious, and by sincere examination of conscience. These are the elements of a complete spiritual program.

The spiritual life will not prosper unless all the necessary means are taken, just as an automobile will not operate without all its essential parts, including four wheels. Some persons fail to make progress because they adopt a partial and not a sufficiently complete program. They may attend prayer meetings regularly, but neglect daily Mass and the sacrament of Reconciliation, or they may receive the sacraments frequently but neglect spiritual reading; or they may fail to practice self-denial or refuse to give up a serious occasion of sin, or pleasures which expose them to the occasion of sin. Rather than seeking to discover, accept and accomplish the divine will, they may besiege God, by all manner of spiritual exercises, to do their will.

IF GOD is our happiness, the better we order our day with this in view, the happier we shall be. Such ordering may take the form of a rule of life that includes our spiritual exercises and the duties of our state of life. The test of use helps to make it practical. In observing it, extremes should be avoided. Inflexibility places a restraint upon the performance of duties and in meeting the unforeseen, such as opportunities for acts of charity or recreation. Excessive flexibility leads to inconstancy, the omission without due reason of essential spiritual exercises, even habitually. Besides providing for social duties and recreation, a practical rule of life contains ordinarily a fixed early rising hour, and a relatively fixed early retiring time.

It will be helpful to many readers to set forth concretely the aforementioned elements of a complete spiritual program.

1. MENTAL PRAYER. A set period of half an hour or at least fifteen minutes of mental prayer daily, preferably before the Blessed Sacrament and early in the morning. Another period later in the day is helpful. As we progress, the spirit of prayer and recollection extends throughout the day.

Speaking to priests with words which ring true for all, Pope Pius XII said: "It must ... be stated without reservation that no other means has the unique efficacy of meditation, and that, as a consequence, its daily practice can in no wise be substituted for" (*Menti Nostrae*).

Speaking to Christians, the Archbishop of Bordeaux, in his pastoral letter of January 25, 1955 on Mental Prayer, says:

> In inviting you to practice it, I would wish to show you that there is no counsel at present more opportune to give, nor one more easy to follow.... This is the practice which I declare to be more than ever indispensable to the men of today. Mental prayer is the only means of meeting the difficulties and complexities of the modern world.

Very helpful is a visit to the Blessed Sacrament during the day to speak with Jesus Eucharistic in one's own words.

2. SPIRITUAL READING. Fifteen or thirty minutes of spiritual reading a day. We have already said much about this necessary practice.

3. DAILY MASS. Daily attendance at the Holy Sacrifice of the Mass with reception of Holy Communion, followed by a thanksgiving of about ten minutes. Sometimes daily or frequent attendance at Mass is impossible or very inconvenient; but almost everyone can receive Holy Communion weekly on Sunday.[1]

It is well to prepare to receive the sacraments with Mary, and to make our thanksgiving in union with her. It is advisable to confess once a week or every two weeks; a moment's thanksgiving at least should follow absolution; often, too, an act of faith in the forgiveness of our sins. The ardent desire for the sacraments increases the grace we receive through them, which may be very great.

---

[1] Mother Loyola's book, *Welcome* (Springfield, IL: Templegate, 1957), is helpful in preparing to receive Our Lord in Holy Communion.

4. SELF-DENIAL. To make the life of the soul secure, it is necessary not only to avoid the near occasions of sin, but also to exercise much peaceful circumspection regarding one's particular weaknesses. This will often entail the sacrifice of legitimate pleasures touching on these weaknesses. The love of God cannot develop in the soul that does not practice self-denial. "Anyone who does not take up his cross and follow Me cannot be My disciple," says Our Lord (Luke 14:27). We must mortify and deny our self-love and the sinful tendencies of our nature (criticism, gossip, impatience, undue severity, coldness, petty lying or stealing, negligence, boasting, idle talk), and the more constantly we do this, even during recreation, the more peace and progress will be ours. In particular, no concessions can be made safely in the matter of purity; the proximate occasion of sin and whatever tarnishes the luster of this virtue must be firmly and perseveringly shunned.

None of the other means will be effective without self-denial. "One thing is needful ... the ability to deny oneself truly for Christ's sake.... If the soul be found wanting in this exercise, which is the sum and root of the virtues, all its other methods are so much beating about the bush..." (Saint John of the Cross, *Ascent of Mount Carmel*, Bk. II, Chap. VII).

IN THE PRACTICE OF VIRTUE, due place must be given to charity toward God and people; submission to the divine will; and humility which is associated with growing self-knowledge, the acceptance of humiliations, the correction of faults and reparation for injuries to others. The more mortified the soul is, the more docile it will be to the inspirations of the Holy Spirit, and the more it will flourish under the wings of the Spirit.

All are not called to follow the counsels of Christ—poverty, perfect chastity and obedience—but all are called to live in the spirit of the counsels, the spirit of detachment from the world, the flesh and self-will.

The spiritual life is a life of love, a life spent with Jesus and Mary, and with the Father. If we are to have them as our companions, we must lovingly think of them or be conscious of them, speak to them or direct our actions by the pure intention of pleasing them. We may renew during the day our morning offering in a few words or in a glance of the mind or act of the will. We may interrupt our work for a couple of minutes to elevate the soul to God while saying such a prayer as that of Cardinal Mercier (see page 313); or we may make a few aspirations when the clock strikes the hour, as some office-workers do. Thus we seek to abide in the spirit of prayer and recollection throughout the day.

Let us repeat that it behooves us to beg Our Lord perseveringly for the graces we need, knowing that God has ordained that many graces be given only on the condition that they are requested of Him. One of the most important of these graces to pray for daily is the grace to remain open to all the graces the Father wishes to give us. Strengthened by the Bread of Life and by our prayer and spiritual reading, we must face manfully the difficulties of life.

We beg God to increase our faith, hope and charity and to grant us the supreme grace of final perseverance: of persevering till the end. For this great grace and for the grace of continence we should pray daily. We need also to pray for good spiritual friends and for a good spiritual director: "A brother helped by a brother is a fortress" (Proverbs 18:19).

We should be careful not to admit to the intimacy of friendship those who are not spiritually-minded; otherwise we shall find it difficult to maintain high ideals or to be true to them. And we should exclude familiarities and license from our friendships.

A good director will help to persuade us of the importance of the spiritual life, will show the beauty and utility of the means of cultivating it, will help us check up on our persevering and effective use of the means, and he will show us how to remove the obstacles that may arise, or those of which we are not conscious. Moreover, if we are candid with him in a spirit of faith, revealing our soul as if to Our Lord, Jesus will give us special graces.

Saturday and Sunday provide more leisure for devotions, and for an increase in the intensity of the spiritual life. A Holy Hour consisting of mental and vocal prayer and meditative spiritual reading may be made profitably once a week. A monthly day of recollection is advantageous, during which we can check up on our fidelity during the previous month, and renew our fervor. When the opportunity arises, we may make a mission, and once or twice a year, a retreat of three or four days.

AFTER LISTING four elements of a complete spiritual program, we have made some further remarks on the practice of virtue: now let us continue:

5. EXAMINATION OF CONSCIENCE. A nightly examination of conscience in which, with the help of the Father's grace for which we ask, we reflect briefly and sincerely on the thoughts, words, acts and omissions of the day, and on the motives which prompted them, thanking the Father for His graces and for what we have done aright, and stirring ourselves to supernatural contrition (in the will), for our faults. Once a day, a particular examen as explained in Chapter 27.

6. ADDITIONAL PRAYERS. Morning and evening prayers, said devoutly, the rosary, and grace before and after meals should be added to our program, and, if we wish, the Angelus.

Vocal prayer renders to God the homage of the body and the soul; through them the soul expresses or is aroused to devotion. To our morning prayer is joined the morning offering. The rosary recalls the mysteries of the faith.[2] The Angelus honors the Virgin Mother while

[2] The Joyful Mysteries: The Annunciation, Visitation, Jesus' Birth, Presentation and Finding in the Temple. The Sorrowful Mysteries: His Agony, Scourging, Crowning with Thorns, Carrying of the Cross, Crucifixion. The Luminous Mysteries: His Baptism, the Wedding at Cana, the Preaching of the Kingdom, the Transfiguration, Institution of the Eucharist. The Glorious Mysteries: His Resurrection, Ascension, Sending of the Holy Spirit, the Assumption and Crowning of Mary as Queen of Heaven and earth. By saying five decades each day, we recall the Incarnation, Redemption and Last Things—thus we may say the Joyful Mysteries on Monday and Saturday, the Sorrowful on Tuesday and Friday, the Glorious on Wednesday and Sunday, and the Luminous on Thursday. If we pause and recall each mystery before reciting the decade attached to it, we will direct our attention to Jesus and Mary in this decade, and we may think of the virtue which this mystery represents and which we wish to practice, and ask for it by our recitation. In each Our Father, we make to the Father the petitions Christ Himself has taught us; in each Hail Mary, we salute her with the words of Gabriel and Elizabeth and beg her to pray for us in the two most important moments of our life, "now and at the hour of our death." In each "Glory be," we center our hearts in the mystery of the Trinity.

recalling the Incarnation of her Son morning, noon and evening.[3] Grace calls down the Lord's blessing upon the food He has provided. With the thanksgiving following meals, it is also a profession of faith, strengthening the soul, so that it begins even now to profit by the promise of Christ: "Whosoever confesses Me before men, I shall confess before My Father Who is in Heaven."

BEFORE CONCLUDING this chapter with a word on consecration to the Sacred Heart of Jesus and the Immaculate Heart of Mary (which epitomizes the spiritual life and the spiritual program), the question of *devotions* deserves attention.

It is devotion, not devotions which counts. We must avoid cluttering up our time and restricting our liberty to perform the duties of our state of life and our essential spiritual exercises by a collection of particular devotions.

It is the quality of our love, not the quantity of our external practices, that makes our worth. When adding particular devotions to our program, we should go slowly, making sure that what we add we can carry out without being overburdened or diverted from what is primary and more important.

With these reservations, we add the following remarks:

The Office of the Blessed Virgin takes about half an hour to say, and may be distributed throughout the day. Fewer will embark on the daily recitation of the Divine Office, available in English in its entirety and in a short form.

The Stations of the Cross have a unique value in arousing love of God, sorrow for sin and genuine devotion for the Person of Christ. They may be made meditatively as a substitute for meditation when, at certain times, mental prayer is especially difficult.

[3] The wording of the Angelus is: The Angel of the Lord declared unto Mary and she conceived of the Holy Spirit. Hail Mary, etc. Behold the handmaid of the Lord, be it done to me according to thy word. Hail Mary, etc. And the Word was made flesh and dwelt among us. Hail Mary, etc. Pray for us, O holy Mother of God, that we may be made worthy of the promises of Christ. Let us pray. Pour forth, we beseech Thee, O Lord, Thy grace into our hearts that we to whom the Incarnation of Christ Thy Son was made known by the message of the Angel, may by His Passion and Cross be brought to the glory of His Resurrection. Through the same Christ Our Lord. Amen.

A picture of Jesus and Mary kept near us will help us to remain close to them. We should try to form a picture of them in our hearts.

Night adoration in the home is a work of reparation for sin made by generous and fervent Christians: those, we mean, who give an example of a truly Christian life by observing Catholic standards of decency in dress, reading, recreation, language, morals, and social justice, and who wish to atone for those who do not, by an hour of adoration and reparation each month in the home.[4]

Concerning the Enthronement of the Sacred Heart of Jesus as King of the home, information may be obtained from the above-mentioned Center. Certain prayers accompany the placing of a picture of the Sacred Heart in the home to designate the family's determination to have Him rule over them. Jesus is thereby given His proper place in the home so that He may have His proper place in the lives of its members. This devotion is highly commended.[5]

The Brown Scapular is a sign of our consecration to Mary. Connected with it are the Promise of Salvation and the Sabbatine Privilege. The great Promise of Salvation is made to those who die wearing the Brown Scapular. The Sabbatine Privilege is the help of Mary in delivering from Purgatory on Saturday of the week of their death those who fulfill its conditions. These are: be enrolled in the Confraternity and wear the Brown Scapular of the Order of Our Lady of Mount Carmel habitually and at the time of death (one must be invested in the scapular by a priest with the necessary faculties); to keep chastity according to one's state of life; to say the Offices of the Blessed Virgin daily, or to abstain from meat on Wednesdays and Saturdays. These last two conditions (recitation of Our Lady's Little Office or abstinence) may be commuted by any confessor.[6]

[4] For information and enrollment communicate with the National Center of the Enthronement, 4930 South Dakota Avenue, N.E., Washington DC.

[5] An account of this is given in *Enthronement of the Sacred Heart*, 364 pp. By Rev. Francis Larkin, SS.CC. (St. Paul, Mn.: Catechetical Guild Educational Society).

[6] The First Saturday reception of Holy Communion stems from her request to the seer of Fatima, Lucy. Its purpose is to offer her reparation for sins (whatever injures the Son wounds also the Mother).

Those who have avoided mortal sin for some time, and have persevered in seeking their sanctification through spiritual exercises, can read profitably Saint Louis Mary de Montfort's *True Devotion to Mary* (see Appendix), and if they desire may make this perfect form of consecration, approved and practiced by the Popes.

Personal consecration to the Sacred Heart offers Jesus love and reparation for sin. By this consecration is ratified the baptismal vow to renounce Satan and all his works and to give oneself to the Father through His Son Jesus Christ (not only for one's own salvation but also for the salvation of others). Fidelity to one's spiritual program leads to the carrying out of this commitment, to comforting the Heart of Christ and to making reparation to Him for oneself and others. The First Friday reception of Holy Communion and the Holy Hour have also the same purpose of offering loving reparation to Jesus. The promises attached to nine consecutive First Fridays, as made to Saint Margaret Mary, are well known.

POPE JOHN PAUL II has repeatedly consecrated the Church and all mankind to the Immaculate Heart of Mary. Each individual ought to ratify this in his own life by a personal consecration to the Most Pure Heart of Mary. In these times, when sin threatens to engulf the entire world in an irresistible flood, the Father has opened to all the Immaculate Heart of Mary as an ark in which they may find refuge and sanctity. Consecration to Mary strengthens and upholds the consecration to Jesus; we are hers, her children and servants, that we may be more surely and truly His. We fulfill this consecration by invoking Mary and by imitating her virtues, by which our minds and hearts become centered, not on Mary, but on Jesus, as was hers. Mary does not want to be an obstacle to our thinking of and loving Jesus, but a help (cf. Ch. VIII, Constitution on the Church of Vatican Council II). By giving her the central place in our lives that God has destined her to have according to His plan, by which we have all graces through her hands, we obtain her assistance in giving the first place in our hearts to her Son and to His Father.

Appendix:

Spiritual Reading

Appendix

Practical Hints on Spiritual Reading & Recommendations

The great law to follow in spiritual reading is this: select that supernatural food of true doctrine which will nourish the soul. This is best accomplished if the book selected is suited to the mentality of its reader.

The maxim "I fear the man of one book" might be understood as the reaction of the devil to the person who masters the spiritual principles contained in one good treatise on the spiritual life, as opposed to the person who reads many books without sufficiently digesting any one of them. However, when we stay with a book so long that it is no longer producing fruit in us, it is time to pass on to another; later we may profitably reread it.

When the assistance of a good spiritual director is wanting (and of course even if one has a good spiritual director), properly chosen spiritual reading becomes a channel of God's spiritual direction, as well as of encouragement and help, and contributes greatly to perseverance in that foremost of undertakings, the development of the interior life. Since many persons will feel the need of specific recommendations to serve this end, certain suggestions are made in the following list of books of proven value. Such proof of value limits these recommendations to books that have been in circulation for some time, yet a few recent titles are included.

The good of the greater number of readers will be served by confining this list to a few suggestions (avoiding the confusion of multiplicity, even at the cost of omission of many excellent titles) and by grouping these titles into categories that will suggest a certain pattern of reading and conform to the continued needs of the readers. Those versed in spiritual bibliography could no doubt devise a better list and each will perhaps prefer his own. Pages 178 to 230 of *A Practical Guide to Spiritual Reading* by Susan Annette Muto (see below) contains an explanatory paragraph about many of the books contained on my reading list, which may be helpful for those wishing further information. But the present list may help the reader to become acquainted with spiritual literature and will allow him to find his own way. Even then, if spiritual reading is to retain its efficacy, it ought to consist in the reading of books that tend primarily to the intensification of the interior life and to its upbuilding.

In keeping with the suggestion that a book of spiritual doctrine be read in alternation with biography, these two types of books constitute the two major divisions of this list. Under Spiritual Doctrine are included the Scriptures and Lives of Our Lord, Our Lady and Saint Joseph, and books about them, since these subjects constitute spiritual doctrine in a special way. The list of biographies is made up especially of lives of the saints, but also includes lives of those who have lived in accordance with their faith or who have followed the leadings of grace, as for example, converts. All such lives can motivate us strongly to follow our own grace, and this the more their circumstances resemble our own. Hence lives of the laity are especially recommended to laymen, the lives of priests to priests, etc.

Ignatius Press in San Francisco, California and St. Bede's Press in Petersham, Massachusetts, have lists of contemporary books of sound doctrine, suitable for spiritual reading.

Some of the titles listed below are out of print in their original editions, but have been reprinted by one or more of the publishers listed here. Those that are available from these publishers are noted next to the title.

Ignatius Press
2515 McAllister Street
San Francisco, CA 94118
www.ignatius.com

Christian Classics
200 East Bethany Drive
Allen, TX 75002-3804
www.thomasmore.com

Sophia Institute Press
P.O. Box 5284
Manchester, NH 03108
www.sophiainstitute.com

Tan Books and Publishers
P.O. Box 404
Rockford, IL 61105
www.tanbooks.com

Daughters of Saint Paul (Pauline)
50 Saint Paul's Avenue
Jamaica Plain (Boston), MA 02130
www.pauline.org

Zaccheus Press
4605 Chase Avenue
Bethesda, MD 20814
www.zaccheuspress.com

I. SPIRITUAL DOCTRINE

1. THE HOLY BIBLE

2. A CLASSIC: This may be read throughout one's life, and is therefore given the prominence of a separate grouping.

à Kempis, Thomas. *The Imitation of Christ*. Available in many inexpensive editions. It is said of this book that one can open it at any page, and it will speak directly to the reader's heart.

3. CONFORMITY TO THE WILL OF GOD: This basic doctrine of the spiritual life deserves special attention and understanding. It is well to read one of these books after one has persevered in the spiritual life for some time.

Caussade, J.P. de, S.J. *Abandonment to Divine Providence*. N.Y.: Benziger Bros., 1952. (*Tan*)

Drexelius, Jeremias, S.J. *Heliotropium*. N.Y.: Devin-Adair, 1912. (*Tan*)

Kearney, John, C.S.Sp. *Learn of Me*. Springfield, Ill: Templegate.

Lehodey, Vitalis, O.C.R. *Holy Abandonment*. Dublin: M.H. Gill & Sons, 1934.

4. LIVES OF OUR LORD: Lives of our Lord help us to penetrate the Scriptures and to form therefrom a true picture of Jesus.

Farrell, Walter, O.P. *Only Son*. N.Y.: Sheed & Ward, 1953.

Fouard, Constant. *The Christ, the Son of God*. N.Y.: Longmans, Green, 1944.

Goodier, Alban, S.J. *The Public Life of Our Lord Jesus Christ*. 2 vols. N.Y.: P.J. Kenedy & Sons, 1944.

_____. *The Passion and Death of Our Lord Jesus Christ*. N.Y.: P.J. Kenedy & Sons, 1933. (*Christian Classics*)

_____. *The Risen Jesus*. N.Y.: P.J. Kenedy & Sons, 1949.

Meschler, Maurice, S.J. *The Life of Our Lord Jesus Christ in Meditations*. 2 vols. St. Louis: B. Herder, 1950.

Kasper, Walter. *The God of Jesus Christ*. (See Section 8, below.) Pages 158 to 198 present doctrine about Our Lord inclusive of the results of contemporary Scripture exegesis and theological development, for those seeking such a treatment, which is somewhat technical.

5. OUR LADY: A book on Our Lady read now and then renews our devotion to her and to her Son.

Alphonsus Liguori, Saint. *The Glories of the Blessed Virgin Mary*. (*Tan*)

Bernadot, M.V., O.P. *Our Lady in Our Life*. Westminster, Md.: Newman Press, 1946.

Brown, Raphael. *Life of Mary as Seen by the Mystics*. Milwaukee: Bruce, 1951.

De Marchi, John, I.M.C. *The Immaculate Heart: The True Story of Our Lady of Fatima*. N.Y.: Farrar, Straus & Young, 1952.

De Montfort, Louis Marie Grignion, Saint. *True Devotion to Mary*. Bayshore, N.Y.: Montfort Fathers, 1954. A book that has a transforming effect on those who have been devoting themselves for some time to the spiritual life. This book is the acknowledged basis of John Paul II's devotion to Mary. (*Tan*)

Fatima in Lucia's Own Words. Her Memoirs. Written in obedience. Very beautifully expressed account of Our Lady's appearances to the three seers of Fatima, by one of them, Sister Lucia.

Fidler, Charles, O.C.S.O. *Father Peyton's Rosary Prayer Book*. Albany, N.Y.: Family Rosary, Inc. Meditations on the rosary with current applications.

Houselander, Caryll. *Reed of God*. N.Y.: Sheed & Ward, 1944. (*Christian Classics*.)

Leen, Edward, C.S.Sp. and Kearney, John, C.S.Sp., *Our Blessed Mother*. N.Y.: P.J. Kenedy & Sons, 1946.

Most, William G. *Mary in Our Life*. N.Y.: P.J. Kenedy & Sons, 1954.

Philipon, Marie Michel, O.P. *The Mother of God*. Westminster, Md.: Newman, 1953. A short work including results of modern theological studies of Mary.

Rahner, Hugo, S.J. *Our Lady and the Church*. N.Y.: Pantheon, 1961. (*Zaccheus*)

Chapter Eight of the Constitution on the Church of Vatican II gives a beautiful contemporary resume of the Church's teaching on Our Lady. For versions see below under Vatican II.

6. Saint Joseph:

Baij, Mother, OSB, Abbess. *The Life of Saint Joseph*. 101 Foundation P.O. Box 151 Asbury, NJ 08802-0151; email: 101@101foundation.com. Said to be dictated by Jesus, this book is inspiring.

Filas, Francis, S.J. *The Man Nearest Christ*. Milwaukee: Bruce, 1944.

_____. *Joseph and Jesus*. Milwaukee: Bruce, 1952. Theological study of their relationship.

Meschler, Maurice, S.J. *Saint Joseph in the Life of Christ and of the Church*. St. Louis: B. Herder, 1932.

Mueller, Joseph, S.J. *Fatherhood of Saint Joseph*. St. Louis: B. Herder, 1952.

Rondet, Henri, S.J. *Saint Joseph*. N.Y.: P.J. Kenedy & Sons, 1956.

7. Books on Prayer:

Dubay, Thomas, SM. *Fire Within: Saint Teresa of Avila, Saint John of the Cross, and the Gospel—on Prayer*. San Francisco: Ignatius Press, 1989. This is one of the finest books on prayer. It shows that Saint Teresa and Saint John of the Cross asked only what the Gospels ask, and explains their doctrine in contemporary language. It contains chapters on friendship and spiritual direction.

Liguori, Alphonsus Saint. *Selected Writings and Prayers of Saint Alphonsus* (formerly titled *Love is Prayer, Prayer is Love*). Adapted by John Steingraeber. Liguori, Mo.: Liguori Publications, 1997.

John of the Cross, Saint. *The Collected Works of Saint John of the Cross*. Trans. Kieran Kavanaugh, O.C.D. and Otilio Rodriguez, O.C.D. Washington, D.C.: Institute of Carmelite Studies, ICS Publications, 1973. A volume of Saint John's writings is available from the Paulist Press.

Teresa of Avila, Saint. *The Interior Castle.* N.Y.: The Paulist Press. Introduction by Kieran Kavanaugh, O.C.D., and Otilio Rodriguez, O.C.D., 1979.

8. OTHER CLASSICS OF SPIRITUAL DOCTRINE:

Aelred of Rievaulx. *On Spiritual Friendship.* Trans. Mary Eugenia Laker. Washington, D.C.: Cistercian Publications, 1974.

Anonymous. *The Cloud of Unknowing* and *The Book of Privy Counseling.* Ed. William Johnston, S.J. Garden City, N.Y.: Doubleday & Co., Image Books, 1973. This book is also available from Paulist Press.

The Art of Prayer: An Orthodox Anthology. Compiled by Igumen Chariton of Valamo. Trans. E. Kaadloubovsky and E. M. Palmer. London: Faber and Faber, Ltd., 1966.

Athanasius, Saint. *The Life of Saint Anthony.* Translated and introduced by Robert C. Gregg. N.Y.: Paulist Press, 1980. Saint Anthony was one of the first monks of the Egyptian desert, and perhaps the most famous. Saint Athanasius, Bishop of Alexandria, was an important defender of the doctrine of the Trinity. This book has had an immense effect on the spirituality of the West.

Augustine, Saint. *The Lord's Sermon on the Mount. Sermons for Christmas and Epiphany.* (Ancient Christian Writers Series) Westminster, Md.: Newman Press, 1952.

Aumann, Jordan. *Christian Spirituality of the Catholic Tradition.* San Francisco: Ignatius Press, 1985.

Bernard of Clairvaux, Saint. *On the Song of Songs.* 2 vols. (paperback available). Spencer, Mass.: Cistercian Publications, 1971. *The Sermons of Bernard of Clairvaux on the Song of Songs* is also available from Paulist Press (1987). Also published by Paulist Press is Bernard of Clairvaux, *Selected Works.*

Bouyer, Louis. *Introduction to Spirituality.* Trans. Mary Perkins Ryan. Collegeville, Mn.: Liturgical Press, 1961.

_____. "The Spirituality of the New Testament and the Fathers." In *A History of Christian Spirituality,* Vol. I. Trans. Mary Perkins Ryan. N.Y.: Seabury Press, 1969.

Boylan, Eugene, O.C.S.O. *This Tremendous Lover.* Paramus, N.J.: Newman Press, 1964. *(Christian Classics)*

Cassian, John. *The Conferences.* N.Y.: Paulist Press, 1985. This is a selection of nine of Cassian's twenty-four conferences. Cassian's *Conferences* were read every day by Saint Thomas Aquinas. They and Cassian's *Institutes* introduced the doctrine of the Egyptian monks of the desert to the West.

Catherine of Siena, Saint. *The Dialogue of Catherine of Siena*. Translation and introduction by Suzanne Noffke, O.P. N.Y.: Paulist Press, 1980.

Chautard, Jean-Baptiste, O.C.S.O. *The Soul of the Apostolate*. Trans. A Monk of Our Lady of Gethsemani. (*Tan*)

Considine, Daniel. *Confidence in God*. Union City, N.J.: Sign Magazine. A booklet.

de Sales, Francis, Saint. *Introduction to the Devout Life*. Garden City, N.Y.: Doubleday & Co., Image Books, 1955.

Diefenbach, Gabriel. *Common Mystic Prayer*. Paterson, N.J.: Saint Anthony Guild Press, 1947. (*Pauline*)

Farrell, Walter and Healy, Martin. *My Way of Life*. Brooklyn: Confraternity of the Precious Blood. (*Christian Classics* and *Tan*)

Francis of Assisi, Saint. *The Little Flowers of Saint Francis*. Trans. Raphael Brown. Garden City, N.Y.: Doubleday & Co., Image Books, 1958. (*Christian Classics*)

Galot, Jean. *Theology of the Priesthood*. San Francisco: Ignatius Press, 1985.

Grou, John Nicholas. *The School of Jesus Christ*. London: Burns, Oates and Washbourne, 1932.

Houselander, Caryll. *The Way of the Cross*. N.Y.: Sheed & Ward, 1955. A new edition is available from Liguori Publications.

Jeremias, Joachim. *The Prayers of Jesus*. London: SCM Press Ltd., 1967. A work of scholarship by a Protestant Scripture scholar. Technical but rewarding.

John of the Cross, Saint. *The Collected Works of Saint John of the Cross*. Trans. Kieran Kavanaugh, O.C.D. and Otilio Rodriguez, O.C.D. Washington, D.C.: Institute of Carmelite Studies, ICS Publications, 1973.

Julian of Norwich. *The Revelations of Divine Love*. Trans. James Walsh. N.Y.: Harper & Brothers, 1961.

Kasper, Walter. *The God of Jesus Christ*. N.Y.: Crossroad, 1984. One of the best works on the theology of the Trinity, as the healing needed by the contemporary world.

Keating, Thomas. *Crisis of Faith*. 2nd. ed. Petersham, Mass.: St. Bede's Publications, 1979. A revised edition, *Crisis of Faith, Crisis of Love* (1998), is available from Continuum.

Keyes, Paul T. *Pastoral Presence and the Diocesan Priest*. Foreword by Thomas A. Kane. Natick, Mass.: Affirmation Books, 1978.

Lallemant, Louis. *Spiritual Doctrine*. Westminster, Md.: Newman Press, 1946.

Laurentin, Rene. *The Truth of Christmas Beyond the Myths. The Gospels of the Infancy of Christ*. Trans. Michael Wrenn and associates. Petersham, Mass.: St. Bede's Publications, 1986.

Leen, Edward. *In the Likeness of Christ*. N.Y.: Sheed & Ward, 1936.

_____. *Why the Cross?* N.Y.: Sheed & Ward, 1939.

_____. *The True Vine and Its Branches*. N.Y.: P.J. Kenedy & Sons, 1938.

Libermann, Francis. *Spiritual Letters to Clergy and Religious*. Three vols. Trans. Walter van de Putte. Pittsburgh: Duquense University Press, 1963, 1964, and 1966.

Marmion, Dom Columba. *Christ the Life of the Soul*. St. Louis, Mo.: B. Herder, 1925. (*Zaccheus*)

_____. *Christ in His Mysteries*. Trans. Mother M. Saint Thomas of Tyburn Convent. St. Louis, Mo.: B. Herder, 1939.

Merton, Thomas. *Life and Holiness*. Garden City, N.Y.: Doubleday & Co., Image Books, 1964.

_____. *The Climate of Monastic Prayer*. Spencer, Mass.: Cistercian Publications, 1969.

Muto, Susan Annette. *A Practical Guide to Spiritual Reading*. Danville, N.J.: Dimension Books, 1976.

Pieper, Josef. *On Hope*. San Francisco: Ignatius Press, 1986.

Pope John XXIII. *Journal of a Soul*. Trans. Dorothy White. N.Y.: McGraw Hill, 1965.

Rich, Charles. *The Embrace of the Soul*. Ed. Ronda Chervin. Preface Raphael Simon. Petersham, Mass.: St. Bede's Publications, 1986.

_____. *Reflections*. Petersham, Mass.: St. Bede's Publications, 1986.

Roberts, Augustine, OCSO. *Centered on Christ. An Introduction to Monastic Profession*. Petersham, Mass.: St. Bede's Publications, 1977. By the former Abbot of Saint Joseph's Abbey, Spencer, Mass.

The Sayings of the Desert Fathers: The Alphabetical Collection. Trans./ Ed. Benedicta Ward. London: A. R. Mowbray & Co., Ltd., 1975.

Stuart, Janet Erskine. *The Inward Life*. Brooklyn: International Catholic Truth Society. A booklet.

Thomas Aquinas, Saint. *The Commandments of God*. London: Burns, Oates and Washbourne, 1937.

Van Zeller, Hubert. *Spirituality Recharted*. Petersham, Mass.: St. Bede's Publications, 1985. The spiritual journey according to Saint John of the Cross with insights derived from a lifetime of spiritual experience.

Vatican II, The Documents of. Ed. Walter Abbott. N.Y.: America Press, 1966. *Vatican Council II: The Conciliar and Post-Conciliar Documents*. Ed. Austin Flannery. Collegeville, Mn.: Liturgical Press, 1980. A later and more careful translation.

Vincent, Mary Clare. *The Life of Prayer and the Way to God*. Petersham, Mass.: St. Bede's Publications. By the Prioress of Saint Scholastica Priory, Petersham, Mass.

von Balthasar, Hans Urs. *Prayer*. Trans. A. V. Littledale. N.Y.: Paulist Press, Deus Books, 1967. *(Ignatius)*

William of Saint Thierry. *The Golden Epistle*. Kalamazoo, Mich.: Cistercian Publications, 1980. William of Saint Thierry was a friend of Saint Bernard. The *Epistle* is a letter to the Carthusians, and noted for its teaching on the spiritual life.

9. CASSETTE TAPES:

George, Eileen. Tapes on prayer and spirituality. Made at home, not of professional quality, but inspired and inspiring. Catalog on request. Also DVDs of her services are available. Meet-The-Father Ministry, 363 Greenwood Street, Millbury, MA 01527.

10. PRIVATE REVELATIONS:

Books of private revelations which have been approved by the censorship of the Church as containing nothing contrary to faith and morals may be read with discretion by persons who have absorbed the principles of the religious life, who realize that gratuitous graces are not of the essence of sanctity, and whose imagination and desires will not be unduly inflamed by such works—and then should be read only occasionally. With these restrictions those who have or develop a taste for such works will be helped by them to realize the truths of faith.

Bossis, Gabrielle. *He and I*. Editions Paulines, 1985. *(Pauline)*

George, Eileen. *Conversations in Heaven I, II, III*. Conversations with Jesus and the Father, taped and edited by Eileen's spiritual director. These may be taken as Eileen's meditations. Meet-The-Father Ministry, 363 Greenwood Street, Millbury, MA 01527.

Marguerite. *Message of Merciful Love to Little Souls*. San Raphael, Calif.: Pope Publications, 1981.

Mary of the Blessed Trinity, Sr. *Spiritual Legacy*. Westminster, Md.: Newman Press, 1950. (*Tan*)

Menendez, Josefa. *The Way to Divine Love*. Westminster, Md.: Newman Press, 1950. (*Tan*)

II. BIOGRAPHIES

Biographies of the saints, or of the fervent or of converts may be alternated with a doctrinal work. They show the doctrine in the concrete and move us to imitation.

Athanasius, Saint. "Life of Saint Anthony." Trans. Sister Mary Emily Keenan. In *The Fathers of the Church*, Vol. 15. *Early Christian Biographies*. Ed. Roy J. Defarrari. Washington, D.C.: Catholic University of America Press, 1952.

Auclair, Marcelle. *Saint Teresa of Avila*. N.Y.: Pantheon Books, 1953. (*St. Bede's*)

Augustine, Saint. *The Confessions of Saint Augustine*. Trans. John K. Ryan. Garden City, N.Y.: Doubleday & Co., Image Books, 1960.

Broderick, James, S.J. *Saint Francis Xavier*. N.Y.: Doubleday & Co., Image Books, 1957.

Buehrle, Marie. *Rafael Cardinal Merry del Val*. Milwaukee: Bruce, 1957.

Bruno, Father. *Saint John of the Cross*. N.Y.: Sheed & Ward, 1932.

Chervin, Ronda, *The Ingrafting: The Conversion Stories of Ten Hebrew Converts*. Petersham, Mass.: St. Bede's Publications, 1988. (*Remnant of Israel, P.O. Box 142633, Irving, TX 75014-2633, 1-888-352-7153, www.remnantofisrael.net*)

Chesterton, G. K. *Saint Thomas Aquinas—"The Dumb Ox"*. Garden City, N.Y.: Doubleday & Co., Image Books, 1956. (*Ignatius*)

Ciszek, Walter J., S.J. *With God In Russia*. San Francisco: Ignatius Press, 1997. The story of a priest captured and held prisoner by the Soviet Union.

_____. *He Leadeth Me*. San Francisco: Ignatius Press, 1995. The efficacy of abandonment to Divine Providence in sustaining him in this situation. His cause for canonization is underway.

Dal-Gal, Hieronymo. *Pius X*. Westminster, Md.: Newman Press, 1954.

Dudon, Père Paul. *Saint Ignatius of Loyola*. Trans. William J. Young. Milwaukee: Bruce, 1949.

Farrow, John. *The Story of Thomas More*. Garden City, N.Y.: Doubleday & Co., Image Books, 1968.

Fatima in Lucia's Own Words. Sr. Lucia's Memoirs. Ed. Father Louis Kondor, S.V.D. (*Available from Ravensgate Press, St. Benedict's Priory, Still River, MA 01467*)

Frankl, Viktor E. *Man's Search for Meaning: An Introduction to Logotherapy.* Trans. Ilse Lasch. N.Y.: Washington Square Press, 1963. Discovery in Auschwitz that the ultimate human freedom is to form one's attitudes, and find the meaning and wholeness of life in a higher dimension.

A Little Brother of Jesus. *Silent Pilgrimage to God: The Spirituality of Charles de Foucauld.* Trans. Jeremy Moisier. Maryknoll, N.Y.: Orbis Books, 1975.

O'Neill, Dan. *The New Catholics: Contemporary Converts Tell Their Stories.* N.Y.: Crossroad, 1989.

Piat, Stephan-Joseph, O.F.M. *The Story of a Family.* N.Y.: P.J. Kenedy & Sons, 1948. The family of Saint Thérèse of Lisieux.

Schimberg, Albert. *The Great Friend: Frederick Ozanam.* Milwaukee: Bruce, 1946. Life of the layman who founded the Society of Saint Vincent de Paul.

Simon, Raphael. *The Glory of Thy People. The Story of a Conversion.* Petersham, Mass.: St. Bede's Publications, 1986. (*Remnant of Israel, P.O. Box 142633, Irving, TX 75014-2633, 1-888-352-7153, www.remnantofisrael.net*)

Suenens, Leon-Joseph. *Edel Quinn.* Dublin: C.J. Fallon, 1954. Story of a young Irish lay missionary, envoy of the Legion of Mary to Africa.

Talbot, Francis X., S.J. *Saint Among Savages.* N.Y.: Harper, 1935. Saint Isaac Jogues.

———. *Saint Among the Hurons.* N.Y.: Harper, 1949. Saint Jean de Brebeuf.

Teresa of Avila, Saint. *Autobiography of Saint Teresa of Avila.* Trans. E. Allison Peers. Garden City, N.Y.: Doubleday & Co., Image Books, 1960.

Thérèse of Lisieux, Saint. *Story of a Soul: The Autobiography of Saint Thérèse of Lisieux.* Trans. John Clarke. Washington, D.C.: Institute of Carmelite Studies, ICS Publications, 1975. Other works about this doctor of the Church are:

Gaucher, Guy. *The Story of a Life.* San Francisco: HarperCollins, 1993.

O'Mahony, Christopher. *Saint Thérèse by Those Who Knew Her (Testimonies from the Process of Beatification).* San Francisco: Ignatius Press, 1989.

Saint Thérèse of Lisieux: Her Last Conversations. Ed. John Clarke. Washington, D.C.: ICS Publications, 1977.

van Kaam, Adrian. *A Light to the Gentiles. The Life Story of the Ven. Francis Libermann.* Denville, N.J.: Dimension Books, 1959. Other works of van Kaam are recommended for those who are interested in a sound presentation of spirituality integrated with psychology, as are the books and tapes of Benedict Groeschel, O.F.M., Cap.

Ward, Maisie. *Caryll Houselander: That Divine Eccentric.* N.Y.: Sheed & Ward, 1962. Her life.

Weigel, George. *Witness to Hope. The Biography of Pope John Paul II.* N.Y.: HarperCollins, 1999. Recommended by Cardinal O'Connor. Cardinal George, Mary Ann Glendon and William J. Bennett, this biography had the cooperation of the Pope and gives an insider's view of his life and teaching.

Cardinal Mercier's Prayer to the Holy Spirit

Holy Spirit, Soul of my soul, I adore Thee.
Enlighten, guide, strengthen and console me.
Tell me what I ought to do and command me to do it.
I promise to be submissive in everything
that Thou permittest to happen to me,
only show me what is Thy will.

Prayer for Priests

O ALMIGHTY ETERNAL GOD, look upon the face of Thy Christ, and for love of Him Who is the eternal High-priest, have pity on Thy priests. Remember, O most compassionate God, that they are but weak and frail human beings. Stir up in them the grace of their vocation which is in them by the imposition of the Bishop's hands. Keep them close to Thee, lest the enemy prevail against them, so that they may never do anything in the slightest degree unworthy of their sublime vocation.

O Jesus, I pray Thee for Thy faithful and fervent priests; for Thy unfaithful and tepid priests; for Thy priests laboring at home or abroad in distant mission fields; for Thy tempted priests; for Thy lonely and desolate priests; for Thy young priests; for Thy aged priests; for Thy sick priests; for Thy dying priests; for the souls of Thy priests in Purgatory.

But above all I commend to Thee the priests dearest to me: the priest who baptized me; the priest who absolved me from my sins; the priests at whose Masses I assisted and who gave me Thy Body and Blood in Holy Communion; the priests who taught and instructed me or helped me and encouraged me; all the priests to whom I am indebted in any way, particularly ....

O Jesus, keep them all close to Thy heart, and bless them abundantly in time and eternity. Amen.

—Rev. Bruno M. Hagspiel, S.V.D.

313

Index